Safe Schools

Crisis Prevention and Response

Michael A. Wanko, Ph.D.

WITHDRAWN

scarecrow
education

The Scarecrow Press, Inc.
A Scarecrow Education Book
Published with the New Jersey Principals
and Supervisors Association
Lanham, Maryland, and London
2001

SCARECROW PRESS, INC.
A Scarecrow Education Book

Published in the United States of America
by Scarecrow Press, Inc.
4720 Boston Way, Lanham, Maryland 20706
www.scarecrowpress.com

4 Pleydell Gardens, Folkestone
Kent CT20 2DN, England

British Library Cataloguing-in-Publication Information Available

Library of Congress Cataloging-in-Publication Data

Wanko, Michael A., 1947–
    Safe schools: crisis prevention and response / Michael A. Wanko.
      p. cm. — (A Scarecrow education book)
    Includes bibliographical references (p.) and index.
    ISBN 0-8108-4175-4 (alk. paper)
      1. School crisis management—United States. 2. Schools—United States—Safety measures. 3. Schools—United States—Security measures. 4. School violence—United States—Prevention. I. Title. II. Series.

LB2866.5.W36 2001
363.11'9371—dc21

2001041792

♾™ The paper used in this publication meets the minimum requirements of American National Standard for Information Sciences—Permanence of Paper for Printed Library Materials, ANSI/NISO Z.39.48-1992.
Manufactured in the United States of America.

This book is dedicated to my extraordinary, lovely wife, Justine, and our incredible son, Jason. Justine, my life partner for thirty years, provides me with love, support, and counsel. Her compassion, knowledge, and understanding have inspired me to attain the optimum levels of performance that are needed in such a demanding profession. Our son, Jason, is always there for us. He is mature beyond his years and knowledgeable in the ways of life. As a result, he required no explanations regarding actions and procedures that needed to be implemented during the crises at our school. Without the love of these individuals, my effectiveness as the educational leader of our school would have been greatly diminished.

Contents

Introduction

As a series of four crises befell my school in one year, I began searching for answers. You can imagine the upheaval and the anguish experienced by not only the school community but also the entire city. As a result, I researched the implications of the whos, whats, wheres, hows, and whys of crisis, crisis management, and procedures to make schools safer. I also honed my skills in managing the stress that resulted from serving as the educational leader of the school. If you do not take proper care of yourself, you will not provide the appropriate care for your students and staff. Service to self might sound selfish, but it is not—it is the only way to provide proper balance in your life and support for your school community.

This book will provide you with enough information to develop a plan for a safe environment in your own school or district. You will have the ability to deal with crises and know what should be done when a crisis occurs. Additionally, you will know when and whether memorial programs are proper and necessary. I have provided forms, checklists, and sample letters to assist in your quest to create a safe and supportive school.

After completing the Crisis Preparedness Checklist you will have a sound idea of where you are and where you need to go to ensure a safe and supportive school for the children entrusted to your care. By following the Three-Prong Plan for safety in your school, you will be able to intelligently decide which course of action is best for your situation.

The results of the Physical Risk Reduction Checklist will provide you with information regarding what steps are needed to design a secure campus. You will know what hardware is necessary to make your school environment safer. As you develop various school climate questionnaires, you will be able to determine what steps are necessary to defuse potential conflicts in the school community.

Further, you will be able to establish a crisis management team in your building. Your team can be trained using the special vignettes included in this book. The vignettes are designed to enhance the crisis team's ability to serve your students and staff. Finally, the bibliography provides a wealth of resources to assist you in the formulation of your individual plan for a safe and supportive school environment.

Three chapters are devoted to understanding perceptions, stress, and creative thinking. Comprehending biased perceptions and past learning experiences will enhance your dealings with students, staff, and parents. By completing the Principal's Job Stress Indicator, you will better discern how you are coping with your employment. The As, Bs, Cs of Taking Control will provide you with a blueprint for managing your life.

I have designed this book to serve as a guide for specific needs in your school. Naturally, I have not provided all the answers for all the questions. Rather, I have shared how we handled the crises in Bayonne High School so we could move forward. I have presented the fruits of my labor, research, and experiences as they related to our situation. This text presents how we went about making our school safer and more supportive.

This book is an outgrowth of the workshops and seminars I began to conduct a year after the tragedies. This was a way for me to spread the word of preparedness. It also was a catharsis for me personally. Until you undergo such horror, it is difficult to understand what one experiences each and every day during and following a crisis. I hope this book will assist you in becoming a proactive administrator in the areas of school safety, crisis management, supportive school climate, and self-empowerment.

Chapter 1

America's Schools in Crisis

I had been a career principal for almost two decades when a series of four crises befell our school community in just one year. None of my training or experience prepared me for such a devastating succession of tragedies. However, by sharing my experiences and the fruits of my research, I hope to prepare others, not only in proper crisis response but also in ways to make schools safer and more supportive.

Through my investigation, I discovered that there are really only two types of schools. I am not referring to public and private or even urban and suburban. Unfortunately, the only two types of schools are those that have undergone a crisis and those that are waiting to undergo one.

If you believe a crisis will not come to your school, you are sadly mistaken. Keep in mind that a crisis can take many forms and can come at any time. A school crisis is an event that is extraordinary, usually unpredictable, but always inevitable. Important to your training is the knowledge that even though the crisis cannot always be predicted, human reactions to a crisis are consistent and very predictable. Remember, crisis does not always come from within. It can infiltrate your student body and staff from events emanating in the community. Therefore, you must be ever-vigilant and keep your Crisis Management Team on the alert at all times.

Whether your crisis is a natural disaster or the sudden death of a student, the manner in which you behave as the educational leader will dictate how, in turn, your staff and students react. Imperative to maintaining safety, support, structure, stability, and control in your school is the ability to anticipate contingencies. You must be proactive in creating a crisis plan rather than reactive to a crisis already in motion. Knowledge of how people will react in a critical situation will make it possible for you to implement a plan that defuses harmful reactions and prevents those reactions from precipitating a secondary crisis.

BEGINNING THE JOURNEY

To begin our journey, let me take you back a few years to a cold and snowy day in the city of Bayonne, New Jersey. My mother was waking me up for school. I looked out the window and pulled the covers over my head to go back to sleep. About five minutes later my mother yelled, "Michael, get up or you will be late for school!" Once again, I pulled the covers over my head and yelled back, "Mom, I am not going to school today!" A few minutes later, my mother walked into my room and asked what was the problem. I told her I was sick and could not go to school. This turned out to be a huge mistake, because my mom, a registered nurse, examined me to determine if I were ill. She concluded that I was fine and could go to school.

I protested and stated that I was not going to school today. My mother then asked me what really was the matter and why I didn't want to go to school. I replied, "The teachers are always giving me work to do. The kids are always making fun of me—and even the custodians give me a hard time." My mother said, "Michael, all that could be true, but the fact remains that you must get up and go to school today—after all, you are the principal."

This is a twist on an old joke; however, on many days, this is the life of a principal—the teachers making work for you, the kids making fun of you, and the custodians giving you a hard time. On these days you might wonder why you chose this career path. Is it really worth the time and effort? Is it worth the time away from your family? Is it worth the stress and turmoil that comes with the territory?

Naturally, numerous rewards greatly outweigh the negative aspects of the job of principal. The grateful students you helped to stay in school. The exhilarating feeling you get at a concert or athletic competition. The joy inherent in helping to shape the lives of the people who will carry the responsibility of the future of the world. We share an awesome responsibility that requires hard work, courage, and determination. It is a calling that we heed with great resolve. However, there will be an occasion when all of your experience will be put to the test during a time of crisis.

As I mentioned earlier, your behavior during and after a crisis will directly determine how students and staff react. You will be the person who brings order back from disorder; provides support to students and staff who are floundering; and maintains safety, structure, and control in an atmosphere of chaos.

PROFILE OF THE SCHOOL AND COMMUNITY

During the 1996–97 school year, Bayonne High School underwent four separate crises. To help you understand our situation, I first need to share some facts about our community and school. The community of Bayonne is a peninsula. Its land border is Jersey City and its water boundaries are the Newark Bay, Kill Van Kull, and New York Bay. In fact, you can see the majestic New York skyline from the east side of town, and you can ferry to the financial district in a matter of minutes. This proximity to the Big Apple affords residents a proliferation of cultural events, entertainment, and gastronomic delights; however, it also presents the community with a host of social, economic, and assimilation concerns.

Because of our location at the southernmost portion of Hudson County, the city of Bayonne is in the center of one of the nation's heaviest drug trafficking routes. Unfortunately, Hudson County was one of the first counties in the country to be designated as a High Intensity Drug Trafficking Area (HIDTA) by President Clinton. Achieving this national recognition was only the beginning of our problems. A natural outgrowth of drug use is the inevitable rise of HIV infection in the population. As a result, our only land border, Jersey City, was ranked second in the number of reported HIV cases by the Centers for Disease Control and Prevention in Atlanta. Only San Francisco reported a higher level of HIV infection in its population.

Naturally, the city of Bayonne is adversely affected by related criminal activities. For example, federal Drug Enforcement Agency intelligence sources indicated that Hudson County had evolved into a major warehouse and distribution center for cocaine on the East Coast. In fact, just recently, DEA agents seized more than 1,350 pounds of cocaine in a Jersey City warehouse. The coke was traced to Mexican drug syndicates.

In 1996, the violent crime index for Hudson County reflected numbers that were almost double the rate for the state. That meant that about one person per each 100 residents fell victim to a violent crime in our county. Again, much of this activity is related to drug trafficking. The number of out-of-town people arrested in the city of Bayonne for narcotics is not only staggering—it is growing.

Family tragedies due to the dreaded Acquired Immune Deficiency Syndrome and criminal activity in the city are two major concerns, but not our only concerns. We now must add poverty to the equation. The last census indicated that almost 10 percent of the Bayonne population exists below the poverty level. Also, about 20 percent of the heads-of-household were women. All indications and preliminary Census 2000 reports show these numbers soaring.

Virtually everyday, families new to the United States are moving into Bayonne. The country that once boasted its ability to serve as a melting pot is now more of a salad bowl. While once it was fashionable to become fully assimilated as quickly as possible into the fabric of U.S. society, now it is in vogue to maintain individuality and cultural diversity. In a community of 62,000, we

have more than fifty houses of worship and numerous social clubs representing a proliferation of cultures. As a result, Bayonne High School, like many
other large secondary schools in similar situations, continuously develops
new programs to respond to the needs of the children of these diverse families. It can be said that Bayonne High School draws its strength from its diversity.

In 1996, the New Jersey State Department of Education (NJDOE) selected
Bayonne High School as one of only two secondary schools in the state to be
designated as a Star School. This declaration is afforded only to schools that
are on the cutting edge of education with identifiable specializations leading
to high student achievement. Furthermore, these schools must also have
demonstrated a history of success. New Jersey is the most densely populated
state (1,000 people per square mile) and boasts more than 600 school districts
serving pre-K to Grade 12 students; therefore, the competition for the status
of Star School is intense.

The following year we were chosen to receive a Best Practice Award from
the NJDOE. Programs awarded this honor were recognized for innovative
strategies that promote high student achievement, address specific educational
needs of students, and yield documented results meeting set objectives.

In 1999, we completed the U.S. Department of Education Blue Ribbon
Schools Program Application. This program was established by the secretary
of education in 1982. It identifies and gives public recognition to outstanding
public and private schools. It also serves as a basis of self-assessment and
planning as well as providing a means of communication and sharing among
schools. Of the twenty-six secondary schools submitting applications in our
state that year, we were one that was chosen to move on to the national judg-
ing. While we were not selected on the national level, the process helped us
to grow as an institution.

Bayonne High School is an urban, four-year, comprehensive secondary
school with an enrollment exceeding 2,100 students from diverse ethnic and
socioeconomic backgrounds. It is the only public high school in the city and
the student population is racially mixed with immigrants from more than fifty
countries. During the past few years almost forty languages were spoken by
the students of the school, including Albanian, Amharic, Arabic, Bosnian,
Bulgarian, Cantonese, Creole/French, English, Farsi, Filipino, French, German, Greek, Gujarati, Hebrew, Hindi, Hungarian, Italian, Japanese, Kiswa-
heli, Korean, Mandarin, Persian, Polish, Punjabi, Russian, Serbo-Croatian,
Slovak, Spanish, Swahili, Tagalog, Tamil, Turkish, Twi, Urdu, and Vietnamese. This number is growing every day.

This is a school steeped in more than 100 years of tradition and customs;
one that has always espoused the values of a solid work ethic, good citizen-

ship, and a sense of morality that supports the community's way of life. The fact that 20 percent of our transfers come from other countries and that about 30 percent of our students come from homes where languages other than English are spoken has not swayed us from our mission.

"The mission of Bayonne High School is to provide students with quality educational programs, and a safe and supportive learning environment, enabling them to maximize their potential thereby becoming healthy, happy, productive, and fulfilled citizens." Students are encouraged to develop a sense of responsibility that enables them to be both self-disciplined and self-reliant. Evidently, we are meeting our objectives. Daily student attendance is about 91 percent and our graduates have attended Princeton, Harvard, Yale, Columbia, Cornell, Brown, Johns Hopkins, Massachusetts Institute of Technology, West Point, Annapolis, and many other prestigious schools throughout the United States.

The sprawling, three-story buildings that make up BHS were divided into houses during the 1970s. Clearly, with a large number of diverse students (at that time the enrollment was more than 3,700) a plan was needed to provide the students with the intimacy of a small school while still furnishing the advantages of a large institution.

The high school is divided into six heterogeneously grouped houses. Each house is under the direction of a vice principal, and students remain in the same homeroom all four years. In this manner the students have the same vice principal, guidance counselor, and homeroom teacher for their entire high school career. With this plan, homerooms accommodate students from all curriculum areas and diverse cultures.

During the first few years, we would receive calls from parents questioning why their child was in a vocational homeroom when the student's curriculum major was college preparatory. It seemed that no matter how much information we supplied to the community and parents, it was difficult to reverse seventy years of recollection of "how things were at the high school."

The Bayonne High School House Plan has developed a cohesiveness in managing a diverse population. It gives students the opportunity to exhibit positive, interpersonal skills and team building. Each homeroom is a true reflection of the community-at-large.

During the past two decades, exemplary programs and new facilities have been created on the 13-acre campus to vigorously take on the challenge of offering the most to the many. In 1986, we constructed an indoor National Hockey League (NHL) regulation ice rink on campus with a four-lane running track, two gymnasiums, a dance studio, locker rooms, meeting rooms, and offices. In addition to adding ten new learning stations for the high school, the edifice provides the community with facilities to meet their diverse needs. Students and community members are thrust together throughout the day and night, as well as weekends, strengthening our cultural awareness.

In addition, 38 percent of our students meet federal eligibility requirements to receive free or reduced-cost breakfast and lunch. In 1997, the American Drug and Alcohol Survey was administered to tenth-grade students at Bayonne High School. Results indicated that during the previous month, almost 30 percent of our students used drugs or had gotten drunk. Further interpretation of the survey data determined that 38 percent of Bayonne High School tenth-grade students were in the moderate- or high-risk categories for drug and alcohol abuse.

VIOLENCE IN THE SCHOOLS

We need only to review the "Indicators of School Crime and Safety, 1998," published by the National Center for Education Statistics and Bureau of Justice Statistics, to learn the horrible truth. According to the publication, students (twelve to eighteen years of age) fell victim to more than a quarter of a million serious violent crimes at school in 1996. Add to this the fact that 5 percent of seniors reported that they had been attacked with a weapon in school makes it easy to conceptualize the increase of violent behavior in our schools. Even more shocking is the report that there were more than 100 violent deaths at schools from 1992 to 1994.

The report went on to relate that 10 percent of all public schools reported at least one serious violent crime during the 1996–97 school year. These crimes included murder, rape, suicide, and physical attack with a weapon. Additionally, 47 percent of public schools reported other less serious violent crimes in their schools.

While the data suggest that elementary school students are less likely to fit these statistics, administrators at this level must still be ever-vigilant of safety issues relevant to this age group. Also, even though there were more crimes reported in urban than suburban communities, students in any school are in jeopardy.

Even your staff is at risk. The same report presented data regarding teacher victimization at school from 1992 to 1996. More than a 1.5 million crimes, including more than a half-million violent crimes, were reported during that time span. If we add all the reported crimes on or near school campuses, it equates to 16,000 incidents per school day, or one every six seconds.

Unfortunately, it appears that the trend of crisis in schools will continue. We just need to look back at the tragedies that occurred involving firearms at schools from February 1996 to May 1998. In fifteen months, a relatively short span of time, nineteen students, three teachers, and one principal were killed. An additional twenty-two students and two teachers were wounded. This spree began on 2 February 1996, in the state of Washington, when a fourteen-year-old boy walked into algebra class with a hunting rifle and killed two students and the teacher.

Major news coverage of Pearl, Mississippi, in October 1997, where nine students were shot, resulting in two deaths, gave way to West Paducah, Kentucky. Here, on December 1, a fourteen-year-old opened fire on his fellow students in a prayer circle at Heath High School—three students were killed and five were wounded, one girl was left paralyzed.

It appears that no region of the country is exempt from school violence. It also is apparent that not all violence occurs in urban schools and that there is no regard for race, color, creed, or economic status. On 19 May 1998, only three days before graduation, an honor student in Fayetteville, Tennessee, shot and killed a classmate who was dating his ex-girlfriend. Only three days later in Onalaska, Washington, a fifteen-year-old boy boarded a high school bus with a gun and ordered his girlfriend off the bus. He took her to his home, where he shot himself in the head and died while she looked on in horror.

On that same day at Thurston High School in Springfield, Oregon, two students were killed. In addition, twenty-two other students were injured during the rampage of the student gunman in the school's cafeteria. The shooter had been arrested the day before for having a gun at school. He was a fifteen-year-old freshman at Thurston High School who was released to his parents' custody after the arrest. About ninety minutes after the shooting, police found his parents shot to death at the family home. The child was found to have three guns in his possession on the day of the shooting frenzy.

Now we come to the gruesome, cold-blooded murders at Columbine High School in Littleton, Colorado. This was a massacre unseen in any school to date. A date that commemorated the birth of Adolph Hitler. A date that was selected by two members of the so-called Trench Coat Mafia. A date that will never be forgotten by the citizens of Littleton—April 20, 1999. The carnage of two students left fifteen people dead. This count included one teacher and the two shooters. One girl was killed because she professed her belief in God. One boy became a victim as he held the exit door open for fleeing students. Another became a casualty because he was black and an athlete. The teacher was shot twice in the chest while directing students to safety.

In all, almost forty people were wounded in the attack. Of that number only seven were treated and released right away. The conditions of the others ranged from critical to good. Of course, I am speaking of the physical conditions of the victims. No one will ever really know the devastating emotional toll that will follow the students, staff, and their families.

Since the 1992–93 school year, there have been 251 school-associated deaths according to the National School Safety Center's *Report on School Associated Violent Deaths*.

Certainly not as tragic, but still disturbing, is the lack of training for administrators and teachers in crisis management. It is a topic that was lacking in my formal undergraduate work. Actually, it was never even mentioned during my graduate work in educational administration and supervision. To be fair, at the time that I was completing work on my degrees (mid-1970s), school crisis was not a hot topic. In fact, the number of violent incidents occurring in schools was not considered huge compared with the community-at-large. Fortunately, I received training in grief counseling while working on my student personnel services certification. Nevertheless, this too, was not nearly enough to prepare me for the realities of crisis after crisis in the school.

However, it has become apparent that as society became more violent, a spillover effect occurred in the schools. What was once the only safe haven in the community, became a place where children and staff became weary of violence and crime.

As a result, the phenomenon of crisis management for schools began to emerge throughout the country. School administrators initiated a review of literature on youth suicide, natural disasters, child violence, hostage situations, and myriad other topics, trying to gain insights for responding to crises. Clues were available in publications from various sources, but there was no definitive source to serve as a handbook for administrators. Given the fact that there are so many variables and types of crises, it is unlikely that one source could ever claim to possess all the answers.

After a quick glance at the references listed in this book, you should notice that great strides have been made in the past few years regarding crisis management. There are many publications covering preparation, coping, and recovery after a crisis. Some districts require training in the area of suicide warning recognition. Others are establishing crisis management teams or disaster recovery teams. Yet, the vast majority of schools have no formal plan to deal with what would appear to be the most common of dilemmas such as sudden death response, evacuation plans, and hostage situations.

Step-by-step guidelines need to be set into policy for school personnel to use when necessary. These policies will guide the school community through tragedies. Sometimes a simple plan needs to be committed to paper that explains the procedures to follow when a faculty member or student dies. Then, as the need arises, there are no mistakes as to procedure. Further, a written policy would ensure that there is uniformity for another occurrence. It also provides a safety buffer for the administrator when faculty members or students begin to demand special or extra accommodations for a particularly popular student or teacher.

Yet, policies are not enough to provide proper crisis management. Many times, once the policy is committed to paper, it is put into a binder and never shared with appropriate personnel. Imperative to proper response is the training of the Crisis Management Team. After the training, the team should meet at least once a year to review policies, procedures, and to update the crisis phone tree.

The entire school community is profoundly affected by the sudden death of a student or faculty member. If the death is violent, additional trauma is felt. Other events are so shocking that their impact on the school routine is inevitable. For example, at the beginning of the 1998–99 school year, a young Bayonne mother took the lives of both of her elementary-school-age children. The incident took place early in the morning at the family's modest apartment. The shocking reports of the knifing not only shook the community, it had a disastrous effect on the normally calm elementary-school population.

Immediately, the districtwide Crisis Management Team sprang into action. Counselors were sent to the school and information was given to families regarding additional services provided by community agencies. Routine structure was maintained at the school and support was delivered to the students and staff. Appropriate programs were instituted to recognize the lives and memories of the slain classmates. Workshops on death and dying were established for the staff and made available to students and families.

Because the community often looks to the school for guidance, proper response is necessary in these situations. Without proper crisis planning, the educational mission of the school can be seriously damaged. Some students can be placed at risk if the trauma is not handled properly. An outgrowth of proper crisis management is appropriate action following the tragedy. Many will find that the school community will actually strengthen as a result of working as a team through the crisis. Teachers, students, and parents will view administrators in a different light. Often administrators will learn of hidden skills possessed by certain staff members that can be tapped in the future.

The crises in our schools are ongoing. The need for safe schools and mechanisms to deal with tragedies at schools is paramount. As a society, we need to address these most pressing concerns. Our youth, like our adults, are more frequently using knives, guns, and other weapons instead of reason or even fists to settle disputes. However, keep in mind that the most common types of violence at schools are still fist fights, bullying, and shoving matches. The media sensationalize the random acts of violence, portraying our schools as unsafe, when in fact, schools are generally among the safest places for a child.

Historically, the school administration followed the law doctrine of in loco parentis. Basically, this meant that school officials had the right and responsibility to act in the place of a parent. Then in 1968, this doctrine began crumbling when *Tinker v. Des Moines Independent School District* found that constitutional rights are not shed at the schoolhouse gate.

During the late 1970s and early 1980s, concerns regarding Fourth Amendment protection for students came to the forefront. Student protection against unreasonable searches and seizures by school officials emerged as an issue. Then in 1985, *New Jersey v. T.L.O.* determined that the vice principal who conducted a locker search was more akin to a government agent rather than to a parental surrogate. This meant that the "reasonable suspicion" standard was now definitively asserted. School officials could, in fact, lawfully search students and lockers upon meeting its two-pronged test: the search must be (1) reasonable in inception and (2) reasonable in scope.

The legal battles continue to this day. During the 1990s, cases regarding student rights resulted in many decisions on search and seizure. Cases ranging from a search of a student's car in the school parking lot, to the use of drug-sniffing dogs and metal detectors in schools were decided. It appears that everyday the job of protecting the rights of individuals while maintaining the safety for all will be a delicate balancing act for the school administrator.

Gone are the years of the principal acting as the sole authority and being able to focus exclusively on educational matters. Today we are expected to be all things to all people. The schools have become social agencies responsible for the care and welfare of their students from morning until night. The pace of the job may seem overwhelming and many times you will serve as a judge, nurse, psychologist, counselor, or social worker. The fact will always remain that you and you alone will determine how the staff and students will react to crisis. Your example will demonstrate to all that safety, support structure, stability, and control are the orders of the day—each and every day—crisis or no crisis.

Chapter 2

The Tragedies That Befell Our School in One Year

The summer, for me, is a demanding time of year, but one that I enjoy thoroughly. For fifteen years, I was responsible for building the master schedule and ensuring that every student received a schedule by mid-August. This ensured that corrections could be made before school began, thus providing a smooth opening. During the past few years I had been training a new student personnel services director in the nuances of scheduling. I also had the services of a vice principal to assist with the procedures. This particular person had worked with our scheduling matrix for a number of years and was invaluable to the process. Therefore, due to the keen acumen of these administrators, I was able to devote more time to the other summer duties of a principal.

It has always amazed me that people who are not educators think that you are on vacation for two months in the summer. They believe that the school will open miraculously in September all by itself. Regardless, we were all working hard to prepare every aspect of our school community for the upcoming year. By all indications, the 1996–97 school year should have been like any other.

SUICIDE FROM THE BRIDGE

On Friday evening, 9 August 1996, at about 11:30 P.M., I received a call from a friend on the police force. He informed me that a teenage girl had jumped from the Bayonne Bridge and was feared dead. She had plunged 158 feet into the Arthur Kill Van Kull waterway. He identified her as a student of Bayonne High School.

By all indications this youngster was a normal teenager. She was an academic student entering her second year of high school with plans to attend college. She had friends at the school and a twelve-year-old sister in a neighborhood elementary school. The family unit was traditional, with both parents working.

At this point I should note that the Bayonne Bridge is the longest single-span bridge in North America. It is the second longest in the world. Only its sister bridge in Sydney, Australia, is longer—by a mere foot. I mention this because over the years the bridge has claimed many lives. It appears that it bears the same morbid attraction as does the Golden Gate Bridge in San Francisco.

The investigation revealed that seven high school students, including this girl, were with four elementary students during the day and into the evening of the tragedy. To this date, it is unclear if she fully intended to jump or was merely threatening to jump and then fell to her death. The police had been summoned to the area, but due to the design and configuration of the bridge's walkway versus the roadway, they were unable to reach the students in time to prevent the tragedy.

The next day, members from our Student Center reached out to the students involved. (The Student Center is located in the high school. It is on the ground level and comprises six offices and a large area for group work. Assigned to the center are a school psychologist, social worker, substance-abuse coordinator, guidance counselor, housing urban development coordinator, and secretary.) Fortunately, all the students involved availed themselves of this service.

An outgrowth of those counseling sessions resulted in one high school student being referred to a hospital for a psychiatric evaluation. Indications were that she, too, was exhibiting suicidal tendencies. She was placed at an in-patient facility for evaluation. Upon her release, the Student Center personnel kept in close contact with her to provide additional counseling if necessary.

The period immediately following the incident was extremely difficult for everyone. The media played the story for days. Monday's story was on the front page. The headline read "Bayonne girl jumps off bridge, rescuers continue search for body." The story incorrectly reported that the girl jumped on her fourteenth birthday. Actually, it was her sister who had just celebrated her birthday.

"Leap from bridge ends a life at 14, Bayonne girl's dad hopes body is found," was the headline for Tuesday's story. Even though the newspaper ran this story, the authorities still had not made public the girl's identity. The interview of the father revealed the heartbreak of the family. "She was a good kid . . . your basic teenager," stated the father. He also added that she was distraught over a boy.

On Wednesday, the headline was, "Boaters asked to help find girl's body." The family pleaded for boaters to help them locate their loved one so they could provide a proper burial. The paper also reported the distance of the plunge and the efforts of the New York Police Department Harbor Unit and its divers.

"Teen's body found near shore," was the lead story in Thursday's paper. "Bayonne parkgoer's discovery ends search," was the subhead for the story describing how a local man found the girl's body. The Hudson County first assistant prosecutor released her name for the first time after a positive identification by a family member. The paper related how the resident spotted the body floating face-up near the shoreline. The reporter chose to disclose every morbid detail about how she was clothed, even pointing out that one sneaker was missing.

The various articles and stories had no regard for the feelings of the family and students involved. The five days it took for the rescue teams to locate the body compounded matters. Also, until the body was recovered, there could be no formal services to provide closure for all the people involved.

Then on Tuesday, 20 August 1996, (nearly two weeks after the tragedy) we were hit with another headline. "Massive injuries from jump killed girl," was the headline, with "Results of toxicological testing still due; grieving BHS students to get counseling," as the subhead. Again, the reporter repeated all the gruesome details, but he did note that authorities said that there were no signs of alcohol or drugs. However, he went on to mention they were still awaiting the toxicological results. The story told of the bouquet of red roses and carnations with a yellow and pink ribbon tied to the guardrail on the bridge. At the end of the article, I was mentioned. I chose to inform the community of the preparations we were making for the beginning of school as it related to this tragedy. Items such as the written statement for homeroom teachers regarding the incident and the availability of counselors for the students were included.

Back at school, in preparation for teacher convocation, we compiled a package of information. Included was the script to be read to students during homeroom and a packet that contained information about suicide crisis and guidelines on how to determine if students are in need of counseling. Teachers were reminded that normal adolescent stresses should not result in suicide. They were also advised that grieving students could experience a wide range of emotions.

Not knowing what to expect, we also contacted the University of Medicine and Dentistry of New Jersey (UMDNJ) which provided us with a resource person for managing violent student death. This person suggested that the teachers refer to their packets when it appeared that certain students were in need of counseling. This was imperative as the contagion factor is always a major risk after a young person's suicide. Also, remember that several students actually witnessed the tragic event. These children needed a close watch and specialized counseling.

In 1985, the New Jersey State Legislative Body mandated that programs with curriculum on adolescent suicide be developed. The initial design was cosponsored by the State Department of Education, the Division of Mental Health and Hospitals, and the State Department of Human Services.

During this time, the multiple suicides in a northern New Jersey community prompted international attention on the state and its response plan for addressing the contagion factor. As a result, the early goals of the state prevention project revolved around postvention techniques to assist schools and communities in the aftermath of youth suicide. The response model developed in New Jersey was used as the basis for recommendations later disseminated by the Centers for Disease Control and Prevention.

Additionally, a program evaluation by a team from Columbia University College of Physicians and Surgeons, determined that most students were well informed about suicide. This suggested that students who held healthy attitudes about life in general did not include suicide as a solution to life problems.

The state provided many workshops, seminars, and training sessions to hundreds of communities to share data about current facts and research on youth suicide. Included was information on how to identify and refer, as well as what to do during the aftermath. This advice covered all grades—kindergarten through high school. A result of the project was the training manual, "Managing Sudden Violent Loss in the Schools." This guidebook is an excellent reference and I highly recommend it. It was authored by Maureen M. Underwood, LCSW, and Karen Dunne-Maxim, MS, RN. Due to the tragedies at our school and my work throughout the country presenting my workshop, "Creating Safe and Supportive Schools—Crisis Prevention and Response," I have had the pleasure of witnessing firsthand the results of the fine work of these two remarkable ladies.

The students in Bayonne, who were witnesses to the tragedy from the Bayonne Bridge, needed specialized counseling due to the firsthand trauma encountered. Some experienced what is referred to as "survivor syndrome" which required other counseling modalities.

These students had stressors that are not within the range of normal happenings. Witnesses to suicide encounter symptoms outside the range of common experiences of simple bereavement. They experience guilt feelings that can take the form of "survival guilt." The students begin to ask themselves questions that produce self-blame, allowing them to believe they might have prevented the suicide.

Whenever someone witnesses that which could be considered a violent death, there are many complications in recovery. The psychological trauma can be overwhelming. Naturally, there is the impact of the suddenness of the death—the unexpected. Any death causes a loss to be felt; however, with a sudden death, there is no time for survivors to prepare. As a result, the grief and shock can be overwhelming.

When someone is suffering from a terminal disease, and is very sick for a long period of time, family and friends have time to adjust to the inevitable. In fact, if the illness is debilitating, and the person is in pain, sometimes the death is seen as a natural termination of the suffering. Anguish of the ill and heartache of the family and friends is commonplace when dealing with catastrophic illness.

Those suffering from the terminal illness must live with the awareness of the impending death. In 1969, Elisabeth Kubler-Ross proposed a sequence of stages for the terminally ill. The five stages that the patients pass through were developed from her interviews with dying patients. Denial is the first stage, followed by anger, resentment, then bargaining for more time, depression, and, finally, acceptance.

It is extremely difficult to watch helplessly as a loved one undergoes pain, suffering, and the occasional dehumanization of a protracted illness. However, there is time to prepare for the phases of grief that follow the loved one's passing.

The students who witnessed the death of their friend, were faced not only with the suddenness of the death, but with a willful disrespect for life and perhaps the guilt associated with enabling the victim. These poor children did not have the chance to say good-bye to their friend. The last memory of their companion is that of her body plummeting to its watery grave. It is not uncommon for students in this type of situation to feel powerless, guilty, and angry. They have great difficulty understanding and accepting the event. Many could experience anxiety, sleep disorders, and somatic complaints.

The natural response to this type of loss is grief. When grieving, there is a feeling of deep sorrow. However, children and adults do not grieve in the same manner. Grief can be psychologically debilitating to both groups. The role of school personnel is to ensure healthy grief resolution. In this manner, the loss will be placed in perspective without permanent damage to the individual who is grieving.

Grief is the intense emotional suffering usually caused by loss. The first stage is protest and yearning. This involves a protest over the loss of the loved one and a need or urge to recover that person. The next stage is referred to as disorganization and despair. Here, the loss is accepted and people abandon efforts to recover the loved one. The last stage of grief is detachment and reorganization, the final emotional separation from the loved one.

It is imperative that educators help the grieving students in a manner that allows for their growth, without interrupting the normal educational program. Remember, in the case of suicide, the loss is unexpected—therefore, helping students becomes especially complex. When mourning the loss of a class-mate, students are especially susceptible to advice given by authority figures or people they have come to trust. Well-intentioned, but poor, advice on how to cope, can be devastating to the healing process. Therefore, it is imperative that the faculty be fully trained in proper grief counseling.

One of the most important concepts to remember is that there will normally be two types of grief to counsel on the student level. For example, the reaction by an individual to a peer's sudden death requires different techniques than the needs of the group. The school climate will be affected as the news of the death permeates the student body. Individuals in need should be sent to appropriate school personnel instructed in counseling. After a short instructor-training period, collective grief activities can be led by the classroom teacher.

Often, after a student death, a spontaneous show of solidarity among various factions occurs. This will result in a reduction of student conflicts and more cooperation among the student body. This is an excellent time for the faculty to open the channels of communication. Care should be taken when developing a group grieving activity especially in the case of suicide. We cannot glamorize or romanticize the violence of the act. Furthermore, not all students will feel a great loss. This is especially true in a large school. Expect that some students will share morbid jokes about the death. These comments allow these students to demonstrate to their peers that they are strong and unaffected by the loss.

The faculty needs to strongly deter these types of morbid joviality. Remember, the students who are deeply grieving will be hurt by these cruel acts and disrespectful comments. Teachers should explain that not everyone is affected in the same manner, however, everyone has a responsibility to respect the grief of others.

As a rule, teachers should be careful not to tell students to think of other things and that by not thinking about it, time will take care of the hurt. If we tell students not to dwell on the loss, we are actually telling them to ignore their feelings. Resolution cannot follow if the child does not move through the grieving process. Also, we are subtly telling them that their feelings are somehow wrong. The result can be confusion about their true feelings.

It is the responsibility of the school to respond to the sudden death of a student. Regardless of the type of death, whether it be an auto accident, suicide, murder, or disease, certain procedures should be followed. Underwood and Dunne-Maxim refer to an approach to resolution of the crisis situation using the principles of crisis intervention theory. They suggest the provisions of Support, Control, and Structure to stabilize a situation until it can return to its precrisis state. It is paramount to maintain what I like to refer to as the S^4C

Stabilization Plan (appendix A). This means that the school needs to ensure that safety, support, structure, stability, and control are maintained.

When dealing with a suicide it is imperative to remember that teenage suicide is not the result of normal adolescent stresses. Rather, it is a compilation of many factors in the life of the child. Therefore, it is crucial not to encourage speculation as to what might have caused the child to commit suicide.

The students and staff will be experiencing a wide range of emotions. As individuals, each imprinted with a unique gamut of life experiences, they may respond differently. Remember, there is no right or wrong way to feel. However, discussions about feelings would be appropriate as one way to express grief. It is also a good idea to establish an area where students can have the opportunity to express their feelings. These areas should have a counselor and crisis team member present. Finally, make sure to meet the needs of any siblings. Remember to check the district roster to determine if siblings are in attendance at another school in the district.

The building administrator needs to verify the suicide with the police. He or she also needs to notify the superintendent and mobilize the Crisis Management Team. Once the team is in motion, a written statement needs to be composed for release to the staff and student body. Be careful to respect the wishes of the family regarding what information is to be released. Information about the death also needs to be committed to paper and sent to anyone who answers phones. This data should not have too much detail, but it must be accurate. Contact the local mental health agency to arrange for outside counseling. You can then share this information with the students, staff, and parent organization. Remember to contact the parents to offer condolences and ask if anything is needed.

SUDDEN DEATH OF A FACULTY MEMBER

That November, just before the annual long weekend break for the statewide teachers' convention, a senior faculty member told a colleague that he was not feeling well. He complained of discomfort in his chest. The following Monday, his wife called the attendance tape stating that her husband suffered a heart attack and was in Beth Israel Hospital.

While hospitalized, his blood pressure went out of control. The medical team decided to insert a stent rather than risk bypass surgery. This decision was reached based on his history of hypertension, which, at the time, was erratic and not responding to traditional medical intervention. The following Friday he was sent home to recover. The next morning when his wife went to wake him up, she got no response. The stent had collapsed during the night and he had passed away. This was a thirty-year veteran of the school, a teacher who was well-liked by students and staff.

To compound this crisis, his two daughters were recent alumni of the school. As a result, there were some students who knew or were friendly with the younger daughter. Once they were identified, we quickly placed these students in a different counseling cluster than the general population. The teacher's current students were also placed in a more intense counseling group.

As with the student suicide, none of us had the time to prepare for this tragedy. However, here at least, the death was not out of sequence. The father of our former students was the one to die, not one of his daughters. As devastating as this sudden loss was, it is even more severe when the death of a loved one comes before its expected time on the social clock.

Other stages for coping with sudden death such as disbelief, protest, depression, and recovery have been suggested by different experts. However, critics question the generality of all stages. They stress the uniqueness of the individual and their life experiences. For example, older people can view death with less resentment and fear than the young.

When a faculty member passes away, I order the flag to half-mast on the day of the funeral. I also assemble an honor guard wherever the funeral services are held. Basically, this consists of the staff members lining up on both sides of the entranceway to the place of worship. We remain there until the casket and family members enter. We then reassemble at the conclusion of the services. In this manner, the casket and family exit through the lines of honor. It is important to note that I first meet with the family to explain my procedures and ask permission to assemble the honor guard. If approval is granted, I then meet with the funeral director to explain the procedures so everyone is aware of them, thereby, assuring the smooth implementation of the assemblage. This is imperative because it would be an injustice to have a gesture of honor and respect turn into an awkward event that would only add to the family's bereavement.

It is a good idea to place a counselor in the classes once taught by the deceased. This person can talk to the students in general terms and then make referrals for the students who are in need. As soon as possible, either through a written memo or by a staff meeting, inform the faculty about the incident. This will assure that everyone has the same accurate information that cannot be distorted.

If some staff members are particularly close to the deceased, it is unreasonable for the building administrator to expect these people to assist with the emotional problems of students. They need to have their own emotional needs met first. Provisions for separate counseling should be made to assist these teachers.

The building administrator needs to be cognizant of the wants of the various groups affected. There will be general needs for the masses and specific needs for individuals close to the deceased. Remember that there will be some individuals who, seemingly, will be unaffected.

Normally, there are numerous requests for staff and students to attend the funeral services. This is a difficult and often awkward situation for the school administrator. You need to determine who and how many people will be excused to attend the funeral. Some options for the staff could be by seniority or members of the same department. Students should be permitted to attend only upon bringing a letter from home seeking permission.

A school representative who was close with the family should be chosen to make contact with the family of the deceased to make arrangements to return personal possessions. This should not be done early in the grieving process. Rather, contents from the desk should be packed and stored to ensure they are intact and whole. Later, the representative can bring up the subject of which personal possessions the family might want returned.

The building administrator should make a visit to the funeral parlor to offer condolences to the family. On a personal note, I offer to send food to the home and I make a contribution to our local chapter of Cancer Care in memory of the deceased. As mentioned above, I also attend the funeral services and assume the responsibility of setting up the honor guard.

HOMICIDE IN THE SCHOOL

Wednesday, 5 March 1997, began as any other day at Bayonne High School. Students were busy gathering books from their lockers and discussing the events of the past night as well as plans for the upcoming day. Some teachers were beginning to welcome students into homerooms, others were providing tutoring, and still others were preparing for the day's lessons. I had just finished greeting students by the main entrance and went into my office for the morning announcements. Yes, all indications were that a smooth opening for the school day was at hand—and then it happened!

At about 8:40 A.M. I received a call from the House Four office that a student had been stabbed. One of the nurses was on the scene and we called 911 to dispatch EMTs and police. As I made my way over the bridge that connects the buildings to the corridor where the incident took place, many thoughts ran through my mind. The health and well-being of the stricken student were of paramount concern.

When I arrived on the scene, I saw students and staff gathered around the fallen child. They were watching the nurse and head football coach taking turns administering CPR and mouth-to-mouth resuscitation, and applying pressure to the wound. With the help of teachers assigned to homeroom hall duty and one of the vice principals, I immediately cleared and secured the area.

I checked on the status of the ambulance via my walkie-talkie and sent for the school engineer to secure the elevator in this building for the paramedics. I then called for a vice principal to stand by the outside entrance to the elevator to direct the EMTs to our area.

We had determined that the student was Aubrey Taylor, a junior. Both the nurse and coach had looks of despair as they worked feverishly on Aubrey while waiting for the ambulance to arrive.

The seconds seemed to pass like minutes, and I began to wonder why the EMTs were not yet on the scene. I radioed the office to check on the estimated time of arrival for the ambulance and was told that they had already picked up a stabbing victim from the school. They informed me that a wounded student had made his way to the Juvenile Aid Bureau (JAB) on the first floor. From there, the JAB officers got the student to the EMTs and he was transported to the hospital. I explained that we were still with a victim on the second floor and needed assistance. We realized a double stabbing had occurred.

As this information was transmitted to me, we were becoming more concerned for Aubrey's well-being. The nurse and coach worked as hard as possible to stop the bleeding and keep him conscious. When the paramedics arrived and took over, I began to brief the police as to what occurred according to my reports. Next, I called the main office and instructed that a general announcement would be made to extend homeroom. This gave us an additional ten minutes to decide what we should do next.

The police contacted the Hudson County prosecutor's office to provide resources and personnel to aid with the investigation. Both police agencies wanted the area cordoned off for an undetermined period of time to conduct their investigation. I contacted my office and had an announcement made that we would be following an assembly schedule. This ensured that students and staff would remain in their homerooms for about thirty-five minutes. By preventing student movement, I was able maintain the crime scene and prevent the majority of students and staff from learning what had happened. This would allow me to give accurate information to everyone at the same time.

We notified the parents of both students and had them go directly to the hospital. I conferred with the investigators on the scene and directed them to potential witnesses. The Student Center is in close proximity to the incident; therefore, we deemed it as the area to be used for the police investigation. This area also doubled as the location to counsel those witnesses who had been traumatized. The center has six counseling offices and a large group area, and is located directly across the hall from the JAB office. Therefore, it was perfect for this emergency use.

As I continued to coordinate the activities of the police with our school personnel, my thoughts kept returning to the injured students and their well-being. Repeatedly, I wondered why this was happening in our school. Shortly thereafter, I received word that the first student taken to the hospital would recover, but that Aubrey had died on the operating table.

I pulled additional staff to further secure the area and went to meet with the superintendent and central office staff. Present at this meeting were the superintendent, school business administrator, and director of student personnel services. We reviewed the option of dismissing school early. All research indicated we should maintain the structure or routine of the school day. Therefore, we all agreed that school should remain open for the entire day for many reasons. First, no one knew who or where the perpetrator was at the time. Dismissing students could place them in danger. Also, the police needed time to investigate the crime scene without 2,100 students milling about the area. Finally, we had the appropriate counseling staff on campus to deal with students who were traumatized by the incident.

A teacher advised us that Aubrey had a sister at the school. She was immediately brought to the Student Center. Once there, the counselors informed her that Aubrey had been stabbed and that he was sent to the hospital where his parents would meet him. She remained with the counselor until an officer from the JAB office transported her to the hospital.

At that point I decided it was necessary to provide the students and staff with pertinent information and set a schedule for the day. Unfortunately, some residents of the city already knew of the tragedy due to the 911 calls and the "grapevine" of Bayonne. This prompted a number of calls to the school seeking information. Therefore, the secretaries and vice principals needed information immediately in order to respond accurately.

The students and staff did not have information and it was necessary to provide them with direction. Therefore, I made a general announcement over the public address system explaining that we had an incident in the school that resulted in two of our students being attacked by an intruder so everyone was to remain in homeroom until further notice.

This gave us the time to create a script that would be read by homeroom teachers in every class explaining what we knew at that point and outlining the procedures for the bell schedule. The statement reads as follows:

> Unfortunately, we have had a grave incident occur at the high school. At this time it appears that a nonstudent from another city entered our building and assaulted two of our students with a weapon. Regrettably, one of the students was fatally injured. Our heartfelt sympathies go out to the family and friends.

Any students who would like to speak to a counselor can obtain a pass from their teacher throughout the school day. All counselors will be in the high school library for the remainder of the day and after dismissal to meet with students.

The police have asked us to have all students remain in their current classrooms. Therefore, you will remain in homeroom during Period 3 and we will resume a normal assembly schedule during Period 4 (11:17 A.M.).

During this same time span, we established a counseling area in the school's library. This facility was staffed by all Child Study Team members from the district and the high school counselors. It was decided to leave the Student Center personnel at their original location. That team comprised a school psychologist, two counselors, and a HUD coordinator.

To assist with the investigation, I met with the police to see what they required. The officers wanted the corridor blocked off and all movement diverted from the lockers. Therefore, I assigned additional teachers and custodians to assist the vice principal in the area, and we then secured the ends of the hall with barricades. The teachers were reassigned from other hall duties and selected custodians were instructed to forgo cleaning duties. Naturally, we had to make accommodations for students who could not get their books or jackets.

As word leaked out to the press, we were barraged with reporters, camera operators, and various trucks to transmit live hook-ups. Every station in the area was trying to get into the school for an interview. Fortunately, we were able to enlist police support to keep these people across the street from the school. However, they were still clamoring for exclusives with everyone and anyone. To control the media, rather than have our actions be little more than reactions to their requests, I sent word via a staff member that I would conduct a press conference at noon in the auditorium. Since it was decided during our central office meeting that I would be the spokesperson for the district, I gave instructions that no one was to speak with the press.

At this point we began to develop plans for the next few days. This included making calls to outside agencies for additional police visibility in and around the school, writing a script that would be read in each homeroom the following day, and planning to have a meeting immediately after school to debrief all staff members.

The police were a great asset in keeping the reporters off school grounds; they stood on the sidewalk using the school as a backdrop as they spoke. During this time I met with the vice principals and director of student personnel services to coordinate the plans for the remainder of the day and the counseling services.

A number of parents who heard of the incident via television and the rumor mill called the school for information. They wanted to know if their children were safe, if school was being dismissed, and in general, what was happening. Many wanted their children released. It was decided that any parent calling to have child released would be required to physically come in to sign the student out of school. Everyone was advised to encourage parents to leave their children in school, where we had a police presence and counselors to deal with emotions. Many of the parents who called agreed to keep their children at school once they learned of their safety and our plans for the day. However, 171 students were picked up by parents on that day—about 8 percent of the student body.

Students who were being counseled in the library were removed by their parents when necessary. Calls were initiated by the counselor to the home requesting pickups. This was done after the counselor completed as much counseling as deemed necessary, and to prevent further contagion. By contagion, I am referring to the spread of hysteria from one student to another.

Before noon, we assembled in the auditorium to prepare for the news conference. I was flanked by the superintendent, director of public safety, school board president, and the mayor. As I approached the podium the questions began to fly. Reporter after reporter shot questions with machine-gun action. I spoke slowly, thinking before answering, being careful to be truthful and accurate while protecting the feelings of the stricken families. There were about fifty media personnel in the auditorium with video equipment, still cameras, tape recorders, pad and pencil. Although I had no prepared script, I was able to inform the public that we had counselors on campus to help students deal with the tragedy.

Questions regarding how everyone felt at the school began the session. I explained that, "Everyone is extremely upset. It is a terrible tragedy. One of my students is gone. It's a terrible occurrence and we are all devastated."

One of the reporters asked if security is lax at the school. I responded, "Our security measures we have found to be quite successful and our history proves that to be so." The follow-up question was, "Are you considering security cameras?" My response was, "At this point we are going to consider all options. We certainly want to avert any tragedy."

Reporters then asked about metal detectors. I stated,

> This is a school of over 2,000 students. We have had a terrific safety record and our students have always been safe and secure here. But I don't think there is any way anyone can prevent a tragedy such as this. One perpetrator—things can happen like this—you cannot safeguard against it. Our hearts go out to the family and the friends of the people involved. This is a terrible tragedy to happen at our school and we are working hard to help those people. We have forty exits and entrances, however, we have an excellent security record. We have a Juvenile Aid Bureau located on campus. We work very closely with them. We have a uniformed police officer right outside the building.

Again reporters referred to the issue of metal detectors at the doors. I responded, "Our safety procedures have been quite effective. If you look at our annual report that must be filed with the state, we have a very low incident of any sort of violence or vandalism."

To this day I am amazed at the media's focus on metal detectors. When the tragedies occurred in Mississippi and other southern states, there was no outcry for metal detectors. It seems that in the north, specifically in metropolitan areas, guns are viewed only as weapons. While in the South and in rural areas, people view firearms as items for sports and hunting.

The remainder of the day was very somber. Of the remaining students, about 10 percent took advantage of the onsite counseling services. At dismissal, we had a police presence around the campus as a way of increasing security and helping with the proliferation of reporters who were trying to get interviews.

After dismissal, I met with the high school administrative team to critique the day and make plans for the next day. I again met with the superintendent and central office personnel as well as the board of education president. Everyone agreed to keep the school day as close to normal as possible. We also had additional counselors assigned to the high school for the remainder of the week. In addition, I received numerous calls from neighboring school districts offering counselors and assistance. However, since members of the local mental health office were already on board, it was decided that we had enough personnel. We also decided to send a platter of food to the Taylor home.

That evening, as I reflected on the day's events, I knew difficult times were still ahead. First, we still did not know who was responsible for the homicide. Reports were still sketchy. Was it a nonstudent, an out-of-town person, or a BHS student? Naturally, safety was of primary concern, however, one could not help drifting back to the anguish of the day.

Later that night I typed out procedures for the vice principals to follow for the upcoming day. This way each would have the "marching orders" in writing for easy referral. The instructions included the entrances that were to be used and those that would be restricted. Everyone was instructed to be as visible as possible and refer students to the appropriate counselors as necessary. Additionally, I composed some thoughts to be incorporated into the script being developed by the director of student personnel services. This prepared statement was to be read by all homeroom teachers to the students first thing in the morning.

As you know, Aubrey Taylor became the victim of a homicide. We are deeply saddened by this great loss. In addition, another student was critically wounded during yesterday's attack. We are hopeful that he will fully recover within a short period of time.

Any students who would like to speak to a counselor should report to their re-
. spective vice principal's office after homeroom.

At this time, we are requesting that all students join in a moment of silence to
honor the memory and life of Aubrey Taylor.

I also made signs for entry the next morning. It was decided that we would
lock down all entrances but three. This meant that thirty-seven entrances
would be closed. In addition to the notices, I needed a plan to ensure that all
locked doors would remain closed and locked.

Upon completing the plans and printing the signs, I turned to the 11 o'clock
news reports. We were the lead story on all the major networks. It was terrible to see, however, I needed to watch to help prepare for the news barrage
that was expected the next day.

Interestingly, some reporters did not seem to care if the information they
were reporting was accurate. They referred to an incident of fog lights stolen
from a car by kids from Hoboken, New Jersey, as the reason for the attack.
These reports were false. In fact, I had to implore a local reporter to print a
story regarding the accuracy of the television reports. My fear was for the students involved in the Hoboken incident and possible retribution by friends of
the stricken students.

Another report on television quoted a family spokesman, who stated,
"They were approached by the young men who were waiting for Akim Gar-
land, neither of the boys from Jersey City were students at Bayonne High
School. John and Jeanne (Taylor, parents of the slain boy) strongly feel this
terrible tragedy could have been avoided if there had been adequate security
at the high school."

As it turned out, there was only one perpetrator. He was a former Bayonne
High School student and current Bayonne Adult Night School student resid-
ing in Bayonne.

Day Two—6 March 1997

After a difficult night's sleep, I arrived at school about 6 A.M. Reporters were
already camped out in front of the buildings. However, the police chief had
assigned about twenty officers to perimeter duty. As I made my way past the
reporters who were clamoring for an interview, I explained that I would supply them with a statement later in the day. Once in my office, I began putting
into place the plan for the day. I gave the signs that I had made indicating entrances and nonentrances to the head custodian for posting. These signs were
posted on all doors except the three decided to be used for student entrance.
"Not a Student Entrance," and directions to the open entrances were listed on
all doors. Staff entered through these doors plus the north center main and

west side annex doors, which were staffed by custodians. I also issued orders to place all doors on panic lock and to post custodians near entrances to close any doors that were not closing properly or were being jammed opened.

The superintendent had assigned three attendance officers to me so that we could cover the three stations designated for entry. Therefore, entrance could be gained only through the center door of the main building and the center door of the annex as well as the north center door on the Thirtieth Street side of the school. Additionally, I assigned a vice principal to these areas to facilitate the institution of the new procedures. Entry ran smoothly, the signs indicated where to go and how to be admitted. However, the press was also on hand filming students and trying to get interviews.

The script that was written the previous day was distributed to all homeroom teachers to be read during homeroom. We ran a regular schedule for the day making an announcement regarding the availability of counselors who were stationed in three areas of the school. Considering the previous day's debriefing, we decided to use the library, guidance suites, and the Student Center as the designated counseling areas. Students in Houses One, Two, and Three were channeled to the library. Students in Houses Four and Five could avail themselves to the guidance suites. The Student Center remained a special area for witness and survivor counseling. Family members and friends within the close circle were also sent to this station.

We had additional personnel from the Mobile Crisis Unit, one of the programs offered by the Jersey City Medical Center for Hudson County. This program uses an ambulance and staff to go to the problem area. For example, if a child is suicidal, the unit will go to the home and bring the child and family to the hospital for proper counseling and care. They are mobile from 8 A.M. to 11 P.M. every day, and have a phone service during the night covered by crisis workers.

Also, the Bayonne Family Counseling Center sent people to assist with the counseling load. This gave us an additional half dozen counselors to supplement our existing staff. By 10:30 A.M. the "rush to counsel" was concluded and we were able to dismiss those additional six counselors.

Attendance for the day was slightly below average and the mood was again somber, yet uneventful. At 10 A.M. I issued the following statement to the press:

The staff and students of Bayonne High School have been devastated by this tragic and senseless occurrence. I have met with Superintendent Richard J. Malanowski and the Bayonne Board of Education to review current security measures. Presently, we have on campus fourteen counselors, six psychologists, administrators, and representatives from the Bayonne Mental Health Mobile Crisis Unit who have set up three areas on the campus for the student body under the direction of Student Personnel Services Director, Mrs. Georgiann Gongora.

Counseling is also being provided, as needed, in the elementary schools. Furthermore, faculty members were informed at a schoolwide meeting yesterday about the services offered through the employee assistance program (EAP).

I have also established a foundation through the student council and faculty association to aid the families in this crisis.

At my administrative or executive staff meeting that morning, I instructed all administrators to be highly visible throughout the day. Also, teachers were to keep a sharp eye and send any student to counseling that they thought might be in need. We sent another food platter to the Taylor's residence and notified the staff that another debriefing session would take place at the conclusion of the school day.

The core team met once again during the day to review past procedures, current practices, and future events such as funeral coverage. We reviewed the newspapers of the day to get a feeling of what would be expected from parents and community members. Naturally, we were in all the local papers, however, we also received a headline in the *New York Times*. "New Jersey Student Is Stabbed to Death in His High School," was the headline in the *Times*. After relating the gruesome details of the stabbing, the reporter wrote, "Dr. Wanko, the principal, said he kept school in session after the incident so that students could seek counseling, and also because a dangerous suspect remained at large."

The local paper, *The Jersey Journal*, printed a screaming headline in red bold letters. "MURDER At Bayonne High." Subheadlines read, "Innocent teen stabbed through heart, 2nd student recovering from surgery, Manhunt for killer, School security blasted, and Victims: A look at two friends." They printed pictures of the two students, and the shocked and bereaved faces of the parents. The front page was covered with reports on various aspects of this story. Another three full pages of articles and pictures were included in this one issue. I was quoted as saying, "I want the students and their families to feel safe." I went on to explain that I had requested six police officers to help patrol the school during the next two weeks and that we were reviewing security. Again I was able to relate that counseling was available for the students and families in need.

It was apparent that regardless of what we would do, the media would continue its barrage on our school. Therefore, we needed to be extremely careful in our procedures for dealing with the press.

Day Three—7 March 1997

By this time we determined that initial counseling had been successful, and we could return to using counselors out of the regular guidance offices. We also discovered that students were beginning to place items of memorabilia and notes in the area where Aubrey was stricken. The core team met to discuss the appropriateness of leaving those particulars intact and procedures to monitor the area. It was decided that since the memorabilia had already been in place, we would leave those items there until a further date. However, we closely monitored the appropriateness of those remembrances and removed some as necessary. Aubrey's homeroom desk was placed in the area, and additional notes and items were placed on it as well as on the nearby walls.

During the day we completed a letter that was to be sent to all Bayonne High School parents and guardians. It expressed our heartfelt condolences to the Taylor family and our wishes for a speedy recovery to the other student who was attacked. We outlined our security procedures and explained that additional measures would be implemented. The new regulations for entry to the school and the use of ID cards that would become effective on Monday, 10 March 1997, were outlined. We also informed parents that increased police presence would be provided. This letter was signed by the mayor, board president, superintendent, and myself.

I spoke with the funeral director regarding arrangements. He was donating his services and the use of his funeral parlor. The fund that I had established on day two garnered more than $3,000 to offset the other expenses. To facilitate transportation of our students to the funeral services, I contacted the principal of the Hudson County Schools of Technology, Bayonne Center, to arrange buses through their motor pool. However, the team decided that it would be best for students to get to the church on their own and that we would provide busing to the repast. There were many reasons for this decision.

By requiring students to secure their own transportation to the funeral we ensured that "bandwagoning" would be kept to a minimum. Those students who were truly intent on being a part of the services would bring in the proper permission requirements. They also would investigate ways to be transported, either by a parent or a friend's parent. This would ensure more adults at the church to assist us with supervision. If we were to provide buses to the church, many more students would decide to attend simply due to convenient transportation.

We were careful to ensure transportation for students that we had identified as "true" in the grieving process. These students were in one of the circles identified after the tragedy. Many were still being seen by one of our counselors; therefore, it was imperative that if they had the desire to attend, they have that opportunity as they moved through the grieving process.

The coordinator of our Housing and Urban Development program (HUD) grant arranged for the repast in one of the housing complex's recreation areas. This ensured that the students would be in one location with our counselors after the service.

Regarding the wake, the team decided that students would be encouraged to go during after-school hours. This was discussed with the Taylors and was partially at their request. We also assigned counselors to the funeral parlor.

That afternoon, I met with the superintendent, school business administrator, and the superintendent of buildings and grounds to review the feasibility of installing video cameras and a buzz-in intercom system at two locations. I then met with the president of a local electrical contractor firm regarding the placement of these units and the importance of having them operational by Monday morning. He met with representatives from Simplex (a company providing fire and safety hardware) to ensure completion. Over the weekend I again worked on the computer developing additional signs for entry as well as procedures for the vice principals to follow.

A New Week

Following this most difficult weekend, I prepared myself mentally and emotionally for the new challenges that would invariably haunt me each step of the way leading toward recovery. Knowing that Bayonne High School would forever be altered by this tragic incident, I also was aware of the need to place a positive imprint on the upcoming decisions and plans implemented. I view Bayonne High School not only as an institution, but as a family. I realized that we must proceed with the business of teaching and learning. As the principal and educational leader of the school, I was the designated person to lead the Bayonne High School family through the many trials and tribulations to be faced on the road to normalcy.

As I made my way through the reporters, I focused on the recovery process that was crucial to the health of our school. I called all vice principals into the main office to hand out and review the procedures I had developed over the weekend. The information sheet that I composed identified the entrances that were to be used by students. A procedure for students arriving late was outlined. Information on the video cameras and intercom systems was also provided. I instructed them to check all fire alarm boxes and to list those that did not have a plastic shield in place. This would lessen the chances for false alarms because when the plastic shield is removed, a piercing local alarm will sound before anyone can actually trigger the schoolwide fire alarm system. I also explained that I would attend the wake at 2:30 P.M., and that the vice principals would attend at 3 P.M. I reminded them to be as visible as possible. Finally, I reviewed the procedure developed to replace student identification cards.

I then met with the director of student personnel services and we composed a script for teachers to read at 10 A.M. on Tuesday, the time scheduled for the funeral service. The script informed students that the superintendent and I were attending the church observance for Aubrey. We reminded students about the counseling services that were available and requested a moment of silence to honor the memory and life of Aubrey Taylor.

We were the headline in our local newspaper again, "On the trail of the killer," was the headline with a composite sketch of the killer. Once again, all the details were rehashed in the article with the reporter writing about a large butcher knife being plunged into the students five times. My heart went out to the parents and families of the poor victims.

That Tuesday the papers ran a story on the arrest. The *New York Times* headline, "Police Make an Arrest in the Stabbing of Bayonne Students," was the most subdued. The local paper covered the front page with a headline reading, "Suspected Killer CAUGHT!" Pictures and quotations filled the page. Sidebars on tighter security and the wake began on page one and continued on a full-page spread with more pictures inside. One reporter wrote that, "A dark cloud has lingered over Bayonne for nearly a week since a killer fled the halls of the city high school—a place everyone thought was safe." Others repeated the details of the horror.

A story on tighter security noted that new procedures were in place, including the video cameras and intercom buzz-in systems. The procedure for students to receive new IDs was covered, but the reporter went on to write that many students were unhappy with the new rules regarding IDs. Another article informed the public about the procedures to be followed for students to be excused to attend the wake and funeral. In this article, I was able to again relate that counseling was available for our students.

I was seated in the front of the church for the emotional ninety-minute service. We wore black ribbons on our lapels in Aubrey's memory. Five preachers were in attendance and one gave a powerful forty-minute sermon blaming the untimely death on evil forces. A choir made up of twelve family members sang, "I Believe I Can Fly," as mourners walked past the casket. The memorial program read, "Aubrey's life was just beginning, be happy in heaven with those of our family who went before to greet you."

On Wednesday, the front page of the local paper ran a huge picture of Aubrey's parents leaving Metropolitan AME Zion Church after the funeral services. Next to their picture, the paper ran a photo of the perpetrator with the caption, "Killer: I was defending myself." Once again, I could not imagine the anguish felt by the parents when they read this paper.

STUDENT DEATH DUE TO ILLNESS

Near the end of May of that same school year an eighteen-year-old junior passed away. She had been diagnosed with osteogenic sarcoma in March

1992. She completed chemotherapy in December 1994 and was to return to school after the winter break. We worked on creating a schedule that would place her classes close to each other because she was limited in the distance that she could walk each day. We even discussed the possibility of a half-day schedule and the use of a motorized wheelchair and assigned aide.

In September of the 1996–97 school year, a physician's request for home instruction was received as this student had to be placed back on active chemotherapy. We assigned a tutor to the home and the student was doing quite well scholastically. When we received the news of her passing we were devastated. Again, a young adult was taken from our high school family. How much more could we endure?

As I mentioned before, when a death occurs out of sequence, it is even more devastating. Some readers might feel that family and friends could have prepared for what seemed to be inevitable. This is not always the case. Just a few years earlier, I had a student who came into our high school with leukemia. In fact, I graduated with the young girl's father a number of years ago. This young lady was able to have a relatively normal high school career. Incidentally, she was on the varsity cheerleading team. She went into remission, graduated, went on to complete college, and is now married with a family. So as you can see, we never know what lot we will have in life.

Also, keep in mind that we are expecting parents and adults to prepare themselves psychologically for the impending loss. Personally, I cannot conceive how one can prepare for, or deal with, the loss of a child. However, the grim reality is that sometimes our young are taken from this earth. This, coupled with the fact that our school community was forced to deal with multiple losses in one school year, affected our capacity to grieve.

When suffering from multiple losses, some people will experience an actual shutting down of the capacity to grieve. It appears that human beings cannot emotionally bear a cumulative loss. We feel numb, and until such time as we can separate the losses and deal with them one at a time, the grieving process is impaired.

I am sure that at sometime everyone has read an obituary of someone in the same age group as the reader. When this happens we are reminded of our own mortality. Imagine when an adolescent, struggling to develop their own identity, learns of the death of a classmate, or, in this case, three classmates in the same school year. The result can be emotionally trying. The adolescent views the loss with caution as it is emotionally challenging. It can appear that they are denying what has happened.

Discussions in the classrooms can help the students cope with the loss of a classmate. The aim of the discussion will depend on the event and the students' immediate needs. These discussions can be led by the students with teachers facilitating only when necessary. Referral to appropriate counselors can be made as the teacher monitors the comments and reactions during the discussion.

Whenever a student in our school dies, I send a copy of the yearbook containing a commemoration on the deceased to the family with a short note. I feel this is necessary so the family can see that we have not forgotten our own and that we acknowledged the contributions and passing of the individual.

Even though the 1996–97 school year at Bayonne High School should have been like any other, it became a year of infamy. Students, staff, families, and the community-at-large were reeling from a series of unexpected crises. School administrators should never be lulled into complacency. Everyone must be ready to spring into action when a crisis occurs so that safety, support, structure, stability, and control are maintained. We must expect the unexpected.

Chapter 3

How We Responded to Our Crises

Imagine—I had spent almost three decades in public education in the same district, and in one school year we underwent four devastating crises. It almost seemed as though we were being singled out to catch up statistically with our sister urban schools. In the urban community, the city of Bayonne had always been viewed as a safe haven. As a peninsula, we are somewhat cloistered—most people do not come to our town unless they have business to conduct. I believe that this is the primary reason that our community has escaped much of the urban blight experienced by other cities in our area.

Now, we were awakened to the fact that we were vulnerable. Certainly, as a large school, we could expect that a staff member could die while in service. Perhaps even a student could pass away. However, no one could ever expect four separate death episodes in one school year.

By death episode, I am referring to a separate event. This is unlike a bus accident or natural disaster, which could claim more than one life during the same event. In these instances, when more than one loss at a time is experienced, schools are thrust into chaos. This phenomenon is due to the overload of not being able to deal emotionally with the group loss. The need to separate the losses and deal with them individually must be met.

My staff and I were now in the position of responding to a series of crises. It seemed that when we were able to recover from one event, we were challenged with another. One of my colleagues commented that she felt that life was a series of tragedies with only some "down time" in between that allows us to recoup our strength and continue. She had lost her husband in Vietnam and witnessed much suffering when she worked as a registered nurse. Her statement seemed to be quite a cynical view of our world, but considering what some people go through in their lives, it is understandable how people become jaded.

CORE TEAM INVOLVEMENT

We developed a core team to serve as the steering committee for crisis management. This cadre of people oversees the Crisis Management Team and develops policy. The team consists of the director of student personnel services, a vice principal, and myself. We meet first to review the episode and then gather with the crisis team as a whole.

Our Crisis Management Team comprises the Core Team Members, a guidance counselor, a nurse, a secretary, two teachers, and a member of the Student Center. The team has a phone chain with home, office, and pager numbers listed. We meet at least once a year to review policy and procedures and update the phone chain. It is inevitable that at the beginning of each year during our first meeting, someone remarks that they hope we never need to be assembled.

Since our first crisis that year occurred before school opened, the response was different. The apparent suicide from the bridge was handled by the members of the Student Center. This staff works year round to ensure that assistance for students in need is always available. The day following the incident, Student Center staff members reached out to the students involved by requesting that their parents have them come in for counseling. Follow-up sessions were conducted at the Teen Center in the local YMCA. Later, after the burial service, this center was also used as a gathering area.

Because classes were not yet in session, it was not necessary to concern ourselves with the placement of a counselor in each class of the deceased. Instead, it was imperative that her name be deleted from each class list. This was done to prevent the inadvertent reading of the name by a faculty member on the first day of school.

Regarding the sudden death of our faculty member, staff members were reminded of our employee assistance program (EAP). This program affords employees access to counselors. If indicated, the service also ensures that referrals to appropriate personnel are completed. However, sometimes just speaking colleague to colleague is all that is needed to ease the pain.

Care was exercised when selecting the substitute to be placed into the teacher's classroom. I wanted a person who was known, compassionate, and respected by the students. Additionally, I assigned a counselor to be present in all the deceased's classes on the first day following the death. The person could answer questions, explain services available to the students, and make referrals if necessary.

The last crisis that year involved the death of a student due to a catastrophic illness. Since the child had been on home instruction since the beginning of the school year, it was not necessary to place a counselor in specific classes.

However, they were made available to meet with friends of the deceased at the normal counseling areas and the Student Center.

COUNSELING STATIONS

No one expects a homicide to occur in their school. By all indications, schools are still the safest places for our children. Nevertheless, homicides do occur in schools. In the aftermath of such a tragedy, students and staff may experience a variety of feelings. The range of emotions can be great. Survivors and witnesses can feel guilt and continued fear. Some may even suffer flashbacks and panic attacks not only at night, but during the day while in school. Everyone can feel anger and experience difficulty with sleeping and eating. Others could experience behavioral problems, difficulty in relationships, and poor academic performance. Providing the opportunity to express grief over any loss is essential to the healing process.

While immediate counseling is primary, it is imperative to maintain a sustained assistance program following the crisis. In most communities the school is the center of the town. It is a place where events are held, performances are conducted, and courses for adults are taught. During a crisis the school becomes the natural center for counseling. The school serves as the grounding force of normalcy and provides services for affected students, families, and community members.

The decision to set up counseling stations following the homicide was based on many factors. The most obvious place was the Student Center. It was already being used by police authorities to question witnesses. We knew that the witnesses needed to be counseled before and after they were questioned by the police. Therefore, the Student Center became one of the counseling areas for the school.

The library was also determined to be a good location for a counseling station for several reasons. Because it is located in a different building from the Student Center, it allowed us to divide the counseling load. It is in a wing with no classes across from its entrances, therefore, we would be able to diminish some of the contagion factor that might occur due to students witnessing upset peers entering for counseling. Last, our library, a beautiful structure with stained glass windows, carved wood, and carpeted floor also offers a soothing view of Newark Bay.

All guidance offices are located in the middle of the complex. This fits well with my philosophy that guidance is the heart of the school. The suite comprises eleven offices with areas for group work and secretaries. However, this area is adjacent to classrooms and directly across from six additional classrooms that could be a contagion risk. Additionally, in the guidance suite each office can fit only about four students with a counselor. This would limit our flexibility to arrange groups of different sizes. Therefore, we decided against using the guidance suite for this particular crisis counseling situation.

I designed the guidance suite complex about seven years prior to the homicide. Before that we had two sets of guidance suites. Each contained five or six offices with a group area. The philosophy at the time was for the counselors serving Houses One, Two, and Three to be in close proximity to those students, while those assigned to Houses Four, Five, and Six would be close to those homerooms.

Over the ten years that the counselors were separated, communications between the two suites began to diminish and some services, such as clerical and secretarial, were often duplicated. Additionally, due to budget restraints we were forced to combine into five houses. When the director of guidance retired, I was assigned to serve as the guidance director for the school. Luckily, I possessed the appropriate student personnel services certificate. I was forced to divide my time between the duties of the principalship and guidance obligations for the next three years. When we were able to hire a director of student personnel services, I recommended that all counselors and the director be in one large suite. The superintendent and board members agreed that it seemed to be the right time to move in this direction. We also expanded the duties of the director and changed the title to director of student personnel services. Now all ancillary services such as the Student Center, Peer Leadership, and the Teen Center are under the direction of one person.

SECURITY AT THE SCHOOL

The day following the homicide, we made many changes at the school. First, every panic bar on all exterior doors was placed in the locked position. This meant that personnel could only exit from any door in the complex. The computer signs that I had made at home indicated which doors would be available for entry. It was decided that only two entrances would be used for student entrance, both on the front or eastside of the complex. Students were directed to one of these two entrances based on their house assignment. Prior to this division, students would enter a building closer to their residence but farther from their homeroom. This resulted in unnecessary traffic in the buildings. By dividing the students by house assignment, we eliminated this concern.

At each entrance we placed two attendance officers and a vice principal. Police were also assigned to assist with the new procedures. Students were asked to show some sort of identification to gain entry. Previously, we had student identification cards containing a photo and homeroom for each student. Therefore, students who had the cards were admitted quite easily. Those without cards had to produce other means of identification. During these rustic days we accepted motor vehicle licenses, social security cards, video memberships, or credit cards. Since names and homerooms are listed on the inside of textbook covers, we were able to use the students' books as another means of identification. Also, students who had their original schedule or a report card could use these as a means of identification. Naturally, if a vice principal recognized a student, entrance was granted.

Concurrently, we began to reissue student identification cards because we really did not enforce the policy for carrying the cards. The equipment was on campus, and we contacted the distributor for additional cards and film. Students had new IDs issued during physical education classes. We chose these classes because some were already assigned to the area (BHS Physical Education and Community Education Center) that contained the ID equipment. In a few days, virtually all students had school-issued identification.

It was not practical to expect a staff of almost 300 to enter in the same manner; additional entrances would be needed. Also, some staff members arrive an hour or two before students. The campus extends three city blocks by one block deep with parking spanning various areas. Therefore, I assigned custodians to another three entrances to form a triangular pattern to the parking areas. Custodians would be at these stations from 6:30 A.M. to about 8:45 A.M. As a staff member approached, the custodian would open the door to allow entry.

We continued in this fashion until the next day, Friday. Meanwhile, meetings were in process with local contractors and security companies. A quick plan was devised to install video cameras at the two student entrances. Monitors would be placed in the main office and by the reception areas. An intercom would be installed at both sectors with a magnetic locking buzzer for entry. Rush orders for the hardware were arranged and everything was installed over the weekend.

To get the word out on the new system, I used the reporters, who were still camped out around the school. When I sent word that I had something new to report, they took the bait and assembled at the designated spot by the main entrance for Houses One, Two, and Three.

The story was how we installed the new equipment to make the buildings safer and the procedures to be followed to gain access. I explained how the system worked and students showed their identification cards. The story ran that evening with a detailed explanation of the procedures. This was an occasion that demonstrated how the media can be a positive part of a crisis situation. Remember, the media has a different agenda than the administration of any school. It is seldom that these two agencies are in concert. Yes, the local papers will run stories on events at the school and highlight certain accomplishments and awards. However, they are in the business of selling papers. They seek stories that are sensational. Then they will milk those stories dry until a new issue arises. Do not be fooled or lulled into a false sense that the reporter is your friend and that you have a special relationship with the paper. Many administrators believe this because they work closely with the papers to highlight achievement. Time can go by without a negative story, and the building administrator feels comfortable with the press.

It will take only one controversial issue to set the administrator right. This could simply be a time when the media takes up the cause of a disgruntled parent. It really is inconsequential if the issue is not of great importance in the total scheme of things. Remember, it is the controversy that will help to sell papers. The media is not concerned with the fallout at the school, any negative impressions that may be cast, or any person who might be affected.

The installation of cameras and intercoms was our "quick-fix" solution. Now we were faced with the realization that our school would never really be the same. Each and every day we would live with the aftermath of a random act of violence. As a result, we were of great resolve to make the school as safe as possible. Keep in mind that the four buildings were erected during different eras. From our oldest section built in 1919, to our newest building constructed in 1986, many intricacies of architectural design are present.

We had many specialists come on campus to critique our situation and make recommendations. Upon review of all these plans, we decided for our application that magnetic panels (mag-locks) should be installed on the interior of all exterior door jams. These panels are about 3-by-11 inches and are connected to a central control station. The corresponding areas on each door received a metal plate of the same dimensions. When the doors shut, the magnets can be engaged. When in contact it takes 1,200 pounds of pressure to pry the door from the magnet.

The entire complex was placed on this system except for the BHS Physical Education/Community Education Center. This is a stand-alone building with its own security system and we decided to keep it separate. The cost of wiring all doors and installing a computerized system to control each entrance was only part of our financial concern. We could not expect only two or even five doors to be enough for a staff reaching almost 300 in number. Therefore, a system of doors on mag-lock with readers had to be researched.

Security is designed to keep intruders out of the buildings. Our system also kept people in the buildings. Remember, with the magnets engaged, doors are locked from the inside as well as the outside. After reviewing many options, we determined that eight doors at strategic locations would be outfitted with readers. These doors could be opened by staff members by using their individual cards, allowing them entry or egress.

Theoretically, if we simply went to a policy of keeping all exterior doors in the panic bar locked position, intruders would be kept out of the buildings. However, we all know this type of procedure is not foolproof. If a door does not close all the way, the panic bar cannot engage. Furthermore, anyone could simply push the bar from the inside to allow an intruder into the building. Also, tape could be placed over the striker and the door would appear secure but actually be unlocked. The list could go on and on regarding ways to compromise this type of security.

Even though it presented myriad concerns we had to overcome, it was clear that a mag-locking system was the way to go for our school. Normally, I tell my staff that there are no problems, just opportunities; therefore, I took my own philosophy to the table as we met with the various experts, consultants, and contractors.

Review after review was conducted regarding the implementation of this type of system. Meetings were also scheduled with personnel from the local fire prevention bureau. This is when it became apparent that the cost of the mag-lock system was not to be our only financial concern. Before we could install a system that kept all doors locked from the inside as well as the outside, the fire alarm system had to be updated. Our current system consisted of the normal pull boxes in prescribed areas and the pneumatic tube system for heat detection.

This type of system comprises a series of hollow tubes. Each tube emanates from a small indicator and runs up the wall to the ceiling and covers a certain area, then returns to the same indicator. This is a closed-loop system. When the temperature rises near any tube to a certain degree, the air in the tube expands causing an alarm to emanate from the indicator. In our system, the various indicators reported to fourteen zones.

A panel with information regarding each of the zones was located outside each building. Additional panels were placed in the main office and the boiler room. When an alarm was triggered, firefighters and school personnel could determine the zone where the problem occurred by simply reading the location on the panel. Many administrators can attest to the efficiency of this system by the number of burn marks on the ceilings in the boys' and girls' lavatories caused by matches held to the tubes.

For a mag-lock system to be initiated, an addressable and compatible fire alarm system had to be installed. This meant that our system had to be totally upgraded. This resulted in more than 1,100 separate addresses or points for our application. Every area in the complex needed its own point or address. Each point had either a smoke or heat detector as the mechanism to monitor fires. The monitor for a particular area is determined by the local fire code. Typically, corridors and stairwells will have smoke detectors. Classrooms and storerooms will have heat detectors. We also installed both audio and visual alarms throughout the buildings.

We now have a state-of-the-art fire alarm system. A computerized monitoring board in the main office will enunciate the location of an individual alarm. Additional monitoring boards are located at the main entrances to each of the buildings. Anyone reading one of the panels can immediately see the problem area. No longer are we restricted to a general location in only fourteen zones. We now have a system that will actually tell us which one of more than a thousand locations has the alarm.

New pull boxes were purchased and all had to be in place prior to installing a mag-lock system. I took this opportunity to have plastic covers with internal battery alarms placed over each pull box to help stem false alarms. In this manner, when someone lifts the plastic, a screeching local alarm is triggered. Normally, attention is brought to the area before the actual alarm is pulled. All pull boxes are coated with a special blue ink that cannot be washed off for a number of days.

To ensure egress in case of an emergency when an alarm is not triggered, we installed emergency release mechanisms at every door. We believed this system was necessary so that everyone could feel they could leave any building at any time. However, the same plastic shields cover all emergency release buttons and an internal alarm will also sound when the cover is removed. Therefore, students cannot sneak out of the buildings without being noticed.

A series of manual override switches in the main office will allow certain doors to be released manually. One of these switches will release all doors. As a final precaution, we placed a special switch on the wall behind the main reception area. This switch is encased in glass and will release all doors throughout the entire complex instantly. There is a small hammer hanging from a chain to break the glass. This allows access to the switch that can release all doors from the mag-locks.

All doors can be programmed to open for special events. For example, if we have a home basketball game, the doors adjacent to the main gymnasium are programmed to be opened for the appropriate time. This is accomplished by the use of a permit which lists the event, date, door access, and times. The secretary brings up a program called Point Control and enters the appropriate data. These special events must be programmed week-to-week as the program works on a day basis, not a date basis. However, the program will allow for multiple days to be programmed, such as, the same day each week for a number of weeks. Care must be taken to remove the data when the event is concluded because the system cannot work by dates, just days of the week.

Part of the new security system was a fresh identification card system for students and staff. As part of the door system, bar-coded photo identification cards for the students were required. This meant that we needed to purchase a new photo ID system. The new program allows us to photograph each student and place the image on a plastic card. As an added safeguard against counterfeit cards, we selected a picture-within-a-picture type of photography. In addition to the photos, the student's name, an identification number, and homeroom designation are included on the cards. Also, each student has a color-coded bar on the top of the card. Different colors are representative of each of our six houses.

Upon entering the complex, students swipe their cards in one of the two readers at each location. In addition to these two areas, we installed student barcode readers at three other areas. One is at the location used for entry for events held in the main gymnasium. A second is at the lobby to the auditorium, and the third is for access to the Physical Education and Community Education Center. Now it is possible to check a student's identification almost instantly at sporting and recreational events, as well as at various cultural and musical performances.

Above the readers are sets of lights—red and green in color. If the student has a valid card and is entering the correct area, the green light will go on within two seconds. If the child is at the wrong location or the card is invalid, red will show. If an administrator wishes to see a particular student, the computer can be programmed accordingly, resulting in a red light.

Instead of sending for a student during the day, a message on the computer screen will come up when an administrator needs to see a particular student. In this manner we can have students brought directly to a particular office as soon as they enter the complex. The computer also has the ability to bring up the picture of the child to check identification.

Incidentally, once the student's picture is taken, it remains captured on the computer board. Therefore, replacement cards can be issued without the need for the child to sit for another photo.

We knew we needed to develop policies and procedures ensuring continuity and fairness. The result was a policy on IDs. Simply stated, "IDs must be worn and visible at all times." The penalty for violation of this rule ranges from a warning to detention, to Saturday School, to suspension. Students who forget their cards are issued a detention. Penalties for repeat offenders are increased accordingly. In any case, students without IDs are issued temporary IDs for the day. If a student loses his or her ID, a replacement fee of $5.00 is charged.

To make the program more palatable, we gave every student a specially designed lanyard to be worn around the neck. Students can have their cards on this lanyard as well as house or car keys. Since this seemed to be a popular trend, we felt that by issuing our own lanyards, students would be encouraged to wear their IDs in this manner. Students who prefer a clip-on type of card have a special snapping device issued.

Another strategy was to incorporate the bar code for use in the school's library. Therefore, we upgraded our library system and students now use their ID cards to check out books. We also combined our Renaissance program with the student ID plan. Renaissance is a national program run by the Josten Company, which recognizes student accomplishment. This accomplishment can be for scholarship, attendance, discipline, or any other criteria that the school administration wishes to recognize. We combined criteria requiring scholastic achievement, good attendance, no discipline referrals, no detentions, and no failures. Normally, three types of cards are issued to students being recognized. We divided the card category by grade-point average. Each card entitles the child to various discounts from local merchants and free admission to certain school events.

For a student to receive these discounts, both the Renaissance card and student ID card must be presented. The passage in the student Renaissance information booklet referring to this policy reads, "Your Bayonne High School photo ID must be presented with your Renaissance card when you make a purchase. Merchants will not honor your Renaissance card if the ID is not shown."

Currently, we are examining the elimination of lunch cards. These cards are issued to students eligible for free or reduced lunch and breakfast. Soon, we will have readers in our cafeterias that will be used to scan the student ID when purchasing food. Adding to our overall safety plan, students could prepay for their food, leaving cash at home.

We still take attendance in homeroom. Future plans will encompass attendance at the port of entry. This change will afford us various opportunities regarding the reconfiguration of scheduling and use of time saved from the existing school day. We are realizing a side benefit that was not really expected from the system. The problem of students leaving the buildings when cutting classes has virtually been eliminated.

A different approach was necessary regarding staff identification. Naturally, we could use the same plastic photo ID. However, a bar-code system was not practical. Rather, we purchased a card system that contained a wire assemblage in the card. Thirty-six wires are embedded in each card. It is the next generation of the Wiegand Format which used magnetic coding similar to an audiotape. This new system uses radio signals instead of a magnetic field. The wires are set in a parallel fashion like an invisible bar code. They are sandwiched within the plastic card, and for all intents and purposes, are the bar code for the card. The card is passive and manufactured with a specific seven-digit number. We purchase the cards already encoded.

Specialized proximity (prox) readers were placed at designated doors. These readers are designed to open the door from either side as they are located inside and outside the buildings. When the staff identification card is placed flat to the reader, a red LED light is lit and a beep is emitted. It is not necessary to touch the reader, in fact, you can even leave the card in your wallet when using the reader.

As the card comes within the short radio field of the prox reader, it picks up the signal and becomes energized. The card actually absorbs power from the field and dissipates it back out to the prox reader. Each wire sends back one bit of information using a binary code (0 or 1). The server can then be programmed to allow entry or exit at specific doors, times, and days.

At this point, it became apparent that many applications could be put to use with this new system. We needed to develop categories of access for staff members. It would be unwise to program every staff member with twenty-four hour access seven days a week. Even though I can review a printout of staff use of the system reporting the time and location of individual use, carte blanche for all staff would be counterproductive to our overall security plan. While it is true that when someone loses a card we can disable it, most people do not notify authorities about the loss in a timely fashion. They believe they will eventually find the card and save some embarrassment. During that time, the security of the complex can be totally compromised. With limited access on most cards, the person finding the lost card will not have free reign of the complex.

As a result, we developed general categories for staff use. However, as we began to commit our ideas to paper, specific category problems began to surface. A general category for teachers was our starting point. We decided that the computer should read these cards as access approved any day that school was in session from 6:30 A.M. to 4:30 P.M. Next were teacher advisors who had their hours increased to 7 P.M. Coaches and advisors had additional time added to the teacher designation for their particular season or meeting days. Distinct categories for custodians were required according to shifts and building assignments. Specifics for cafeteria workers with earlier entrance and exit times were also developed. An executive code for my administrative team was also designed. This code was the easiest to develop. It allows access twenty-four hours a day, seven days a week at any reader location for various programs and emergencies. When we were finished, we had about forty different access code categories.

If a teacher needs to come into a building during the weekend or on a holiday, they can have their access code adjusted. The same holds true when overtime is required for custodians. The procedure we devised for this application was a simple form requesting the time and date of access. After I approve the request, a secretary enters the program, adjusting access for the time and date requested. Again, the card is passive and only sends back information as to the card's number. Therefore, the teacher and the card do not need to be anywhere near the computer for the application. This makes the system user friendly. The system is also flexible, allowing for a teacher to request additional access as needed.

For added safety and convenience, we built a reception desk, equipped with a monitor and intercom, at the main entrance to the complex. We also assigned personnel to this location to monitor the doors and let people in and out during normal operating times. We have programmed this set of doors to remain off the system during school days up to 11 P.M. These doors are kept on panic lock so entry cannot be made. However, if a staff member loses a card, egress could be made from these doors even if the person assigned to the desk is not at the post.

At any time we can invalidate anyone's card, regardless of whether they are a student or staff member. For example, students who are on suspension have their cards listed as suspended. When they are swiped, the red light will flash. A message on the computer screen will indicate that the child is on suspension and should not be granted access.

If a staff member loses a card, we can place the number of that card into a red flag category. The card will be read, but access or egress will not be allowed. In this manner we have a chance of catching the person trying to use an unauthorized card. Another option is to delete that card from the system and issue a new one. If we choose this option, the number cannot be reassigned, whereas if it is red-flagged in the computer and the card is recovered, we can reassign that particular number. In either case, anyone finding a card that has been reported lost will not be allowed access.

A final note on door security is necessary. The computer system that runs the locking mechanism has a battery backup. The company estimates that the system will maintain its integrity during a power failure for up to ten days. We also designated one door to remain off the system at all times. This door is located in the building that houses the computer system. Therefore, if there is some sort of failure that keeps all doors locked we can still enter the building to rectify the situation.

SECURITY PERSONNEL

A decision had to be made as to whether we would go the way of our neighboring cities and hire a uniformed security company. Many schools have adopted this approach. Some believe we should not be in the security business. Others feel that an outside professional firm can do the job better than board personnel. In either case, these districts set aside a specific amount of money for a security firm to police the buildings.

Personally, I know of some high schools that have even gone to the next level. They have hired retired police officers as security guards and permit them to actually carry weapons while on duty in the schools.

We decided on a more subtle approach, no uniformed guards and no weapons. Instead, our security crew consists of one attendance officer, three permanent substitutes, and two secretaries. One secretary is full time and one has a split assignment. Naturally, the vice principals and I float in and out of the security mode as needed. The full-time secretary is stationed at the main building reception area. We built a large desk at this location that contains a monitor, the intercom and buzzer system, a phone and walkie-talkie, and one of the manual override switches to release all doors.

Of the remaining four people on the security crew, two are assigned to the areas for student entry from 7 A.M. until about 9 A.M. We rotate these assignments to keep everyone fresh and alert. As students enter the buildings and swipe their cards, security personnel monitor the red and green light system. If a child's card comes up red, an additional swipe is attempted. Failing to see a green light at this time, the student is brought to the secretary assigned to the security computer terminal.

At any red light status, the student's picture automatically is brought up on the monitor and a visual check can be made. The computer operator then moves to the cardholder status. This allows the operator to view the message regarding the cardholder's status. This message indicates if the student is at the wrong entrance, is on suspension, has an invalid card, or needs to meet with the vice principal. Actually, it is almost impossible for a nonstudent to compromise this system.

Everyday during the last class period, the secretary assigned to the security system enters the appropriate data. Each house office sends a list of suspensions, home instruction placements, and any off-roll notices. The secretary brings up the message file and reviews all postings. She then removes any student's name who is returning from suspension or home instruction. She also enters the names of students who are being placed on suspension or home instruction and the corresponding time period. She also keys in any messages from the administration regarding specific students. Naturally, a back-up person is essential, as this procedure dictates which cards are read as valid.

Because these two entrances serve as the only ports of entry, late students are assigned detention right on the spot. This eliminates making the student even later by necessitating a visit to a house office to be processed.

The personnel at the doors also have walkie-talkies and hand-held metal detectors or wands. At present, we randomly move the wand over backpacks, pocketbooks, and students. Perhaps one in every twenty are checked in this manner each morning. Immediately following the tragedy at Littleton we increased this procedure to about every five students. When we receive security-sensitive information through the grapevine, we increase wand usage accordingly.

I have witnessed demonstrations of walk-through metal detectors and various other metal detecting devices. I have also been at demonstrations of various X-ray equipment. For almost every device invented to make us safer, a device or procedure to counteract the new apparatus is developed. When we reviewed our options, we decided to use wands for our screening mechanism. We felt that installing walk-through detectors right away would be too imposing. Furthermore, it could create a false sense of security. Walk-through detectors can be fooled, and many people might become complacent or lax throughout the school day. They would believe that no weapons were present in the school and lower their guard. Perpetuators would then have a distinct advantage in any given situation.

Most important, we know that metal detectors cannot identify hateful emotions and feelings. As a result, we have placed more emphasis on programs designed to reach students who may be disaffected. In this manner, we can attack the problem of school violence that results from a negative climate at its roots. We strive to keep the lines of communications open at all times. Students need to know that they can speak to any faculty member or peer mediator as needed. The message is clear—confidentiality is the order of the day. Share your innermost feelings at no risk of disclosure or embarrassment.

Students know information is always kept confidential. However, the rule of confidentially is breached when the safety of that particular student is in question. If the student has information on another student or group of students who are planning to harm others or themselves, we can still spring into action and preserve the anonymity of the student with the information. More and more often we are witnessing the swing of the pendulum where the unwritten code of silence is broken when fellow students are at risk. It is not uncommon for students to approach a favorite teacher or counselor with information regarding the safety and welfare of others.

A colleague of mine is the principal of a large South Jersey high school. He told me of a student in his school who approached a trusted teacher with a story of a fellow student making a bomb to blow up the school. The teacher contacted the principal who notified the police. A search of the student's locker came up empty, so the police went to the student's home. There, they discovered the makings of a bomb. Whether he planned to blow up the school was not known. However, due to the efforts of a courageous student, the other students, and staff of this school were spared what might have been a horrific act. This incident verifies my contention that visibility of administrators and security personnel encourages students to share this type of information.

With this in mind, the attendance officer and three permanent substitutes assigned to the security team begin making their rounds after the morning entry procedures at our school are completed. Basically, this consists of walking the corridors to supply the administration with additional sets of eyes and ears. Since each vice principal and I have walkie-talkies, we decided to give a separate channel to the security team. In this manner they could keep in constant touch with one another without cluttering up our communications.

We did not want to give the impression of a prison, so we decided against uniforms for security personnel. Rather, I purchased shirts and jackets with the Bayonne High School logo for this group. Students are repulsed by an ardent authority figure clad in an imposing uniform. The crew also serves as greeters and guides for visitors to our school.

A special relationship is forged with this type of system. Students are met by security personnel the first thing each morning. They are greeted in a friendly manner and exchange pleasantries. Throughout the day, security personnel walk through the complex and its outer perimeters to assist students with various concerns. It is not uncommon for security to visit the cafeteria and eat with the students or sit on one of the benches placed about the buildings to discuss last night's game. At the end of the day, security is stationed in front of the school, ensuring a safe and orderly dismissal.

When we scheduled breaks and lunches for security, care was taken to ensure that we had adequate coverage for cafeteria periods. When I became principal, one of my initiatives in scheduling was to create a closed lunch program. As an urban school, with our closest neighbors only eight feet away, I felt it was imperative to be good neighbors. To prevent students from loitering on neighboring property, a closed lunch program was essential.

To develop this type of initiative, many variables must be addressed. First and foremost, the school must have an area large enough to feed the students. In our case we could fit about 750 students in our three cafeterias at any sitting, therefore, we needed three lunch periods to accommodate our enrollment.

The next step is to decide if lunches are to run for the full period or be staggered. We tried both systems and found that for the best accountability and least amount of hall traffic, a full period for lunch would be best. At this point we wrestled with a system to account for each student at lunchtime. To assure this accountability, we decided it would be best to actually assign a specific seat for each student. Computerized sheets were developed listing each seat at every table in each cafeteria.

Students are allowed to eat with friends; however, at the predetermined time, they are required to return to their assigned seats for attendance. They are also responsible for the cleanliness of that area. As a result, many students choose to stay in their assigned area so they are only responsible for their own cleanup. Our closed lunch system has worked extremely well for almost two decades.

Seniors were given a privilege about five years ago. It was at this time that I remodeled the smallest cafeteria, converting it into the Senior Lounge. Through various donations, I was able to add air-conditioning, round tables, a CD jukebox, vending machines, and an area for a fry cook. After checking in with the teachers assigned to lunch duty, seniors can sit at any table. A teacher is assigned to the Senior Lounge every period of the day as well as before school. This assures that students can come to the lounge during a study period to have a snack, work on an assignment, or just relax anytime during the day.

Each cafeteria has two to four teachers assigned according to student enrollment. The security crew members station themselves in the cafeterias during lunch periods and I assign a vice principal to every cafeteria period to supplement the teachers. I try to make the rounds to every cafeteria each lunch period. Visibility is one of the many keys to a successful program of school safety.

In 1999, the city of Bayonne was awarded a $1 million grant for three years to increase the role of the Community Oriented Policing (COP) program. This grant (COPs In Schools) allowed eight officers to be assigned to both the public and private schools in our city. Bayonne High School has two police officers from this program assigned to the campus every school day. Their role is not one of police security, rather it is one of police presence. We do not call on these officers for normal situations. We only call for their assistance when we would normally need police assistance. For example, if a fight breaks out, we follow our normal procedure to quell the disturbance. If it rises to the level that we would have summoned the police, we can now simply radio to one of the officers already in the complex for assistance.

Prior to the school year these officers were trained to serve as chaperones for various trips and activities. They also are present in the cafeterias providing positive visual impact on the students. Even though we have an assemblage of up to 300 students eating lunch together in one of three cafeterias at the same time, the atmosphere is cordial and inviting.

At dismissal time, I stand in front of the main entrance to the campus. Vice principals are also assigned to areas outside the perimeter of the school. This is now supplemented by the security crew and the officers from the COPs In Schools program. Within twelve minutes, virtually all students who are not involved in an after-school program for that particular day exit the campus in an orderly manner. Keep in mind this is an urban school situated in the middle of the city on a major avenue.

APPROPRIATE POSTCRISIS ACTIVITIES

There is a myriad of information regarding appropriate postcrisis activities. It is paramount for the school administrator to review all information on the crisis and to meet with the crisis management team to determine if some sort of activity is necessary or appropriate. For example, whenever contemplating a memorial program, the concept of church and state as it applies to school activities must be considered.

In the case of our first tragedy of the 1996–97 school year, the student suicide, it was not appropriate to conduct an activity. As noted before, it is not fitting to conduct a memorial service for a suicide. We cannot glamorize or glorify this type of behavior. Copycat suicides could occur if we memorialize the tragic event. If the crisis team believes that some observance is necessary due to specific concerns, the program should be very low profiled. Extreme care must be exercised so as not to make the suicide attractive. Do not have a program that would serve to mystify the event.

However, it is still incumbent on the administration to develop and implement some sort of itinerary for students. This could be as simple as setting up counseling stations. In our case, since school was not in session, we sent counselors to the wake and service. We also sent out notices that the counselors would be available at the onsite and offsite Student Centers if needed.

Any sharing of information must also be carefully executed. Large group gatherings, such as an assembly program shortly after the tragedy, will only serve to heighten emotions.

After school personnel decide what will be done, notification to the student body should be made as soon as possible. This will bring about three results. First, the student body will know that the faculty is caring and that counseling is available. Second, it will prevent students from devising makeshift memorials for their fallen comrade. Third, students will have a program designed specifically for them. This should also halt bothersome calls to the home of the deceased. Regarding this last result, it is imperative for the administration to discourage students from seeking information directly by contacting the family of the deceased. Therefore, have appropriate and accurate information available and accessible to the student body.

Our second tragedy during the same school year was completely different from the first. Even though the sudden death of a faculty member is an unexpected occurrence, the teacher did not commit a violent act. It was an involuntary event which, nevertheless, resulted in a loss for the school community. Normally, when a colleague dies while still employed or even just recently retired, faculty members usually rally to establish a memorial fund. This could be in the form of a donation to the school or a scholarship in the memory of the deceased teacher. In both cases the memorial serves as a catharsis for the faculty and a somewhat long-term remembrance for the deceased.

Over the years we have done both. Money is collected and placed in a school account set aside for this use. Usually, a close friend of the deceased or a member of the same department will present the scholarship at the dedication program.

If the crisis is an act of violence in the school, a different approach is dictated. Our third tragedy that school year was the homicide. One of our students was killed and another was injured due to a random act of violence. A natural outpouring of grief and anger was to be expected. Almost immediately, a makeshift shrine was established. When this occurs, the administration is wise to let it run its course. Keep a vigilant eye on the items placed at the shrine and decide when it would be appropriate to remove these items so as not to cause an emotional response.

In our case, notes, poems, and other writings were placed on the wall in the area of the stricken student. Flowers and other types of memorabilia were also in the assemblage. At one point, the student armchair from Aubrey's classroom was also placed at this spot. We checked the area throughout each day to ensure that all items were appropriate and in no way offensive to anyone. We also informed the family regarding the sanctuary and invited them in to view the shrine and decide what items they would like. As educators, we knew it would not be appropriate to leave this shrine in place for a long period of time. We met with the family to discuss the necessity of returning this area back to a normal corridor. The students were informed, in advance, that the shrine would be removed. They were made aware that some items would be given to the family. This way we met the needs of the students who were still grieving as well as those who had moved past the grieving stage.

The core team decided it was appropriate and necessary to mark the passing of our student for many reasons. First, it was a homicide that occurred within the school. Next, all indications led us to believe that Aubrey was merely coming to the aid of his fellow student and cousin, an act of selflessness that had resulted in death. Finally, many students not only felt the loss but felt violated and fearful.

We needed to decide what type of program would meet the needs of the largest number of students. Providing an agenda that was meaningful and acceptable to large numbers is not an easy task. Care to prevent the out-spilling of emotions at such an event also had to be considered. The team decided on an antiviolence assembly with a tree planting ceremony.

As there is no one place in our school that can accommodate the entire student body, we were faced with a decision regarding who should attend the program. After much reflection, we decided that all freshmen would be the target group. Due to their age, and the fact that they would be with us for another three years, we felt the most impact and longest lasting impression could be achieved with this class.

Much planning went into our memorial. We decided that a specific day would be termed as Aubrey Taylor Day. The day 21 May 1997 was selected and a full program was developed. The date was eleven weeks to the day of the tragedy. We felt this was an appropriate waiting period. Conducting the program too soon after the loss would cause undue emotional trauma. Waiting until the next school year would be insensitive. Looking ahead, we knew that a one-year memorial would be in order. Having two programs in the same year would not be appropriate and perhaps counterproductive to the healing process.

Scheduling the event was also a concern. Normally, when conducting programs, we run an assembly schedule. This means that a particular class or grouping of students by homeroom would be invited to the auditorium or gymnasium for the specific event. Five minutes from each period are removed and added to the homeroom time. As a result, the assembly schedule allows for a forty-six-minute homeroom.

By having the program first thing in the morning, students who became depressed might be listless for the remainder of the day. Yet, by scheduling the program in the morning, we could channel these students to the appropriate counselor. However, we wanted to conduct a tree planting ceremony after the assembly program. Logistically, moving students out of the building and back to class before the end of the period would be nearly impossible. Furthermore, the time to run both programs would probably exceed two class periods. We were faced with a dilemma.

The core team decided that an afternoon program would be best. We would not lose two class periods and the tree planting ceremony could run as long as necessary. Furthermore, we could then provide a gathering area with counselors and refreshments after the ceremony. To address the concern of students becoming depressed, we spoke with the presenter about an upbeat program.

Student input was sought to develop the program. The core team thought the program should be short but tasteful. I would begin the program with opening remarks and we chose an antiviolence speaker. Detective Steven Mc-Donald, a decorated New York City police officer, seemed to be an obvious choice. Detective McDonald was a New York City police detective who was shot while on duty and paralyzed. On 12 July 1986, he was on routine patrol in Central Park when he spotted three teens acting suspiciously. When he approached them, one youth pulled a .22 snub-nosed pistol and fired three shots into McDonald.

McDonald miraculously survived the attack. His heroic fight for life became national news. Even though he survived, he remains a quadriplegic. His recovery spanned nine months at Bellevue Hospital in New York before he could be moved to Craig Hospital in Denver. While at the Craig Hospital, he learned to speak again and operate a wheelchair with his mouth. Detective McDonald speaks to audiences bringing the message of nonviolence and forgiveness.

Another example of his selflessness was witnessed firsthand by all of us when we were negotiating his payment for the program. I was telling Detective McDonald about our Project Graduation, a program that offers our students a totally drug-, alcohol-, and smoke-free environment following the graduation ceremony. Detective McDonald was so impressed with the program, he donated his entire stipend for the program to offset some of the project costs.

In the midst of the memorial program, it was very moving to witness our students glued to their seats, listening to a fellow human being who would never again have the use of his arms or legs. This person, like Aubrey, demonstrated selflessness and compassion for all humanity. After McDonald's inspirational words, the director of student personnel services explained the antiviolence pledge that was to be distributed to all students during their eighth period class the next day. I briefly explained the tree planting ceremony that was to follow the assembly. Then, I closed the program with a few remarks and we dismissed the students.

During the tree planting ceremony, I served as the master of ceremonies. After some brief remarks, I introduced the mayor and superintendent. They gave appropriate statements and a representative from the Taylor family spoke. Students and family members placed flowers at the base of the tree we had just planted.

When choosing the location for the tree, we took into consideration the section of the school where the tragedy occurred. We also wanted to ensure that the area would be visible yet unobtrusive. The north section of lawn outside the annex building (Houses Four and Five) was selected. After the ceremony, we brought those in attendance to the Student Center. Here, we had counselors available and served light refreshments. Mr. and Mrs. Taylor attended both the assembly and tree planting ceremony.

I then called together the core team to review the next day's program. We developed an antiviolence pledge that was given to the teachers at the program with instructions. The pledge was read to the students who were at the assembly program. Teachers followed up during homeroom the next morning, reviewing the pledge and its meaning.

Members from the Student Center and guidance counselors went from class to class to read the pledge with the students. In this manner we were assured of the proper interpretation by a trained professional. Also, a certified counselor was on hand in case a student was in need. The students were not required to sign the pledge in class. We did not want to create a hostile environment nor place any student in conflict. Rather, we suggested that they take the pledge home and discuss it with family members. Then, if they decided to commit to the pledge, they could sign it and place it in a prominent place in their home.

A few days later, Mr. and Mrs. Taylor approached me regarding their desire to establish a scholarship in the memory of Aubrey. I reviewed some options, set up the criteria, and had moneys donated for the award. Donations came in quickly and the Taylors came to the program to present the award.

Because Bayonne High School is so large, we do not grant awards at graduation. However, all award winners are listed in the graduation program. To acknowledge student achievement, I developed an awards banquet to properly recognize these hard-working students.

We rent a local catering facility and provide three tickets to every award winner. A complimentary ticket is given to the person or organization granting an award. We present approximately eighty awards, so we normally have 300 people in attendance. It is an exhilarating event. Students are dressed in their best, and proud parents boast of their children's accomplishments. The sponsors for the awards share pleasantries with the winners and family members. Patrons explain the establishment of the awards and learn about the current winners. An exchange of various concepts, work ethics, and values results because of this program.

Many presenters are graduates of Bayonne High School, so positive role models proliferate the dinner. Board of Education members, the superintendent, and the mayor attend, which adds to the pomp and circumstance of the event. Performing groups from the school are on hand to showcase their talents and provide entertainment for the evening. Overall, it is a great night.

In establishing the Taylor Award, it was decided that part of the criteria would be an antiviolence essay. Applicants must write a 500-word essay on the following topic: "How can I use my education to help create more understanding and less violence in our world?" The family wanted the award to be open to all seniors at the school regardless of race, major, or career goals.

COMMUNITY SUPPORT

Throughout our recovery, community support was omnipresent. However, I cannot stress the importance of the concept that when a school crisis hits, you will make the difference. You will be thrust into the limelight. During and after our tragedies, I received numerous letters, notes, and phone calls expressing support and offering condolences and resources. The amount of support was heartwarming and unexpected. Many expressed their concern for my well-being and offered prayers for my continued strength in mind, body, and spirit. Letters from parents, students, politicians, teachers, and principals from surrounding schools came in daily. I even received notes from various vendors and lawyers who had provided services in the past to our school. These fine people provided me with the support needed to survive those trying times.

Many of the letters and notes were from people I had never met—people who had seen me on the evening news or read about our tragedy in the papers. It is a great comfort to know, firsthand, that humanity is really alive and well in a world that is seemingly full of such turmoil.

Other letters were from parents, students, fellow administrators from around the state, community leaders, and members. One letter written by a mother expressed her feelings that I knew how to handle the painful situation in the best possible way. She noted that she was a witness to all the good things that Bayonne High School offers and that her daughter, who was one of our students, received a great deal of attention. She concluded by saying, "KEEP IT GOING, you have the support of the Hispanic Community, wishing you the best."

The principal of a parochial high school in our county wrote, "Just wanted to let you know that my thoughts and prayers, and those of the Prep community have been with you and all at B.H.S. The week has reminded me of how vulnerable we are. If I can be of any help, please don't hesitate to call. May the days ahead be good ones for us all."

A letter from the all-girls' academy in our city expressed their heartfelt sorrow at the tragedy. The principal stated, "Dr. Wanko, I realize how hard you work to make your school an excellent institution of learning and it is unfortunate that such a crime could have been committed in Bayonne and in your school. Please know we shall remember you daily in our prayers."

The brigadier general commanding the Military Ocean Terminal in Bayonne expressed his knowledge that it was a very difficult time for me but wanted me to know that the parents and students of Bayonne High School are fortunate to have my leadership.

The superintendent sent a note as follows:

Your steadfastness and leadership skills came to the forefront these past tragic days. In the midst of our most trying times, you demonstrated the necessary decorum and decision making that helped students and staff "get through." By doing so, you helped me administer to the needs of the entire district. I am proud to have you on my staff.

One letter, from a senior at our school, conveyed his gratitude for the way in which I handled the tragedy. He expressed how it really hit home when an adult "that is looked up to by the students" expressed his emotions openly. He went on to say that he thought I was a great principal who showed much concern for the students and faculty. Furthermore, he expressed his appreciation of my not announcing the details of the tragedy until the family was notified. He went on to express his thankfulness regarding my dispatching vice principals to each homeroom to explain the situation. He felt this was a very humanistic gesture on my part. While all these comments were helpful to me during that terrible time, his statement, "I still feel safe at Bayonne High School." gave me additional strength to continue each day.

However, without the support of my wife of thirty years, Justine, our son, Jason, and my extended family, I do not know how I could have functioned at the level needed to maintain the safety, support, structure, stability, and control necessary to lead the students and the staff of Bayonne High School.

You also will be able to pick up the pieces and continue to move forward. All your hard work to achieve status and recognition for your students and school will not disappear due to a crisis. Everyone will be able to continue to grow due to the leadership you exert during and after the tragedy. Always keep in mind that you must be strong, as everyone will be looking to you for guidance and stability.

Although we had undergone four separate and distinctive crises in our school, we survived. Actually, when I reflect on that horrific year I can say that we more than survived. In a sense, we actually thrived. Our student body and staff came together and nurtured a stronger bond. The community came to our aid in our time of greatest need. My fellow administrators from around the state provided support on many levels. The parents and various parent groups of our school all rallied to ensure that the healing process could be achieved. The board of education and my administrative team worked very hard to return our school to normal. Everyone who learned of our trauma expressed their condolences and offered sentiments for staying strong and moving forward. I, as the educational leader of the school, was overwhelmed by the genuine support and concern offered by the community-at-large. This uplifting response provided me the strength and stamina needed to lead our Bayonne High School family onto the next restorative plateau.

Chapter 4

Factors That Affect School Safety

As I began to travel around the country speaking on safe schools and responding to crises, I would solicit ideas on what educators believed were necessary to create safe schools. In different regions of the country, slight nuances to the equation were evident. However, certain common factors were repeated and became universal to the basic ideas of what would constitute a safe school.

Concern was always expressed about the increase of violence in our culture. From the print media to evening newscasts, our children are exposed to a proliferation of violent episodes. Add to this the violence portrayed in the movies and video games and it is no wonder that aggression is rampant in our society.

While in high school and college, I remember watching the news and witnessing the atrocities of the Vietnam War. This was what I consider to be the beginning of the caustic, irresponsible behavior of the media, when sensationalism was chosen over good judgment. From this point on, many newscasters continued to push the envelope to enjoy higher ratings.

If it was acceptable to broadcast human slaughter during dinnertime in America, why should anything else be off-limits? No longer does the press respect the sanctity of the individual. In the 1930s and 1940s, the public never saw a photograph or newsreel of President Franklin D. Roosevelt in his wheelchair. Even to this day, many people are still not aware of his polio affliction. Yet, during the past two decades, broadcasters have flocked to portray our leaders in awkward situations. For example, in the 1970s they would clamor for film of President Gerald Ford falling. A few years later, when presidential candidate Bob Dole fell from a stage, it made all the network news programs.

When a fight breaks out between two professional athletes during competition, more airtime is often given to the fight rather than to the results of the competition or highlights of the event. Children watch their sports idols settling their disputes in a violent confrontation. If a sports team wins a national championship, the celebration that follows can result in a riotous situation. In 1993, when the Chicago Bulls won the NBA championship, two people were killed and almost 700 were arrested during the celebration.

The message being sent to our children is quite clear—violence is an acceptable way to resolve conflict. Until we, as a nation, decide that violence cannot be accepted in any form, our children are at risk to physical harm from a variety of sources in their environment. This risk is not confined to the schools, but rather it is pervasive in society. Schools are a microcosm of the community. If the community is violent, chances are violence will be experienced in the school. We cannot be expected to undo the culture of our society. How much can be done in six hours a day? Even when the school rules are clear and understood by all, disorder results when students believe that violence is acceptable in society.

Virtually every school administrator can relate a story about parents who encourage their children to fight. Normally, this tale is heard when two students are suspended for fighting. One or both sets of parents blame the other child for starting the fight. They explain their child's involvement as natural. "I tell my son not to take any garbage" or "Fight back whenever you feel threatened," are some of the usual comments expressed by the parents.

THE GOALS OF SAFE SCHOOLS

Goals have been set and achieved. Goals have been fixed and never realized. If we set achievable goals we will never go beyond our reach. On the other hand, if we reach for the stars, we may fall short of our goals. If we believe the traditional, that a goal is the end toward which effort or ambition is directed, setting goals should be easy. I always tell people that a goal is simply a dream with a timeline. It is imperative that when setting goals, we also set parameters. In the general sense, the dominant goal of school safety should be creating and maintaining a positive school climate. Goals should be expressed in short statements because simplicity and brevity will allow everyone to understand and strive for the same objective.

Goals for a Safe School Environment

- To ensure that the school is free of violence and crime
- To create a positive and welcoming school climate
- To maintain this type of atmosphere at all times

- To remove all fear and intimidation
- To maintain a drug-free environment

When these goals are met, schools become places where teachers can teach and students can learn. The climate will promote the success of students, allowing them to reach their fullest potentials. The professional staff can best serve the student population when fear and intimidation have been removed. If everyone feels safe and secure at school, all can concentrate on the business of teaching and learning.

Unfortunately, this is not yet the case in all of our schools. A review of the *Indicators of School Crime and Safety*, which was published by the National Center for Education Statistics and Bureau of Justice Statistics, in October 1998, points out this fact. By combining their reports of thefts and violent crimes occurring on or near school campuses every year, a number approaching 3 million is achieved. Keep in mind that it is not only our students who are at risk. Of that number, nearly 250,000 are crimes committed against teachers. Breaking down this number to a daily occurrence, it equates to almost 16,000 incidents per school day. A further breakdown reveals that one incident occurs every six seconds. Imagine employees in corporate America working in settings where they are prone to such a staggering rate of crime. Immediate corrective action would be taken by employers to maintain a cadre of competent employees.

Think about coming into work everyday in fear. You would certainly seek employment elsewhere. Our students normally do not have this luxury. Many are forced to attend a school that is considered to be dangerous. This danger could only be a perception, or it could be based in truth. The results of the label will remain the same—students living in fear.

In 1999, the U.S. Department of Justice released statistics regarding our students living in fear. They estimated that every day 100,000 students bring guns to school. Furthermore, they reported that 160,000 students miss class everyday because they fear physical harm. These numbers are quite disconcerting. All of these particulars translate to problems in schools.

Some of our children turn to drugs, cults, or gangs to either escape or gain recognition. Often this is the only way they can feel successful or accrue an identity. It appears that our juvenile justice system ensures that children younger than eighteen are always given the benefit of the doubt, they are easily paroled or go unconvicted when caught in an illegal activity. As a result they are solicited as perpetrators for crimes by career criminals. School must be the safe haven for our children. Sometimes it is the only place that can provide support, stability, and control. It should be a place where children can experience that feeling of belonging and importance. A place where their efforts can be recognized.

IDENTIFYING SAFE SCHOOL FACTORS

What constitutes a safe school environment? Why is one school considered safe and another viewed as menacing? Certainly, perceptions play an important role in how the community views its schools. However, many schools are not only perceived as safe, but their annual reports on vandalism, violence, and drug abuse reflect this perception. On the other hand, some schools are assumed to be unsafe due to their location. Their reports can attest to their safety, but the perception due to proximity labels them as menacing. Many factors can serve to determine if a particular school is a safe haven for its students and staff.

Environment of Surrounding Neighborhood

Individuals bring a variety of experiences that influence their participation in the school community. This multitude of prior learning experiences sway their participation in either a positive or a negative manner. Students bring all kinds of baggage to school everyday. Even in what appears to be the best of family units, various forms of trauma can be present. In 1999, I remember sitting on a state panel discussing the problems of school violence when a young man in the audience addressed the panel and identified himself as a student of a prestigious school in a very wealthy community. He spoke about his feelings and those of his friends, explaining that they would rather live in smaller houses and be able to spend more time with their parents. He lamented that he hardly ever saw his parents, as they worked long hours to maintain a certain lifestyle. These young people felt abandoned by their well-to-do families. Paradoxically, the parents believed that by working long hours they would counteract the negative aspects of spending time away from the family unit.

Unfortunately, this concept is very common. Parents seem to forget that material possessions are not the really important things in life. Children need their parents to spend time with them. They also need to have boundaries set by the parents. When the expectations are set early and clearly, the household can thrive. Responsibility must be given to the children and be accepted by the parents. The parents must welcome the responsibility to be available to their children. Perhaps they do not need a $400,000 house in the best neighborhood. A modest home in an average community will serve the family better if the parents can be home to spend more time with their children.

This is exactly what this young man was expressing at the panel discussion. He wanted his parents at home to share with him the everyday joys and sorrows of growing up in America. He did not care that his house was valued at nearly $500,000. He wanted his parents to spend more time at home.

The extra cars and all the so-called advantages he was afforded would be given up immediately for a better relationship with his parents.

People are quick to mention that it is not the amount of time spent with the child, rather, the quality of time. The time has come for us as Americans to review this philosophy. I believe that more time spent with children is better. Some of this time could be as inconsequential as sitting in the same room with parents and children engaged in separate activities. It may not be quality time, but it is time spent together. Our children need to be with adults for longer periods of time. Nothing can replace the benefits of a loving home life.

On the other hand, we in schools are faced with a proliferation of problems brought into the schools. Some students have been victims of severe physical abuse. Others have been raised in abject poverty. Naturally, they present unique challenges. They come to schools without proper nourishment and can become ill more often than children who are properly fed and have warm homes with running water. They have a feeling of insecurity and bring a sense of hopelessness to the school. As a result, many children could be distrustful of schools. To these students the need to belong is essential. Administrators need to address this need if they hope to develop a positive climate and be proactive in creating a safe school environment.

Drug Activity

Drug activity in and around school can have a profound effect on the safety of students attending the school. It is imperative that the school administration aggressively attack the drug problem in the school. Programs to educate students on the harmful effects of addiction need to begin in the primary grades and continue through twelfth grade. Outside forces are constantly bombarding our youth and luring them into the drug culture. Drugs are seductive and children can easily become addicted, resulting in aberrant behavior thus compromising the safety of the school. Money is needed to support a drug habit. Crime is the obvious way that this money can be obtained.

More difficult for administrators is the spillover of drug activity around the schools. The government recognized this problem and established "Drug-Free School Zones." This was a well-intentioned movement to help protect our children. However, when viewing the signs that designate these drug-free zones, I often wonder if postings should be placed at the end of the zones. These signs would read, "End of Drug-Free Zone—Resume Selling Drugs." As ludicrous as this may sound, think of the concept. Rather than making the penalty for all drug dealing more severe, the government specified a school zone for harsher rules. Why not make it more severe for all drug sales? We seem to be losing the so-called War on Drugs. We need to attack the problem at its roots, so that everyone in society can be safer.

Our culture cannot espouse that it is acceptable to use drugs for recreational purposes. We cannot send the message to our children that it is acceptable for those of celebrity status to use drugs. Impressions that the rich and famous can use drugs and not suffer the consequences need to be quelled. If not, everyone in our culture will be doomed to suffer the consequences of this type of attitude.

Community Crime Rates

Another factor that negatively affects school safety is a high community crime rate. If drugs are a problem in your community, the crime rate will escalate. Even if drug trafficking is not rampant around your school, the crime rate can still be of concern. Unfortunately, this is an area in which you, as the school administrator, have very little control. It is a factor that is not malleable by school personnel. Consequently, you must develop a good working relationship with the local police and various community groups. Working together as a team is the only way you can hope to attack the problem of community crime rates and prevent the spillover effect on your school.

As the building administrator, you can meet with neighborhood groups to work together to find solutions to combat community crime rates. Often the school is the place for these groups to meet. Invite personnel from the police and fire departments to attend meetings. If there are stores or small businesses around the school, invite the owners to these meetings. These business people have the same interest as you—creating a crime-free area. Similarly, clergy members are usually willing to attend and lend support. Try to supply refreshments and have agendas for the meetings written beforehand. While you have little control over the crime rate surrounding your campus, you can still attack the problem by mobilizing the neighborhood.

Presence of Gangs or Nonstudents

Gangs can compromise school safety. This adds to the possibility of a nonstudent presence in and around the school. The problem of nonstudents entering schools has become an increasing concern because while some of these "visits" could be for legitimate reasons, most are clandestine in nature. Even though schools keep doors in the panic lock position, students have devised many ways to gain entry. By establishing a strict dress code, nonstudents can usually be identified quickly. Naturally, in smaller schools the presence of a nonstudent is noticed quickly. In larger schools identification of these trespassers becomes more challenging. Mandatory wearing of an identification badge can assist in these instances.

To combat the gang factor, you need to first identify the gangs who are in the school and in the community. Visible signs are relativity easy to determine. For example, paraphernalia such as clothing and graffiti can indicate a gang affiliation. Clothing can include bandannas, belt buckles, caps, shoelaces, and certain styles of clothing. More subtle signs are the colors worn by gang members. More obvious and extreme is the use of tattoos to show affiliation. Finally, members can communicate to others with slang, slogans, and the flashing of signs.

Care must be taken to discourage gang activity. A strong dress code will help to lessen the perception of gangs. It also deters and diminishes the concept that a student becomes someone important when joining a gang. If the students cannot flaunt their membership by sporting their colors in school some of the gang allure is diminished. Watch for patterns of congregation. Gangs are territorial in nature. Members will try to claim a portion of the school or campus. They will mark this region with graffiti and congregate in that area. It is relatively easy to discover these areas in the school. Take note of the group that gravitates to a certain area. If it is truly a claimed territory, other students will not trespass to that sector even when the gang is not occupying the turf.

Once you have identified the gangs, call in the leaders. Inform them that you are aware of their gang and that you and your staff will be monitoring their activities. Review the school rules and policies prohibiting gang activities. The next step is to meet with the parents of the gang members. Provide information about the gang. Review the school rules and consequences regarding negative gang activities. Try to solicit parent support in curtailing disruptive gang pastimes. Do not be surprised if parents show disbelief regarding their children's membership in gangs. Also, do not be alarmed if a parent was a member of the same gang and fails to see the harmful effects of membership.

Currently, the dominant gangs are ethnic in nature. White "stoner" gangs are growing. This group is drawn to heavy metal music. Male chauvinistic attitudes are promoted. They are a recent phenomenon as compared with other ethnic gangs. However, young people are drawn to the group for many of the same reasons as the well-established gangs, such as the breakdown of family values. Adolescents need to belong, feel wanted, and be valued. When these needs are not met in the home, children will look elsewhere.

Punk rock began as a movement of social rebellion in England during the 1970s. American punkers oppose acceptable American values. They too, are growing in certain communities.

Hispanic gangs descend from Spanish-speaking cultures. Usually a team approach is used in these gangs for leadership purposes. Occasionally, as the situation dictates, a member with a specific talent will assume the leadership role.

The late 1930s saw a proliferation of black youth gangs. They originally organized around street crime activity. The Crips became the dominate black gang during the 1970s but are rivaled by the Bloods. It is not unusual for these groups to deal with narcotic trafficking. Local affiliates of the Crips and Bloods can be prevalent in some communities.

Cities with large Asian populations can expect the rise of Asian gangs. These gang members are more difficult to identify. They adhere to a strict code of silence and do not wear distinctive clothing. Usually, they have experienced leadership, are well-structured, and are profit-motivated.

Included in the Asian crews are Chinese, Samoan, and Vietnamese gangs. The Chinese groups, who originated from the respectable social organizations called Tongs, are the oldest. Samoan gangs mark their turf and wear gang clothing. The Vietnamese groups often victimize their own people. This is because many law-abiding Vietnamese distrust police authority and do not come forward regarding gang activities.

Then there is the proliferation of gangs that are unique to your community. It is not unusual for adolescents to form gangs in their own neighborhood. Occasionally, these neighborhood gangs can reach out to a larger area and allow membership to like-thinking youth. Make no mistake, these home-grown gangs can be just as dangerous as the well-established national groups with local affiliations.

Be aware that the female affiliation in gangs is escalating and their violent acts are on the rise proportionately. Membership is usually open to children as young as nine and adults up to about forty years old. When dealing with gang members, understand that this is their culture. It is their family unit and their mode to acceptance as a person. Finally, cooperation with law enforcement is essential to reduce gang activity in and around schools.

Nonstudents can affect your school safety plan. I am referring to the group of adolescents who are not in gangs or schools. Usually, this category of youth travels alone or in small groups and likes to congregate around the schools for many of the same reasons as gang members. Many are former students who have quit or have been expelled. Some may be alumni. Their attraction to the campus is normally due to their friends still attending the school. Others are there to conduct illegal activities. Remember, you are housing potential customers for all types of illegal activities and products.

Design of Facilities

The design of the school and campus will dictate how your safety plan evolves. It is unreasonable for the building administrator to suggest that the physical layout of the campus be altered in a cost prohibitive manner.

Naturally, an argument could be easily made that money should not be an issue when dealing with student and staff safety. However, as with all budgetary matters, a fine balance between the good of the school and the demands placed on the local taxpayer must be considered.

For new school construction safety factors should be considered early in the planning. It is easy to change ideas on the blueprints. It is very difficult to get a change order approved by a board of education during construction. Again, the cost factor will become pivotal.

Once the building administrator determines the areas of the school and campus that are breaches to security, careful planning to create a safer environment can ensue. Some corrections to existing facilities could be as simple as adding lights to the roofs of buildings. The added lighting around the perimeter of the buildings and on the grounds will deter vandalism and prevent groups from gathering.

Installation of security cameras and intercom systems can be accomplished quite easily and relatively inexpensively. Burglar alarms can also deter potential perpetrators. To make these alarms even more effective, they should be visible. Post signs noting their presence as an additional deterrent.

Some administrators have removed all pull handles from the outside of entry doors. Only the visitors' doors retain handle hardware, thereby deterring people from trying to enter the complex from other areas. The installation of fences around the campus can divert unwanted visitors. Fences can also serve as guides for visitors, channeling them to the proper entrance.

Many schools use security gates in hallways to cordon off sections of the building. This concept must be reviewed with the fire department to ensure that proper egress is afforded to the student and staff. Normally, this type of hall gate is used during after-school hours or when school is not in session.

Remember, when considering the facility issues to make your school safer, reflect on the perception of your school. Ensure that the school is safe without making it look like a military compound. For example, if you decide that fencing around the school is necessary, soften the visual impact of the fence. Plant shrubbery and trees to cover as much of the fencing as possible. The school should still be inviting and maintain its history as the center of activities for the community.

SAFE SCHOOL STRATEGIES

During the past ten years, many strategies have been developed to ensure a safe school environment. Some of these concepts are new, others are recycled, and some are combinations of old and new. As the building administrator, you need to review all options before developing your total safety plan. Many strategies can be implemented immediately and without much financial burden. Other strategies will require a change in board policy. Still others will require training of personnel. If construction or installation of equipment is part of your plan, expect some disruption of the school routine.

Regardless of the strategies you choose, much work on your part will be necessary to assure fruition of your plan. Teachers and support staff may be asked to change their routines numerous times or have more expected of them. As the educational leader of the school, you need to set the example regarding the importance of these changes. Some faculty members will resist change even when its value is obvious. Others will join you wholeheartedly with great enthusiasm. A third group will just stand by to watch what happens.

That is why it is essential for you to plan carefully. Appoint as many staff members as possible to various committees when designing the safety plan. If each committee member convinces just one or two colleagues regarding the value of the program, the word will spread like wildfire. The more people who buy into the concept, the easier it will be to introduce the changes necessary for success.

School Curriculum

The school curriculum is a powerful tool to aid you in your safety plan. It is also one area that is very much under your control. Naturally, the principal must follow state and federal mandates regarding curriculum, however, much leeway is afforded the creative administrator. A strong family-living course is essential in providing proper values to our youth. Your social studies curriculum is another vehicle that can be used to extol the virtues of this country.

Our first attempts to develop curriculum that would assist in creating a safe and supportive school came in the way of offering various courses such as ebony culture, American social issues, and ethnic cuisine. In addition to the standard Spanish, French, German, and Latin languages, we offered four languages that were reflective of the population at that time. Imagine a school offering Hebrew, Polish, Italian, and Russian. We then took it to the next level by offering Japanese and courses in conversational Spanish, Italian, and French.

It was hoped that by learning about differences, the student body would not only accept diversity, but become fully immersed in other cultures. Students could discuss differences in open forums, sample foods from various cultures, and speak to one another in a language other than their own. The obvious result would be less confrontation among students.

As we progressed, it became evident that other avenues needed to be explored. Therefore, we developed courses such as transitional English and expanded the traditional English as a second language (ESL) program to include classes in social studies and the sciences. The infusion of specially designed courses to ease the transition to the United States has been quite successful. Foreign-born students could feel comfortable and less threatened by their new environment. The physical education program was also modified to provide a rotating elective program and team-building activities.

Although there were no real concerns regarding the performance of students in the physical education curriculum area, it presented an arena where student-to-student acceptance could be fostered. The plan was to bring students together and encourage them to work together as a team. As part of the freshman curriculum, we infused a segment of cooperative games and adventure activities.

Freshmen enrolled in physical education are divided into small groups of eight to ten students. This lowers our section size for PE 9. Normally, each section hovered around forty to fifty students. Now that number has a range of twenty-five to thirty.

After a few days, the teacher has a good handle on the diversity of the student population assigned to a particular section. At this time the instructor divides the students into smaller groupings, being careful to maintain a reflective cross-section. The students are then assigned a variety of tasks that require cooperation, interaction, and an emphasis on nonverbal communication. Thus, we have assurance that at least the spoken word could not be used as a cultural bias. After two weeks of activities, the students are brought to our on-campus High Adventure Course, which won us our first Best Practices Award from the New Jersey Department of Education.

This is the only urban school in the state that can boast such an extensive array of outdoor elements on campus—all assembled in a courtyard. For example, a thirty-foot climbing wall is attached to the side of the school. Other elements are the suspended log, spider web, nitro crossing, ten-foot climbing wall, barrel roll, cargo net, porthole, teeter-totter, tire traverse, tension traverse, and the fidget ladder. Here, students are graded on successful completion of each task as a team. When the youngsters realize that each is dependent on the other, amazing results in the area of student-to-student acceptance are noticed.

During the past few years, we have developed an award-winning life-skills course offering: *Family Living and the Developing Child*. This course affords our students excellent opportunities to learn strong family values. Students study relationships and personal responsibilities. They are exposed to the pitfalls of poor decision making. They are taught the steps necessary to make proper choices in their lives. Morals, traditional values, and clinical information on child rearing are presented to the students. The course is taught by a health educator who is also a registered nurse. This teacher serves not only as an instructor, but as a confidant and advisor to these students. Every year we exceed the enrollment parameters for this offering. As the budget allows, we will expand this program with the hope of eventually making it a requirement for graduation.

Service Learning can teach students proper values and the ideals of service to others. By requiring a service learning component for graduation, we have made sure that our students will learn more than just subject matter. It provides our students with another connection to the community, thereby, providing us with another piece in the safe school puzzle. Adults see students in another setting, one that demonstrates that adolescents can be caring and committed to the community. Students learn that adults have attributes other than authority. The stereotypes held by both groups can be changed to support for one other.

Establish Clear Student Expectations

The most obvious strategy is to establish clear student expectations. When students, parents, teachers, and administrators know what is expected of each other, a well-run school is the result. The same is true for a safe school. When developing the rules and regulations for student conduct and safety, make sure it is a collaborative effort. When all the stakeholders are involved, they can claim ownership of the resulting policy. They will buy into the total package when they know why the rules were established. They will understand the mechanics and comprehend the consequences of violation.

Most schools publish student and faculty handbooks. These handbooks contain rules, regulations, and consequences. Information such as phone numbers, personnel listings, school history, and various other facts concerning school life are included. Although well meaning, most of these handbooks are written in a negative mode. They list the possible offenses and then present the disciplinary action that will result from violations. It would be just as easy to write these publications in a more positive vein. For example, a statement such as, "No running in the halls" could be phrased as, "Walk at a normal pace in the halls."

Distribution of expectations is essential for your safety plan to be successful. Listing an expectancy in a booklet that fighting is unacceptable and will result in a harsh penalty is necessary. However, if the handbook is not in the possession of the students, they could plead ignorance.

Many years ago I began the policy of a summer mailing. I compile an assemblage of information and send it to all students and parents/guardians at their homes. In this packet I provide an overview of student expectations. The individual student schedule is included as well as pertinent information on student services, a school calendar, phone numbers of various offices, and other types of general information.

Each year we conduct an onsite eighth-grade "Bridges to High School" Day. All eighth graders and their parents are invited to Bayonne High School for a special program. The program is run by the BHS ambassadors during the normal school day so that an accurate picture of our daily operation can be experienced. The program begins in the auditorium with performances by various musical groups. Next, an overview of the curriculum and a review of student expectations are provided. This is followed by skits about high school, growing up, and the student coping services we provide. The ambassadors conduct campus tours that are followed by an activities fair and refreshments.

After the elementary school visits, ambassadors serve as big brothers and sisters for elementary students who would like to spend a full day at the high school. These visitors follow the same schedule of the assigned ambassador so they may acquire a genuine feel for the school and its offerings. Incoming students learn the rules and regulations of the school and the manner in which they are expected to behave. Due to the ambassadors' efforts, they also feel connected. When everyone knows the expectations and feels as if they are part of the school family, fewer conflicts occur and school safety is enhanced.

Prior to the opening of school, we conduct an orientation program for students new to Bayonne High School. This is normally done in August on a nonschool day. The incoming freshman class and all transfer students are invited to attend. Students have a chance to meet their vice principal, counselor, and other teachers involved in various activities. After I greet the students at a general gathering in the auditorium, students are divided into smaller groups to review expectations. Student ambassadors guide the new students through their schedules and show them points of interest and areas of importance. We end the day with a barbecue and an activities fair. In this manner, new students have established a support network prior to the first day of school.

To elicit firsthand feedback, I meet with the freshmen in small groups. The vehicle for this gathering is simple. I select one period of the day each year for my visit. The visits are conducted during this same period throughout that school year. I do not select any period when lunch is served. If I did, 30 percent of the freshmen would still be in large groups during those periods.

I take the time to go to their classes because small group meetings allow for more interaction. It would be easier for me to meet with the entire freshman class in the auditorium, however, this would result in a sterile situation. Students would not be as willing to share concerns in a group of 500 peers. By visiting classrooms, I reduce this number to about twenty-five students. This results in a more personal approach.

First, I explain that my visits are designed to improve the school community. I cite examples of suggestions that have been implemented such as menu changes for the cafeterias, new lockers, and renovated toilet facilities. After the preliminaries, I ask the students to imagine that they are king or queen for the day. As such, they could change anything at the high school. Many times specific rules are questioned during these visits. I respond to the queries and solicit ideas for making the rules more effective. Most of the time, the students react in a positive manner. Usually, students are more compliant when the reason for implementing the rule is known.

Divide Large Schools

Another strategy to create a safer school is to divide a larger school into smaller schools. This concept has been around for many decades, and was highlighted in the National Association of Secondary School Principals publication *Breaking Ranks—Changing an American Institution* in 1996, as a notion to increase accountability, provide for individuality, and maintain safety. The concept is simple—smaller is better. The house plan, a school-within-a-school concept, affords students the intimacy of a small school, while providing all the facilities that a large institution can offer. As a result, students receive the best of both worlds.

There are many types of school-within-a-school plans. Administrative teams in schools with populations of more than 1,000 should establish a committee to review this concept. This committee should be composed of teachers, administrators, support staff (such as secretarial, custodial, food services, transportation, and maintenance), parents, community groups, chamber of commerce members, and students.

Prior to the implementation of the house plan or school-within-a-school concept, students of Bayonne High School were assigned to certain areas of the complex according to the curriculum major that they selected. In a sense we were segregating students according to majors.

In the mid-seventies, with a population of 3,500 students, we moved to a house plan. Preceding the change, we sent a team to visit many schools who had instituted the concept. After review of the scholastic data and the information collected by our visits, we designed our plan. We could not develop a plan that would involve construction, rather, we needed to create a plan that could be retrofitted into our existing layout.

This presented many problems unique to our school and student body. The plan we developed established six houses on our campus. The school and its buildings were divided by geography. An equal number of staff members and students were divided among the houses (approximately 600 students and thirty-five instructors per house). Custodians were also divided in a like manner. A house director was appointed as the leader for each house, and small offices in each location were constructed. Finally, a secretary was assigned to each house office to complete the staffing plan.

The first few years were difficult as teachers and students became accustomed to reporting to a new leader in different areas of the campus. To facilitate the change, we conducted many meetings before implementing the plan. These meetings were held for faculty, support staff, students, parents, and the community-at-large. Since most of our parents and many of our staff graduated from the school, this type of change was difficult to accept.

Everyone on the original team worked very hard to make the transition as easy as possible. However, as with any change in a high school, it normally takes about four years for it to be fully accepted. After four years there is no longer a class of students left in the school who knows the old system. Then, as an entire new class of students moves through the school, the old system becomes totally foreign to the student body. Now, two decades after the implementation of our house plan, it has become a common concept accepted by students, faculty, parents, and the community.

The benefits of this plan are many. The vice principals get to know the students assigned to their houses. The students develop a closeness to the teachers, counselors, and vice principal in their house. Students no longer feel as though they are lost in a sea of humanity. They become individuals of worth. Self-esteem is raised and a camaraderie between students and staff is developed. All of these factors help to establish a safer school.

The ability to know students by sight is a safety factor that cannot be overstated. Behavior is improved when the students know that they are recognized by the administration and faculty. It is more tempting for some students to misbehave if the chance to be apprehended is nonexistent. These students think twice about violating the rules simply because someone on the staff might recognize them.

The Bayonne High School House Plan has developed a cohesiveness in managing a diverse population. It gives students the opportunity to develop positive, interpersonal skills, and team building. Each homeroom is a true reflection of the community-at-large.

Embrace Diversity

Schools that have a multicultural student body need to embrace and celebrate their diversity. We are so diverse that no bilingual courses are offered,

as the number of students in any given language is always below the federal requirement of twenty. We have innumerable programs that enable us
to maintain our quest of embracing diversity. Many of these programs also
serve to reduce violence, vandalism, drug abuse, and other problems prevalent in today's secondary schools. We have found that by welcoming diversity, many of these problems have diminished. When our students leave us
to begin the next phase of their lives, they are better prepared to function in
a divergent population.

Everyone needs to belong, yet we all feel the need to be proud of our heritage. Unfortunately, in some schools these differences cause a division in the
student body. Remember, like students tend to gravitate together. Unless the
administration recognizes the need for expression of a rich cultural heritage,
the chasm among these groups will grow. Ultimately, disagreements and even
fighting can result. By chartering specific groups or clubs to recognize various
cultures, a school sponsored vehicle is then provided for cultural expression.

When these groups are sanctioned by the school, a crossover begins to occur. It is not unusual in our school for 20 percent of a cultural club to be of a
different background than that of the chartering group. Almost 30 percent of
our Latino Dance Club membership is derived from non-Hispanic backgrounds. Students learn about different cultures by attending and participat-
ing in meetings. Throughout the year these clubs conduct various activities,
that are open to the entire student body, to radiate information about their specific interests.

Create Programs to Foster Conflict Resolution

Whenever you gather large groups of adolescents, many against their will in
one complex, conflict seems to be inevitable. I like to refer to our population
as the Bayonne High School Family, and as in any family, disagreements can
occur. The way that those misunderstandings are handled, dictate if the disagreements will escalate to violence.

To lessen the chances for violence, many types of programs can be infused
into your school. Peer mediation can be very effective. It is based on a simple concept: kids will listen to kids. Care must be taken to provide proper
training for your peer mediators. Safeguards for the sessions must be pru-
dently crafted. If you structure the program well, amazing results can occur.
Our peer mediators have proven to be very successful.

Other organizations that we have chartered have also proven prosperous in
our school. These groups foster open and positive communications. Peer
Leadership is a program that has been in existence for a number of years.
Members learn to communicate in positive and effective ways. They actively
seek opportunities to initiate understanding, tolerance, and respect for people
of all cultures and ethnicity.

ERASE is an acronym for End Racism and Sexism Everywhere. This program is designed to eradicate the negative feelings and ideas held by individuals in regard to all types of prejudice. They meet twice a month to plan activities that promote the positive aspects of a diverse community.

Our Student Center Club provides students with a comprehensive array of activities to promote a safe, culturally enriched, and cooperative school atmosphere. Members serve as conflict mediators, peer tutors, and Student Center hosts. Members also attend recreational and cultural field trips and perform psychodramatic skits depicting typical adolescent concerns.

The Ambassadors' Club promotes the values and ideals of the school and disseminates information about the academic program, campus life, sports, and school activities. Specially designed uniforms sporting our school crest are issued to each ambassador. Staff members nominate students to be ambassadors. This group of nominees is then interviewed by the advisors and a vice principal who, in turn, makes the final selections. Members must be academically successful and hold the virtues and qualities promoted by the school. They promote a sense of school spirit, loyalty, and respect.

We also chartered the Student Self Advocacy Team (SSAT). Its goals are designed to protect student rights through advocacy and empowering students to take charge of their destiny. Members learn to discover their hidden abilities, interests, and talents. Initially, the organization attracted classified students with learning disabilities. Membership has now spread to students with physical disabilities and other medical concerns. Students without any disabilities have also joined because they share common concerns regarding student rights. During the 2000–2001 school year we received a Best Practices Award from the New Jersey State Department of Education for this program.

SPHERE is the acronym for Students Promoting Humanity and Equal Rights Education. Students created this program with the hope of including all adolescents in the school. It is designed to make all students comfortable with their educational institution. Members encourage their fellow students to take personal pride in the school. They advocate respect for the school and the people inside it. By taking personal pride, it is hoped that violence will be eliminated and involvement will bring about a safe environment in the school. They sponsor forums on antiviolence and communications. Additionally, they developed the Adopt-A-Homeroom program. Upper-class students adopt a freshman homeroom to make students comfortable in school and acquaint them with activities.

The student council of any school can be a driving force to foster a safe school environment. Our group of dynamic students works at our freshman orientation and serves as hosts for various school functions. They spearhead the Spirit Committee which meets every week to make and post signs of upcoming events at the school. They also work to elicit the support of all students for all activities. Other activities sponsored by the student council have been The Day of Respect, Homecoming, Spirit Week, Lock-Ins, and the annual Valentine charity flower sale.

Enhance Interagency Cooperation

Establishing a good working relationship with local agencies cannot be overstated. Schedule meetings every other month with representatives from the police and fire departments, Division of Youth and Family Services (DYFS), Chamber of Commerce, and mental-health organizations. These groups can provide valuable services to students, parents, and staff. Each group can furnish verbal accounts of the services they provide for the community and the vehicles through which particular needs are met. Try to meet with each agency separately. This will require more time on your part, however, the personal relationship you develop with them will be returned many fold to your students.

A technique that can help to develop a strong interagency relationship is to provide office space for some of these agencies. We have provided space for the Drug Abuse Resistance Education (DARE) and Community Oriented Policing (COP) police officers. For more than four decades we have provided an office for the Juvenile Aid Bureau (JAB). Some principals do not like a police presence in the school, however, I have found this practice to be quite beneficial and actually symbiotic. The high school administrative team knows the JAB squad and vice versa. We are not just voices on the phone, each group is familiar with the other.

Over the years, we have developed an excellent working relationship with the juvenile officers assigned to the office at the high school. A procedure to share information has evolved that assists both the police and school personnel. Open communication is the key. If a problem arises that requires assistance from the police, we receive an immediate response from the JAB officers.

The space afforded to the DARE officers is in an ideal location. Fortunately, I was able to assign them to an area within our student activities center. This was the old guidance suite in the main building. With a little work, we were able to convert this space into offices for advisors to the yearbook, school newspaper, and student council. An additional office was assigned to the DARE officers. There is also a large group area in the middle of the offices. As a result, the students who are working in these offices and group area are exposed to the police in a different venue. It is not unusual for a student to ask an officer for an opinion on an item earmarked for the yearbook or school newspaper.

For the duration of the COPs In Schools grant, I am providing space adjacent to the Senior Lounge for these three officers. This allows for a police presence in three buildings of the campus. I provided all of these officers with our walkie-talkies. We do not expect these officers to respond to normal problems in the school. However, in the instances when police would have been summoned to the campus, we use the walkie-talkies for a quick response.

Usually, the local fire department does not seek office space in schools, but there are occasions when they would like to be on the premises. For example, during Fire Prevention and Awareness Week it is a good practice to offer a temporary area for fire personnel. This section can also be used for students to display their work done in preparation for Fire Prevention and Awareness Week.

I have also developed a program with fire officials to provide discipline and education to students who pull false alarms. Whenever students involved with false alarms or bomb threats are apprehended, a ten-day out-of-school suspension is mandated. During the suspension, these students are assigned to spend time at two locations. One is the Student Center where counseling is provided and the other is at the local firehouse. Here, the culprits learn the day-to-day operations of the fire department. They witness the dangers of responding to alarms. Prior to being readmitted to school, they are also required to write compositions on fire safety.

I have found this program to be quite successful. The number of false alarms in the school has dropped drastically over the past ten years. Even during those trying times following the tragedy at Littleton, Colorado, we were spared the rash of false alarms imposed on our neighboring schools.

As the principal, it is incumbent on you to develop ties with DYFS and local mental health organizations. Establishing good working relationships with these agencies are essential for your school community. There will be times when you need to refer a child or parent to either of these agencies. It is much easier to accomplish goals if both parties know the person on the other side of the phone.

The local chamber of commerce can aid your safety plan in many ways. For example, when you develop a safety drill for your school, you will need to move students to alternate areas. There might be a natural disaster that strikes the school, a gas leak, or a hostage situation. In any event, safe and secure areas must be designated in advance. Once these areas are established, movement of your students can be accomplished in a safe and orderly fashion. If there are no other schools in close proximity to the school that needs to be evacuated, the chamber of commerce can aid in finding locations that can be used for this purpose. Officers of this group can serve as the agents to facilitate agreements between school officials and building owners. Sometimes a natural site such as a movie theater is overlooked by school officials.

Create a Climate of Ownership and Pride

Each year I select a theme to assist with developing pride in our school and we develop activities that revolve around that topic. For example, one year I chose "Celebrate Diversity" as the theme. Prior to that year, "cultural tolerance" seemed to be the buzz words used by many schools. Yet, I felt it was demeaning to our students. Cultural tolerance sent a message that we would just tolerate someone who was different. I wanted to send a message that was much stronger and more powerful. The message was that we considered our greatest strength to be our diversity. A missive that we, in the Bayonne High School community, embrace differences and learn from everyone. A directive that a view different from your own is just as important as your own.

For the 1999–00 school year, I took another approach regarding the selection of a theme. I sent a cross-section of students to Camp Anytown. This program is run by the National Conference for Community and Justice (NCCJ). At this weeklong program, the students learn communication and leadership skills. They also select projects to bring back to their schools. These projects are designed to combat concerns voiced by the students. Our team presented me with three topics from which I selected the year's theme, "Look at me, See within, Understanding will begin." The shortened version was placed on signs and posters read, "Look, See, Understand."

Everyone should feel like a key part of the school community. If all have ownership, a feeling of pride will result. If the stakeholders possess pride in the school, a safer environment will ensue. I assign various areas of the school to different clubs and teams. It becomes their responsibility to decorate and maintain these areas. It is here that meeting notices and practice dates are posted. Additionally, newspaper articles on the accomplishment of the group or an individual in the organization grace the area. These display areas go virtually untouched by graffiti or vandalism. Students take pride in the area and spread this feeling of ownership to the rest of the student body.

Our Ecology Club plants various shrubs and flowers at different times of the year throughout the campus. The Art Association paints a mural depicting harmony or other topics related to working together for the common good. The Environmental Club takes water samples from the bay behind the school to test for bacteria. The Spirit Committee designs and hangs signs that advertise upcoming school events. They then place these signs throughout the school for all to see. Members of the National Honor Society and the Ambassadors Club serve as peer tutors. We even have a student group that posts all messages on the outside marquee.

To add to the overall esprit de corps of the school, the building administrator needs to practice Management by Walking Around (MBWA). This concept certainly is not new, however, it speaks to the issues of positive climate and ownership. By being a visible entity, the students and staff realize that you care about the school. Reports and other paperwork can be done after the students and staff leave the building. Spend time talking to kids in the cafeterias and the corridors; greet them in the morning as they enter the school; stand outside the building at dismissal to ensure that you are the last person they see before going home for the evening.

Form Partnerships with Businesses and Parents

Another approach that will affect school safety is the implementation of partnerships for schools. These affiliations can become an important key for success in your safety plan. The partnerships can be formal, as through the local chamber of commerce, or informal, such as individual parents working in the school. Parent groups can also be enlisted for safety planning regardless of their affiliation to a specific school club, sport, or activity.

In addition to partnerships with the local police, fire, and mental health agencies to provide services as needed, relationships with business and industry can be quite beneficial. Students can witness the opportunities available in the partnering business. Many who thought that there was no chance to be successful in life can gain a new perspective. Especially helpful is an association with a company that has a number of alumni from your school as employees. Students meet and speak with people who were just like them a few short years ago. The goal to become successful without resorting to crime is reinforced by these partnerships.

If students see only criminal activity as a means to success, they model this behavior. Positive role models from your partner organization can change a child's perspective. Administrators should work hard to forge these associations. The company paired with the school can provide not only monetary gain, but human resources can be made available. This results in more adults in the school.

Since 1988, Bayonne High School has been in a partnership with International Matex Tank Terminals (IMTT). The headquarters for this worldwide industry is in New Orleans; however, in the early 1980s the company came into Bayonne. They purchased land with existing ports in the industrial section of the city. During the past twelve years, they have contributed more than $150,000 in the way of grants for programs designed by the students and staff. They also serve in a job-referral capacity by providing employment for our students. Additionally, they provide chaperones for trips to sporting events, and specialists who come into the school to share their expertise.

One program that they have funded over the past decade is the Broadway Scholars Program. This program allows a group of students to attend a Broadway play in New York. They also provide a $100 award each month to local restaurants for the teacher of the month program. Our annual Senior Day program is also funded by this company. This program places half of the senior class against the other in various competitions. It allows our seniors to be kids again, if just for the day. Music and a barbecue are provided. Additional money has been granted for AP testing, various educational software programs, as well as music and art supplies.

This type of partnership establishes a strong community tie with the school. As a result, school safety can be enhanced. Periodic visits to the school by the partnering agency also provide additional adults in the building.

Parent involvement to assist in creating safe schools is easy to understand. First, anytime adults are in the building, student behavior is affected. Add to this the fact that students know the adults, and the effect is even stronger. Usually, the children of parent volunteers and their friends are on their best behavior when they know parents are in the school.

The volunteer parents can serve in many capacities. For example, covering the reception desk is a task tailored for volunteers. Assisting in the office, answering phones, and other such tasks sometimes are better left to the professional staff. Parents used as chaperones works well only in conjunction with lead teachers who are comfortable working with parents.

Likewise, some schools have been very successful in using parent volunteers for safety patrols, tutoring, school-beautification programs, career advice, and as aides in bilingual classes. A careful review of the needs of the school population and the talents of the parents should be conducted before entering into a large-scale parent volunteer program.

Target Troublemakers

Any seasoned school administrator can tell you that only a small percentage of young people create most of the problems in our schools. A disproportional amount of time must be spent on these recalcitrant students. Some of these problems occur because a small number of unspecified children do not want to be in school. Our forefathers believed that compulsory education was necessary to make our country strong and prosperous. However, as well-intentioned as these motives can be, when children do not want to be in school and your efforts to entice them to learn have failed, frustration ensues. Then misbehavior occurs and the pattern is repeated. To stop this behavior, it is essential that the sharing of information on juvenile offenders takes place, and to establish a good working relationship with the police. Reach out to other schools in the area and develop an alliance that will facilitate the movement of this type of information when students transfer from school to school.

Some would argue that these children should come into new situations with fresh slates, without preconceived opinions about their behavior. While this argument has merit, the building administrator needs as much accurate and timely information on potential problem students as possible. The principal has the responsibility to maintain a safe and secure environment for all students.

In more than three decades as a public school educator and leader, I have seen a great number of troubled students who were on the path to prison or an early grave. I have witnessed many of these same students become happy and productive citizens after graduation from high school and college. I believe that this turn-around came about because we kept a vigilant watch over these students. We constantly met with the parents or guardians, and many times the probation officers of these students. We channeled this group of adolescents to the proper counselors who could meet their individual needs. By holding the line, providing proper counseling, and making the students accountable for their actions, a change in behavior occurred. Yes, it would have been easier to repeatedly suspend these students, however, suspensions alone would not address the problems.

Identify the chronic offenders in your school and develop plans to address their needs. Early intervention can result in positive results. Repeated suspensions with no services provided to the student will virtually ensure a continuous pattern of misbehavior.

Establish a Vibrant System of Co-Curricular Programs

Bayonne High School can boast more than eighty clubs and activities. This extensive array of organizations is the result of an active student body and devoted faculty members. Most clubs are advised by faculty members with no remuneration. We will charter a new organization when only ten students show an interest in a specific area. The students then approach teachers who they believe share the same interests and ask them to serve as advisors. At that point a constitution for the group is drawn up and the student council recognizes the group as an official organization of the school.

Many of these clubs revolve around our diversity. For example, some of our groups have included Bible Club, Culinary Art Society, Ebony Culture Club, French Club, German Club, Italian Club, Karate League, and Spanish Club. These clubs meet to learn about the specifics of a particular culture or activity. In this manner, students are immersed in diversity from many different sources. Interclub meetings are scheduled to encourage the clubs to work together for a common goal or activity such as our annual homecoming celebration.

Our Ebony Culture Club conducts an annual Kwanzaa celebration that is attended by students from virtually all backgrounds. Parts of the festivities include an explanation of the holiday and some of the historical contributions made by African Americans. Students and faculty in attendance learn about the African culture. We all know that knowledge is power and these clubs spread knowledge. When everyone in the school is well-informed regarding the different cultures that comprise the school community, harmony results. This understanding translates to fewer confrontations between the students and consequently, a safer school.

For a number of years, we conducted an International Night celebration. This evening provided an opportunity for various cultures to showcase their heritage. Parents, friends, and members of the community came to share in the evening's festivities. We made a special effort to invite members from our senior citizen housing complexes in the city. This allowed the city's elders to see our students in another light. Ethnic foods from around the globe were enjoyed while entertainment was provided by various student groups dressed in native costumes.

Open the School to the Community

A safe school concept that goes unnoticed by many administrators is to make the school more open to the community. At first, the idea seems to compromise the security of the complex. It would be very easy to lock down the building after school to maintain security. However, I contend that using and keeping the school open enhances security. First, remember that it is the community in which the school is located that supports the school. The community provides the money to construct and maintain the buildings. They provide the funds to hire the staff members and purchase supplies. We are dependent on the community for our entire existence.

We should make sure that the taxpayer receives the best value for every dollar spent on public education. This does not only translate to the education of the young people in the community. It needs to extend to the community-at-large. Learning is a lifelong process—womb to tomb. Establish a strong community education program in your school. Make the school available to various community groups for meetings. Keep as many adults around the campus as possible. Evening classes for adults have become very popular. It is a practice that will keep the building in operation and provide you with many sets of eyes and ears. Try to schedule courses for adults immediately after school. Some of these twilight courses enjoy high enrollments.

Administrators who realize the benefits of more adults in the building during normal school hours are creative in scheduling. Many times it is possible to schedule a community education offering in your building when a classroom is open. For example, we have offered daytime courses to women who are interested in rekindling a career or learning a skill to begin a new occupation. However, we did not just offer keyboarding and computer training. We have offered welding, plumbing, automotive technology, television production, and an array of other courses, thereby dispelling stereotypical roles. Sometimes it is possible to use the day school staff as instructors. They can be allowed to teach during their preparation or lunch periods for additional stipends.

All the strategies we have implemented helped to make our school safer. Our plans to embrace and celebrate diversity in Bayonne High School as a means of making our school safer has been quite successful. We have demonstrated that a nurturing learning environment can be provided when cultural diversity is embraced. Students are taught that all cultures have something to offer. Each student learns from the other when exposed to a special type of food, a different article of clothing, or an unfamiliar custom. They can also feel comfortable keeping their own diversity and unique traits as individuals, since each is respected for who they are.

Over the years we have witnessed a decrease in bias incidents and fewer suspensions. Our anger management and peer mediation have resulted in fewer physical confrontations. As cultural barriers are erased, there is less conflict. Nevertheless, the spirit of the individual is maintained and embraced for what can be offered to school as a whole. Students and staff embrace diversity and use it to teach each other how to become true members of a global society.

In a five year period from 1994 to 1999, the incidents of vandalism, violence, and drug abuse dropped 72 percent at Bayonne High School. The financial cost of vandalism dropped from $30,818 in 1994 to $490 in 1999. The installation of the mag-locks and video cameras at entrances certainly helped; however, the change from a negative climate to one of acceptance and caring cannot be overlooked in the quest for a safer school.

Chapter 5

Crisis Preparedness

Now that you have an idea of the problems facing our schools today, it may behoove you to take stock of your school and devise strategies to create a safer environment. Many things can be done immediately to enhance school safety; others will require a change in board policy. Some will require extensive planning and a substantial financial investment. In this chapter you will be able to quickly assess your readiness to cope with a crisis. You will also receive clues as to which strategies you can implement when developing a safer school community. You will also acquire information on how to establish a Crisis Management Team (CMT) for your school or district.

CRISIS PREPAREDNESS CHECKLIST

To assess crisis readiness in specific schools or districts, I developed a Crisis Preparedness Checklist (appendix B). This instrument highlights areas that are necessary when generating a successful crisis management plan. It is a self-administered, self-scoring device that provides a rating to place your school or district in a particular range. Each item is rated as one point. A total of thirty points or above indicates that your school or district is well prepared to deal with a crisis situation. If the score is in the thirty to twenty-four range you are prepared for a crisis; however, a review of the blank areas should be conducted. If the score is twenty-three to seventeen, the school or district is considered to be doing well, but more work and training are needed. Finally, if the score is below seventeen, the staff in the school or district needs to start working immediately to create an environment that is safe and supportive. The following is a description of each of the forty items and their relevance to a safe, secure, and responsive school.

Definition of Crisis for Your School

The first item highlights the necessity of developing a working definition of *crisis* for your school. Remember, that the event is extraordinary and usually unpredictable. What could be considered a crisis situation in one school or district may not necessarily be classified as a crisis in another. Furthermore, the crisis can occur outside the school and carry over into the building.

Crisis Management Team

The next point asks if a Crisis Management Team is already in place. It is imperative to establish this team early in your planning. Do not wait until the entire plan has been developed. Many times the members of the team can provide valuable insights into the creation of your total plan. Tap their resources early on in the process. If a crisis befalls your school before the total plan has been developed, at least you have a group with whom to meet and review the actions that need to be taken.

Training of Crisis Management Team Members

Once a team has been selected, conduct training as soon as possible. Since it is impossible to predict when a crisis will hit your school, speedy setup of your program is necessary. The training of the team can be done in-house or by outside consultants. I have developed vignettes for crisis team training that can assist you in this quest (appendix C). A review of the board of education policies on crisis response should be part of the training. These policies will determine what action is to be taken when responding to specific situations.

Person in Charge During Crisis

The selection of the person to chair the operation during a crisis could be a difficult task. This individual needs to have a working knowledge of the school and be able to maintain composure during difficult conditions. Also, it is a good practice for every member of the crisis team to be familiar with every duty. In this fashion of cross-training, if an individual is absent or cannot rise to the occasion during the actual crisis, a trained person can assume the role.

Written Policies and Procedures for Handling a Crisis

I cannot emphasis enough the importance of developing a plan and committing it to paper. When in the midst of a crisis, it is too late to try to write out the marching orders. When there is a written policy adopted by the board of education, it not only provides the guidance necessary to implement the plan, it protects the members of the crisis team. A written policy also provides you with the perfect tool for training team members. Procedures can easily be reviewed and upgraded as needed.

Crisis Phone Chain

Every school has an emergency-closing phone chain. The procedures for placing this chain into action are reviewed each year by the principal during an early faculty meeting. The chain should be updated throughout the school year. The same holds true for the crisis phone chain. When anticipating an emergency closing for inclement weather, staff members are normally placed on alert. During an unforeseen tragic event, crisis team members may not be a phone call away. Therefore, in addition to the home phone numbers, list the office and pager numbers of the crisis team.

Evacuation Plan

Your evacuation plan needs to address when and to where students and staff will be moved. Different situations need to be covered in the egress plan. For example, when conducting a fire drill, it is good practice to close a particular stairwell or exit as though the fire was in that area. In this manner, the students and staff will be able to practice using the alternate egress plan. List the possible scenarios such as a gas leak, bomb threats, hostage situations, and so on, then map out the egress for that particular situation. Many times the egress will be the same or similar, however, particulars may dictate different plans for your school.

Alternate Site for Students

Once the decision is made to move, everyone needs to know where they are moving to and what procedures to follow to arrive safely at the predetermined destination. Urban or densely populated districts can easily use other schools as receiving areas. Because distance is a factor in suburban and rural districts, the transportation department must be involved when developing plans for relocation. Be creative in developing sites. Talk to business people as well as educators about possible locations for your students during an emergency.

Bomb-Threat Procedures

Every building administrator needs a written procedure for response to a bomb threat. Have this plan reviewed by the local police and fire departments. If you are in an area that is close to police with a canine division, make contact as soon as possible. These officers will come into your school to demonstrate the effectiveness of their units. The dogs are trained to sniff out explosives, weapons, or drugs.

Floor Plans in the Hands of Police Department

When the tragedy hit at Columbine High School in Littleton, Colorado, the police did not know the layout of the school. They had to rely on staff and students to give them directions to various sections of the complex. While rescuers were gathering information, students trapped in the school were calling for help on cell phones. This conceivably could compromise the rescue mission. Exchanges could be overheard by terrorists and exacerbate the crisis.

Floor Plans in the Hands of Fire Department

As important as it is to have your floor plans in the hands of police, it is even more important to have a set of plans with fire officials. There could be some situations that will require the assistance of firefighters that are not deemed full-crisis situations. When the professionals on the scene are prepared with detailed plans of the buildings, a safer and quicker response is possible. In both cases you should meet with the police and fire personnel to review the plans before a crisis strikes.

Spokesperson to Deal with Media

As with the crisis team leader, the spokesperson must be knowledgeable and able to maintain composure during difficult conditions. Above all, no matter how hurtful it is to the school or district, the truth must be told. Deal with the situation honestly from the start. If this person skirts the issues, the information will get to the media via other means, thereby creating additional problems. Only *one* person is to be designated as the spokesperson for the school or district.

Listing of Community Agencies with Contact People and Numbers

A list of community agencies needs to be compiled and maintained. The names of the contact people, their phone numbers, fax numbers, e-mail, and pager numbers should be included on this list. When the crisis strikes, you will have a complete directory of resource people to contact and deploy as needed. It is also a good idea to meet with these people once a year to review their involvement in various crisis situations. These agencies should include organizations such as community mental health, women's health, YMCA, YWCA, public health, family counseling, individual counselors, social workers, psychologists, and psychiatrists who are willing to serve during a crisis.

Procedure to Notify Staff

Early and proper notification to the staff is necessary to make your operation as smooth as possible. However, problems can arise. We certainly do not want the students to know all the nuances of the plan, but it is important for the staff to be knowledgeable. The type of crisis will determine how the staff is notified. Something that requires immediate evacuation must be done over the public address system because speed is essential. When speed of information is not crucial, either written or verbal instruction via administrators or lead teachers can be effective.

Method for Sharing Information

How you share information is crucial to maintaining control and structure in the building. There will be occasions where a script is written and all homeroom teachers will simultaneously read the message to their students. Other occasions will dictate that a message be announced via the P.A. system. Still others will necessitate a letter to the home of every student. Some situations might require a combination of notification procedures. It is suggested that when dealing with sensitive issues, the P.A. should not be used since many people deem it an impersonal method of communication.

Determining What Information Is to Be Released

Information to be released must be accurate, timely, and compassionate. Enough facts to ease troubled parents must be provided, however, too much information can cause confusion. By providing essential information, you will help to reduce anxiety and the number of calls to the school by frantic parents. Care must be taken regarding the families of victims when deciding what is to be released. It is also recommended to include information concerning where people can go to get help or supplemental data.

Procedure to Release Information

As with all crisis programs, planning is essential. The same is true for the procedures established to disseminate information. These procedures can be as simple as placing notices in the bookbags of elementary students or as high-tech as e-mail to the homes. Contact with the local cable company can provide a fast and efficient way to deliver messages. Writing statements for press distribution helps to get items across that might not be covered in the press conference. During a crisis it is a good idea to establish an information center away from the affected area. It should be staffed with a member of the crisis team or other personnel so that accurate notifications can be relayed to interested parties as needed.

Plan to Cover Classes in Emergency

If teachers are pulled from an area for any reason, procedures to maintain proper coverage for their classes must be made. Written plans to double assignments or move students to larger group areas can be accomplished quite easily. It is more challenging to find coverage for students who must remain in classrooms until the conclusion of the crisis. At these times think about using ancillary staff to assist in coverage. It is better to have a noncertified, yet trained employee in charge of a class, rather than leaving the children to their own devices.

Law Enforcement Liaison

This person needs to be selected and be onboard from the beginning stages of your crisis management development process. An officer who has been trained in the DARE or COP programs would have discerning insights for the needs of students and staff. Nevertheless, the selection of this person needs to be done carefully, and the building administrator needs to work diligently to establish a good working rapport with the liaison. Keep the officer informed of weekly events to ensure open communications. In this manner, each of you will get to know the other so a bond will be created before a crisis.

Designated Counseling Area for Students

When in a crisis situation, the need for a predetermined area to counsel students cannot be understated. First, review current counseling areas to determine if they would be suitable to handle what might be a large volume of students. Determine if private areas can be established to keep contagion at a minimum. Remember, the counseling conducted during a crisis will be done on a triage basis. Find areas that can be used as alternate sites in case the designated counseling areas are unavailable due to the crisis itself.

Designated Counseling Area for Staff

Many times when developing a total crisis management plan, the administration forgets the needs of staff members. We tend to view our professionals as a cadre that can do what has to be done, regardless of the situation. While this is probably true most of the time, there will be some residual fallout during and after a crisis. A private area needs to be established where outside professionals can meet the needs of staff members.

Designated Meeting Area for Parents

During a crisis many parents will call the school for information, many others will actually come to the school. As the volume of parents will be greater than usual, it is prudent for the principal to have a site where these parents can assemble. It is easy to imagine a main office jammed with parents clamoring for information. An overflow of parents into the halls will naturally have an adverse affect on nearby students. Therefore, choose an area that is somewhat secluded from the student body to meet the needs of anxious parents.

Referral Process for Additional Counseling

The initial rush for counseling will dissipate after a few days. Most students and staff will be eager to get back to normalcy. However, there will be a small number of students and staff requiring additional counseling. Some might require long-term treatment. The response portion of your crisis plan should address these needs. Contact local mental health agencies for a listing of services. Also, persuade the local board of education to institute an employee assistance program (EAP) if one already is not in place. Consider in-house counseling, it can be helpful in certain situations. However, this decision should be made by your counseling staff according to the individuals in need.

Accountability System to Determine the Whereabouts of Students and Staff

During a fire drill all teachers must take their roll books with them to assure student accountability. The same must be true for accountability of students and staff during a crisis. Copies of these lists need to be held in an area where they can be easily retrieved at a moment's notice. Clear instructions for the staff regarding roll books and seating charts need to be established. In the same manner, the administration needs to maintain a directory and master schedule of staff members.

Forms to Assist in Crisis Management

One of the tasks that helps to crystallize crisis management for your team is the construction of scripts, checklists, and classroom activities to be used as needed. Generic scripts regarding the loss of a student or staff member can be quickly tailored to meet individual situations. Checklists need to be developed so that items will not fall through the cracks. During a crisis it is very easy to forget a simple procedure that might keep the situation from escalating. By devising checklists for all members' responsibilities, you eliminate the guesswork. If a lead member is not available to perform assigned duties, replacement personnel will have a checklist to guide the efforts. Finally, packets of classroom activities to direct student attention in a positive vein are necessary. Careful selection of this material can assist students and teachers on the transitional road to normalcy.

Crisis Response Practice

Successful athletes, musicians, and artisans must practice for countless hours to enhance their skills. Crisis response is no different. Once your plan has been developed, conduct a safety drill with your response team. After a critique, try the plan again with a specific scenario involving the student body. Invite the police and fire departments to participate and try to videotape the drill. Conduct a review of the drill with your team and representatives from the police and fire units to fine-tune your response.

Legal Review of Crisis Policies, Practices, and Forms

It is imperative that you comply with all written elements regarding your policy and procedures for crisis management. This is not only good practice, it can save the building administrator from possible legal actions. All procedures need to be reviewed by the board of education council. Having the procedures adopted as policy by the board of education will also provide additional protection for the administration. This will also ensure that student and staff rights are not violated by any of the procedures.

Annual Crisis Management Team Meeting

The Crisis Management Team needs to meet at least once a year to review policies. The team leader should update the phone chain and review procedures for notification. During these meetings review and critique crisis management events that have occurred throughout the country since the last gathering. Much insight can be gained by examining the actions or inaction of other districts. As outside observers, the crisis team can take an analytical look at each step taken and relate the actions to specifics at their own school.

Annual Staff In-Service for Updates

Just as the Crisis Management Team needs to meet and review policy each year, the entire staff needs to be trained annually. Turnover in personnel and the amount of information that each staff member is required to retain necessitates this review. Naturally, this in-service needs to be conducted early in the year because a crisis can strike at any time. In addition to providing the necessary information to make the plan work, conduct an annual in-service that emphasizes the importance of crisis preparedness.

Fully Stocked School Crisis Kit

Every school has a first-aid kit and an oxygen tank. A school crisis kit is now also an essential weapon in the arsenal for safe schools. This kit should contain items such as: a mobile phone, walkie-talkies, binoculars, flashlights, batteries, candles, matches, paper, pencils, index cards, markers, poster board, masking tape, caution tape, duct tape, scissors, knife, utility knife, hammer, nails, screwdriver, saw, plastic water containers, large plastic bags, pails, first-aid kit, blankets, water purification materials, rope, and string. The kit should be in an area that is accessible during emergencies. Also, be careful that staff members do not "borrow" items from the kit. Ensure that it is always fully stocked.

Site Communication Systems Evaluation

In addition to the daily check of your communication systems, a complete and thorough review of all systems must be conducted annually. The public address system and intercom system should have maintenance or service contracts. Meet with the field representative and discuss the necessity for updates to the systems. Keeping these systems in good working order can prevent many problems. Be sure to have the phones and walkie-talkies checked. Batteries for the walkie-talkies, while rechargeable, normally only last two years. Make sure an adequate supply of extra batteries are on hand and always keep at least one fully charged. Teachers should be encouraged to immediately report that the communication system in their room is not functioning properly. Finally, if your phone system requires that a nine be dialed first for an outside line, place stickers on all phones indicating that the emergency number is 9-9-1-1.

Fire-Alarm System Evaluation

The normal twenty or so fire drills conducted each year not only train students and staff in proper egress, if done properly they also test your system. Meet with fire officials and discuss the possibility of pulling alarms in different areas of the building for drills. This will check that particular pull box and the connection to the fire department. Also, have fire personnel inspect the system each year and ask for recommendations for possible upgrades. When dealing with the safety of children, the financial costs should be inconsequential.

Sign-In Center for Support Personnel on Campus Established

Find an area that is accessible yet away from the core team decision-making area. This could be the reception area of the school or a section of the main office. The area needs to have phone access and should have someone from the crisis team as a contact person on hand. Keep a sign-in book noting the date, time in and out, name, phone number, and affiliation of each support person. Place a bulletin board or easel in a visible area to serve as a message center.

Procedure to Identify At-Risk Students and Staff

When a crisis strikes, some students and staff will react in a manner that might be considered excessive. This could be due to many factors. For example, a similar crisis might have been experienced by those demonstrating the disproportionate behavior. The staff needs to be in-serviced regarding the warning signs that will normally be displayed by these individuals. It is good practice to develop a referral form that can be used by the staff. This will provide a record and serve as a tool for the counselors who will be working with the students. The administration also needs training so they can identify staff members who might need counseling.

Incident Reporting System in Place

Accurate and timely incident reporting is crucial. Forms are required by state agencies for federal reporting. In addition to these mandated reports, it is good practice to develop an Incident Fact Sheet for internal use (appendix D). This form will contain information in a narrative style with a factual framework. A copy of this form should be sent to the superintendent as soon as possible. The superintendent should then share this information with board members. In this manner, everyone will be apprised of the situation quickly before reading about the incident in the local papers. Outline the procedures and categories necessitating implementation of a response to serve as guidelines (appendix E).

Contingency Action Plan to Deal with Disruption and Vandalism During Crisis

When in a crisis situation, chaos can ensue if proper administrative action is not taken. The building administrator needs to be proactive in these situations. Contingency action plans need to be developed prior to the incident. Disruption can be caused by concerned parents arriving at the school, media personnel swarming around the campus, or students deciding to leave the building in droves. People will react differently in crisis situations, however, many human emotions are consistent and predictable for certain situations. Develop plans for as many scenarios as possible that could happen in your school.

Procedure to Release Students

It is only natural for parents to become upset and concerned when a crisis strikes. The instinct to protect our children is great. Some parents will be hysterical and demand that their children be sent home. Others will run immediately to the school to pick up their children. Procedures need to be developed in two areas to ensure an orderly and effective release of students. First, a general format needs to be established for the discharging of students if an evacuation is deemed necessary. This would include the route to follow, the procedures for accountability, and the sites where students will be housed. The second format includes the procedures employed when a decision to keep school in session has been made. In this case, students should be sent to a holding area to be counseled and await pickup by the parents/guardians. No students should be sent home by themselves. We even encourage parents of adult students to abide by this process.

Debriefing Process

Every day at the conclusion of classes, the principal needs to meet with the staff and conduct a debriefing meeting. This will help to quell the rumor mills that accompany such occurrences. Accurate information should be shared at this gathering and time for questions needs to be provided. A factual review of the events should be presented in sequence. Be careful not to interpret the data, just report the facts. Even if some of the information is embarrassing to the school, district, or administration, the truth must be shared at these debriefing meetings. Eventually, the facts will be known, therefore, it will serve every-one's best interests to be candid at all debriefings.

Follow-Up Procedures

A critique needs to be scheduled after the crisis has passed. This must be done as soon as possible while memories are still fresh. These meetings will serve as a place to brainstorm, thereby improving the total crisis management plan. Part of the review procedure should include the paper documentation of the crisis and the actions taken by the administration. Letters to the home, articles in the local papers, and perhaps even a town meeting should be considered as vehicles to inform the parents and community-at-large of the crisis management process. Counseling services as well as referral services need to be provided and maintained for those traumatized by the event.

Possible Memorial Programs

Not all crises dictate that a memorial program be conducted. For example, in cases such as suicide, memorials are not recommended. However, a decision regarding the appropriateness of memorial programs needs to be made shortly after the crisis has been dealt with and normalcy is restored. The Crisis Management Team should review the crisis and develop a plan to conduct the memorial if deemed appropriate. It is better to be proactive in this regard rather than having to respond to a swelling of the masses to memorialize victims. Student leaders need to be called in as part of the planning process. Their involvement will demonstrate that the needs of students have been addressed.

WRITING A CRISIS MANAGEMENT PLAN

It is imperative that a policy be created to guide the administration and staff during and after a crisis. By committing to policy the procedures to follow, stability and order can be maintained. The plan needs to be developed in a manner that will take into consideration all the particulars of your school.

The first section of the policy should include events that rise to the level of crisis for your school. These would include events such as: sudden death, suicide, homicide, hostage situations, terrorist threats, and any other natural or man-made disaster that can impact the school. Also, cataclysms that hit the community can have a spillover effect on the school, therefore, plans to deal with those types of situations also need to be developed. Information regarding human reactions to traumatic events can be useful in developing responses for the crisis management team.

State in the policy that the superintendent of schools is the person to determine, on a case-by-case basis, when the crisis management plan is to be implemented. In most instances, this determination will be made based on information received from the building principal. Board of education members need to be informed as soon as this determination is made.

The policy should also contain a list of personnel on the Crisis Management Team. A district team as well as building-level teams need to be defined. Normally, the district team will comprise the following: central office administrator, principal, vice principal, guidance counselor, child study team member, and a community mental-health professional. The district chair could be a principal or a central administrator, however, if you have a director of student personnel services, this person should serve as the district chairperson.

Each school should also establish a building-level Crisis Management Team to deal with emergency situations. The building principal should serve as chair and the group can include the following: vice principal, guidance counselor, nurse, secretary, teacher(s), community mental-health person, and a PTA liaison. When the team is selected, it should meet and review plans to manage specific events. Reviews of various scenarios need to be conducted as each individual situation will require specific actions. Require that the teams meet at least once a year individually, and at least each semester at the building level to review plans and organize general responses and policies for the schools.

Depending on the size of the school, you might like to establish a core team. This team would be composed of only three or four members and serve as a sounding board during the crisis. It will allow you the flexibility of meeting quickly with trusted and informed personnel to advise you on strategies for response to events not reaching the crisis level.

Many functions will be executed by the Crisis Management Team. The prime directive is to maintain safety, support, structure, stability, and control in the school. Some sample goals for the team are to:

- provide proper support for the students and staff.
- communicate with the staff, students, parents, and community, providing them with accurate and timely information.
- establish groups to allow students and staff to grieve.
- provide counseling to students, staff, and parents in need.
- develop the criteria for memorials.

These broad goals can serve as an excellent guide when developing your specific policy. The team needs to provide a nurturing and supportive environment for the students and staff. However, this must be balanced with order and control.

Next in your policy should be a section dealing with procedures to assess needs during and after the crisis. The needs could be divided into student, faculty, support staff, and parents. All these groups need the following:

• Information on the event (death and/or disaster)
• Information about community resources
• Information regarding the crisis plan in action

The students, faculty, and support staff will need additional considerations including the following:

• Allowance for grieving and a place to mourn
• Personnel on campus to provide counseling
• Support and additional needs met based on individual situations

Faculty members need information on how to recognize students in need. They should be provided with data to prepare them for various student reactions. Guidance in structuring school activities should also be provided. It is a good idea to reach out to the parents and supply them with information on children's reactions to similar situations.

Stabilization of the situation is crucial during a crisis to ensure that you do not glamorize or dramatize the event. Be careful in your response. Doing nothing in a traumatic situation can be as harmful as doing too much. Facilitating the expressions of grief in a controlled and organized way will help everyone handle the tragedy. Remember that staff needs should be met if you expect to help the students.

Establish a procedure to gather accurate information. Devise a plan to communicate to the students, staff, parents, and the community. Various sample scripts can be developed to keep on hand for use as needed. In the policy, designate who will be the spokesperson to deal with the media. Make it clear that this will be the only person with that responsibility. Everyone on the staff needs to know that media inquiries are to be channeled to this individual.

The policy can also clearly define procedures for attendance at funeral services. This would include the number of people on staff who would be allowed to visit. It can also establish the procedures for the selection of staff to attend. Procedures to provide counselors at wakes and funerals also need to be addressed.

When to call in outside assistance can also be outlined in your policy. Provisions for in-servicing teachers before they meet with students need to be established as well as plans for briefing and debriefing the staff.

The final section of your policy needs to address the implementation of your plan. Procedures such as the hand delivery of sensitive information, and the establishment of a hotline needs to be clearly defined. Also, the manner in which you make contact with the affected families and the proper way to become informed of their wishes needs to be established. How and where you are to establish counseling areas should be outlined. The procedure to contact the parents of distressed students for pickup, and additional counseling services should be covered. Also, the procedure to excuse students at parent request needs to be examined carefully. In most cases a designated separate area with a requirement of parent or guardian physically coming to the school is the best method.

All this information can be incorporated into your policy. When a draft is completed, meet with the Crisis Management Team to review and fine-tune the document. Throughout the crisis remain visible. Keep in contact with the crisis team and make family contacts. Reassure students, staff, parents, and community members since you will be the person they look to for guidance.

Preparation is absolutely essential to assure effective response to a school crisis. The crisis plan and materials as well as the crisis kit need to be in a safe yet accessible place. They must be in a constant state of readiness. All members of the Crisis Management Team need to be fully cognizant of their responsibilities and be able to carry out their responsibilities under dire circumstances.

ESTABLISHING A CRISIS MANAGEMENT TEAM

Once you have completed the Crisis Preparedness Checklist and have written the policy for your Crisis Management Team, you can establish the formal team. Prior to the selection of these members, you have been working with people in positions of trust that have advised you on the creation of the Core Team. Many of these same people will serve as the basis for the full Crisis Management Team. The expertise and knowledge they have gained while creating the policy make them uniquely qualified for this duty. However, reach out to others on your staff to become members of the team. Also, schedule visits to other schools that have demonstrated the effectiveness of their team by responding to a crisis in their school.

New people with fresh ideas coupled with tried-and-true procedures will result in a CMT for your school that can effectively meet any crisis situation. The goal of maintaining safety, support, structure, stability, and control for your students and staff can be achieved with the proper planning. Crisis Management Team members must be able to perform difficult duties during times of extreme stress.

Once the team has been selected, training in areas of crisis management, grief counseling, and general interpersonal relationships needs to take place.

It is also of great benefit to have one person of the building crisis team from the central office, another building, or a local community health agency. This will provide an "outside" perspective when developing responses to your tragedy. This person will not be directly affected by the crisis and can present a degree of objectivity.

Naturally, team responsibilities take precedence over normal job responsibilities. That is why I suggest that the principal or vice principal serve as team leader at the building level. They will have the authority to change assignments and coordinate team activities. At times decisions must be made immediately; therefore, the team leader needs authority to respond accordingly.

In New Jersey, the State Department of Education has established a cadre of experts who provide guidance to local Crisis Management Teams. Check with officials in your state for similar programs and keep their numbers handy. These experts are only a phone call away and will come into the district as needed. Due to their experience, training, and specialized knowledge, they can easily provide the objectivity that could be lacking due to the intense emotionality of the situation.

DUTIES OF THE CRISIS MANAGEMENT TEAM

Many duties will fall upon the Crisis Management Team. It is wise to develop a checklist of duties that will guide the response; otherwise, members of the team will be pulled in all directions trying to be all things to all people. Specific duties for members need to be explained, and members should be able to assume various roles as dictated by the tragedy.

As you develop specific scenarios for your school, choose the precise numbers and locations of crisis stations for each situation. It is advantageous to design a plan that affords more and smaller locations. If possible, keep each area to a maximum of ten students so the situation can be controlled and contagion kept to a minimum. Be creative when searching for these areas in your school. For example, a large music room could be divided into sections with portable room dividers. Perhaps the music room has separate rehearsal booths that can be used for private counseling. Let the team members roam the building seeking out these areas so that a number of possible locations can be designated in advance.

Each of these areas needs to be covered by a member of the team. Even though outside counselors might be performing the actual duties with students, it is imperative that a recognizable school person be present. Ownership of the tragedy is a powerful emotion. Students and staff can easily resent and resist help from an outsider who has no knowledge of the persons involved in the event. By the same token, when dealing with a student death, make sure that one of your counselors sits in all the classes of that student. Classmates will be faced with an empty chair in each of these rooms. The same holds true if a faculty member is the deceased. Remember, the deceased was a part of the daily schedule and the empty desk or chair will serve as a reminder of the tragedy. These students may need a professional to help them explore their feelings regarding the loss.

The team will also need training in the procedures to identify students who are in need of counseling. This training will then be transferred to the entire staff by way of an information sheet that lists symptoms to watch for in their students. Students who knew the deceased will be most affected, however, students who have experienced similar loss yet did not know the current deceased can also experience an intense grief reaction.

When dealing with a student death, immediately check your roster for siblings. Also check the district listing for siblings in other schools. Then move to girlfriend or boyfriend. Teammates, classmates, members of the same clubs, performing groups, or other such school activities need to be viewed as students who may be more traumatized by the loss. Other groups who need to be reviewed are members in the same grade level, neighbors, and students who have recently lost a loved one. Review your records and identify students who have been previously preoccupied with death or suicide. Through interviews, try to determine if the deceased had so-called enemies, as these students will probably be experiencing guilt as well as grief.

Another duty of the team will be to contact the family of the deceased. This is one of the most painful tasks to perform. Normally, this task falls on the principal or superintendent; however, by assigning a member of the team to assist with the task, the agony can be diminished. After the anguishing news is delivered, and condolences on the loss are expressed, try to determine the family's wishes. You need to obtain information on what is to be released regarding the death and the viewing of the deceased. Collect the belongings of the deceased and keep them secure until you determine an appropriate time for their return to the family. ·

Each day a debriefing meeting needs to be conducted. Throughout the day, decisions will be made, sometimes without input from team members. A meeting with the team for a short period of time each day is essential. A general meeting for the entire staff needs to be conducted after the team has reviewed the events of the day. When presenting to the entire staff, be truthful, provide factual information, and respond to questions accurately. If you do not know an answer, tell your staff you will seek it out for your next debriefing. After the initial crisis, arrange to meet with the Crisis Management Team for a critique of the response. This meeting should take place about a week after the tragedy.

The role and responsibilities of the Crisis Management Team are varied and complex. Only through careful planning and training can you hope to respond effectively during and after a crisis. Even with proper planning and training, situations can arise that will present a problem for which you have not been prepared. The ability to think on your feet and act with calm, deliberate, and measured actions will result in the proper response by the Crisis Management Team.

Chapter 6

Planning to Create Safe Schools

The ability to plan effectively is paramount to creating safe schools. Planning for a safe and supportive school is an ongoing process. As you place one plan into effect and work with it for some time, you will discover nuances that would make the plan work better and make the school safer. Therefore, any safety plan will be an evolving strategy, similar to the ongoing curriculum revision process.

A comprehensive approach to the development of your safety plan is necessary; nonetheless, as the building administrator, you also have countless other responsibilities vying for your time. However, the fact remains that you are the person responsible for creating a safe and supportive educational community—a place where teachers can teach and students can learn, free from fear and intimidation.

The National Association of Secondary School Principals (NASSP) in conjunction with DynCorp published *Safe Schools: A Handbook for Practitioners* in 1995. This is an excellent resource to assist you in creating safe and secure learning environments. The format is a loose-leaf binder with step-by-step instructions for assessing security and developing action plans. They developed a five-step process for creating a safe school. Some of their concepts are universal to the process of development and review of plans for any safe school.

The strategy that I created is a Three-Prong Plan that accomplishes the same goal—a safe school environment. The three components of the plan are as follows.

1. Pinpoint problems.
2. Develop objectives.
3. Implement a plan of action.

In addition to the three components of the plan, it is imperative that you infuse an element of harmony to make your school supportive as well as safe. The roots of school violence are emotions fueled by hatred and ignorance. By assuring an open and supportive climate in the school, you can combat the problem at its origin. Furthermore, when a crisis hits the school, you will be ready to provide the support necessary to work through the tragedy. The support component of the plan will become an ongoing process. Once all needs have been addressed immediately following the crisis, additional counseling will be appropriate for some students and staff. Support should be a natural and ongoing component of any school environment since there will always be issues that need to be addressed.

HOW TO PINPOINT SCHOOL PROBLEMS

The NASSP handbook notes that the first step to building a safe school is to identify threats to security. The handbook divides these threats into two sources: security problems and climate problems. This division is advantageous because it defines, in simple terms, the areas of concern. Violence can pervade the climate of schools and cause negative events to escalate into damaging episodes. Violence can also be the result of random mayhem. In the latter, the school merely serves as the location for the event. However, the episode will still devastate the school, leaving everyone feeling violated.

As in any plan, if the design is to be successful, the principal must examine the school environment and climate. I had not yet been exposed to the NASSP handbook when our crises struck. Nonetheless, we reviewed these same two areas since it seemed to be the natural course of action.

Immediately, we reviewed all breaches of security on the campus. As was noted in chapter 3, we developed a plan to secure the campus with high-tech physical mechanisms to make the school safer. We conducted a thorough review of the complex with police and fire officials on hand to offer suggestions. Additionally, I reviewed all of the incident reports for the past three years to see if any patterns or similarities of events could be noted. These reports are required; however, some administrators are reluctant to complete them for each incident. They are fearful that a less than desirable picture of the school will be painted when the annual reports are issued.

Do not fall prey to this practice. First, it is a violation of the local, state, and federal reporting process. Second, these incident reports can provide you with valuable clues to the areas of your campus that are a threat to security. They can reveal patterns of bias, gangs, drugs, and weapons in the school. Furthermore, these reports will memorialize the time periods and locations of the incidents. To summarize, the first step in your security plan is to identify factors that affect school safety.

Physical Factors

As mentioned, there are many factors that affect the safety of schools, however, the division of climate and security problems is an excellent way to proceed in developing your plan. Complete the Violence, Vandalism, and Drug Abuse forms for each and every incident. Review these reports every three months to discover if patterns are developing. When developing your initial plan, review the past three to five years so that an accurate account of problems can be assessed by the team responsible for creating your safe school plan. I have constructed a reporting instrument that is easy to complete and will properly memorialize the incidents for your review (appendix F). This prepared form incorporates the following: the type of incident, who was involved, what was involved, where it occurred, when it happened, and how many times it occurred.

Once you have charted the types of events, locations, and times, you can start to develop strategies to combat problem areas. Magnetic door locks, video cameras, identification cards, security personnel, metal detectors, fences, and walls are the easy part of the solution. These items only require a monetary commitment to be implemented. The way these solutions are viewed will determine if they can be an effective part of your plan. Only if the students, staff, and parents buy into the physical changes will the alteration be successful. It is imperative that you include all stakeholders in the planning process so they can sense ownership of the plan.

Meet with students, staff, and parents to discuss the plans to upgrade the physical security at the school. Go to community groups to explain the reasons for the changes. Write press releases with the particulars of the plan. Invite photographers from the local papers into the building to take pictures of the hardware while it is being used by the students. As the building administrator, you must sell the program to everyone.

I made a formal presentation to our board of education explaining all the plans we hoped to incorporate. Because we had just undergone a crisis in the school, there was unanimous approval for our security plan. If you compile the statistics from your incident reports there will be very few questions regarding the implementation of your security plan. Everyone wants our students to be safe.

Climate Factors

A 1982 article by S. C. Purkey and M. S. Smith for *Educational Leadership* titled "Too Soon to Cheer?" revealed that a consistent finding in the studies of school effectiveness was that a safe and orderly environment was paramount for learning to take place. Unfortunately, even a single act of violence inside a school can destroy the years of work spent creating a safe and orderly learning environment.

After the suicide from the bridge but prior to the homicide, we conducted a climate survey with our students. We called this instrument a Student Opinion Survey and asked for honest responses to help make our school better. We placed a statement in the instructions that all responses would be kept confidential. A four-point rating system was employed with responses of: I agree a lot, I agree a little, I disagree a little, and I disagree a lot. Providing an area for comments encouraged students to tell us more about our school and their experiences as students. We reiterated that no one would know how they answered, and that only answers of the students as a group would be reported.

The questionnaire was divided into six sections: (1) Expectations and Rules, (2) Conditions in the School, (3) Classes and Courses, (4) Teachers, (5) Students, and (6) What You Get Out of School. A section on sex, race, types of courses, activities, and future plans was also included. This instrument provided us with a feeling for the climate of our school at that time. Again, the survey was administered prior to the homicide during the 1995–96 school year. Three months after our tragedy, we conducted the same questionnaire (during the 1996–97 school year). In just that short span of time we had made major physical security changes and instituted numerous programs to provide support to students and staff. The result of that work is reflected in the comparison of the two surveys.

Bayonne High School Student Opinion Survey

Categories	1995–96	1996–97
Expectations and rules	45%	78%
Conditions in school	46%	80%
Classes and courses	42%	72%
Teachers	60%	81%
Students	60%	71%
What you get out of school	62%	75%

A comparison of the surveys reveals that we did a good job in creating a supportive atmosphere in the school for our students. Climate in the school is an important factor in creating a safe and supportive school environment. Students need to feel good about themselves and their schools. Their interactions with fellow students and staff will have a direct impact on the climate of the school.

The conscious decision to embrace our diversity, create programs to foster conflict resolution, and create a climate of ownership and pride in the school was working. Our students now perceived that their school environment was safe and supportive. The next step was to transfer this feeling to the parents and community-at-large. This was not as easy as one might think. Remember, parents set the tone in the homes. All the positive work we do in the schools can be dashed by unwitting comments at home. Parents exert great influence on their children's perceptions. The parents want what is best for the children and they want them to be safe. It is easy for them to buy into a hysteria frenzy when their children's safety is in question.

Forums such as Parents' Night, Back-to-School Night, and Parent-Teacher-Student Association meetings were used to educate the parents about our new security. These venues, along with the news releases and mailings to the home, bombarded the households with positive reinforcement. We provided information on security and our new student groups designed to foster the support that is necessary to complete a safety plan.

It has been estimated that every hour an individual commits a hate crime somewhere in the United States. These crimes are the result of poor perceptions. Bias is a human condition, however, our country has made major progress in outlawing discrimination. Our schools have been integrated as well as our neighborhoods. Yet, FBI statistics suggest that 40 percent of bias crimes target blacks and 13 percent are antiwhite, with the greatest growth in hate crimes being committed against Asians and homosexuals.

As part of our safety plan, we encouraged our students to become proactive. In the face of hatred, we do not accept apathy, as it will be viewed as acceptance. We try to collect ideas from everyone, and encourage everyone to get involved. In this manner, we unite to create a diverse coalition. Our students are encouraged to exercise their First Amendment rights to expose and denounce hatred. We have moved past teaching tolerance as we believe that connotation is demeaning. It fosters an attitude of just accepting others. We foster a concept of embracing diversity as that celebrates differences. Student groups examined issues that divide us and work against discrimination on all levels.

Schools are microcosms of their communities, and as such will have different needs and strengths. However, all schools need to develop a complicated set of interwoven factors designed to create wellness. On the top of the list is the feeling of community and ownership. Pride, discipline, and parental input are also necessities. Consideration and care for every person in the school must be present and the facilities must be well-tended and maintained.

PHYSICAL RISK REDUCTION CHECKLIST

To assist in creating a safe school environment, I developed a Physical Risk Reduction Checklist (appendix G). I recommend that you make copies and distribute them to the administrative team, the facilities committee, and the head custodian. To allow sufficient time, give them a week to complete the form. Allow for a thorough walk-through of the campus. Then meet with the Crisis Management Team and facilities committee to review the completed forms. Critique the omitted elements and decide which ones you believe will enhance security for your school. Given the current situation, assess the items checked and determine if they are satisfactory. Develop an action plan to incorporate the omitted items identified as integral. Then upgrade as necessary those items already in place to complement the overall safety plan for the school.

Barrier or Fence Around Campus

Although sometimes impractical, consideration must be given to the possibility of surrounding the entire school and grounds with fencing or a similar barrier. I have visited schools that have built very attractive walls around the entire perimeter that encases the school and the athletic field. Some have erected attractive fencing and landscaping to create a pleasing atmosphere. If finances are a concern, consider planting holly or other prickly leaf bushes to discourage unwanted intruders.

Areas to Hide Eliminated

Invariably, there are certain areas around the school that can conceal illicit behavior. These hiding spots can be inside or outside the building. A review of incident reports can reveal some of these clandestine meeting areas, while student surveys and interviews can help to discover others. A tour of the complex with the head custodian will reveal still other potential trouble areas. Areas such as the spaces below stair landings can be enclosed to provide storage areas, thereby, solving two concerns at once.

Proper Lighting of Campus and Trimming of Foliage

An element as simple as proper lighting can eliminate many safety concerns. Perpetrators do not want to be identified. Install proper lighting to deter activity and congregation. Lights with timers can be placed on the roof of the building or in the ground shining upwards to highlight the architecture of the structure. Large bushes or trees with low branches can provide great cover to criminal activity. Keep all foliage well trimmed to provide visibility for administration, security, and police. This practice will also serve to enhance the attractiveness of the school environment.

Signs for "Drug-Free School Zone" Properly Posted

Although ignorance of the law is no excuse, the posting of "Drug-Free School Zone" signs is necessary to assist with your total safety plan. The signs are required to properly prosecute offenders. The message needs to be clear, drug dealing will not be tolerated in or around the school. Remember that there is a certain amount of crime associated with drug trafficking. The elimination of drugs in and around the school can only enhance school safety.

Video Cameras in Strategic Locations

Extra sets of "eyes" can actually mean the difference between violence and nonviolence in a school setting. Video cameras in strategic locations provide an excellent deterrent to illicit behavior. Just knowing that one might be caught on videotape can serve to prevent criminal acts. The installation of cameras in areas such as corridors, stairwells, cafeterias, and the perimeter of the building will result in student demeanor that is supportive of one another.

Security Personnel or Police Presence (Patrol Car or Foot Officer)

Whenever possible, the employment of security personnel will enhance your school safety plan. If the board of education is resistant to hiring security, try to convince them to employ a cadre of permanent substitute teachers. These teachers will be assigned to the school regardless of absences. When their services are not needed in the classrooms, they can be used to patrol the halls and campus. In this manner, you will at least have sporadic security coverage. Also, contact the local police department and request the assignment of a patrol officer to the perimeter of the school. If they cannot provide this service, request that a patrol car be assigned to spot-check the school as a part of regular rounds.

Restricted Access to Parking

If a parking lot is provided for staff and/or students, precautions must be taken to ensure security. First, divide the areas keeping staff and students apart. Next, develop policies to assure that access to parking is restricted. This can be accomplished by the use of parking decals and traffic ordinances regarding the use of the lots. Add these areas to the daily patrol for security checks. By maintaining high visibility of personnel in these areas and limiting vehicle access, criminal activity will be deterred.

Locking Windows and Doors

Securing the building is a task that sounds simple; yet can be difficult to accomplish. Simple procedures such as locks on all doors and windows can have a profound effect on the overall safety of the complex. However, locks are not foolproof. Many buildings have been compromised simply because someone forgot to lock the windows. This procedure should be part of the daily routine for teachers and custodians. If you expect to maintain secure buildings, locks on every door are a must. When conducting safety drills, teachers should lock the windows and doors to classrooms while keeping everyone away from both.

Master Key System

A system that allows for easy entry by approved staff is necessary. Depending on the size of your complex, develop a system of grandmaster, master, and submaster keys. The principal and head custodian will each have a grandmaster key that operates all locks. Vice principals and custodians assigned to specific areas will be issued a master for that wing. Staff assigned to smaller areas can receive a submaster for that particular area. Individual teachers will have separate keys for their rooms.

Procedures for Distribution and Collection of Keys (New and Former Employees)

Extreme care must be taken when developing procedures for the distribution and collection of keys to sensitive areas. Systems where teachers have individual keys for their rooms diminishes the problems associated with lost keys, only one room will need the locks changed per loss. Individuals who lose a submaster key will require a series of lock changes, but not as many as the loss of a master key. If the grandmaster is lost, substantial cost will be incurred. Keys need to be signed out when issued, collected during the summer break, and turned in when employment is concluded. Occasionally, when a staff member leaves, the situation could dictate a change of locking mechanisms.

Exterior Doors Designed for Egress Only

Virtually all schools have a panic-bar locking system on exterior doors. These doors can have the bars "dogged down" to prevent entry from the outside while still providing egress from the inside. To enhance this system, the outside pull handles can be removed to make it even more difficult to enter at these locations. Remember, students and staff must be able to leave the building in emergency situations that require evacuation.

Restricted Entrance Areas Secured by Personnel

Most security plans will have designated entry areas for students and staff. The number of entrances will be dictated by the enrollment at the school and the amount of security sought. The student entrances need to be supervised by personnel to monitor who is coming into the building and to oversee what they are bringing in with them. If more than one entrance is to be used for students, plan to divide the students according to grade level or homeroom assignment. This can ease congestion and enhance security. Staff entrances need to be designed in a manner that will allow only approved personnel to enter.

Entry and High-Risk Areas Secured with Reinforced Doors and Jams

Perpetrators will attack entries that seem to be penetrable. The installation of metal reinforced doors and jams will be a visible deterrent to perpetrators. They are also more difficult to compromise. This type of door system will also provide safety for students and staff when teachers are to "lock down" their rooms in certain crisis situations. Remember, these doors will also present a "fortress" appearance to the students; therefore, encourage teachers and students to hang signs or decorations that will provide a warm atmosphere for everyone.

Individual Classrooms Secured with Locks

Locks on every classroom are a must not only for safety, but also for security of supplies and equipment. When unoccupied, locked classrooms will deter vandalism and prevent students from congregating in areas that are unsupervised. Also, when a situation arises that requires teachers to secure classrooms, locks are essential. If perpetrators are roaming the corridors, many times they will try to enter classrooms to wreak havoc. More often than not, when the doors are locked, the criminal element will seek the path of least resistance and move to another location.

Door Hinges on the Inside of Doors and Nonbreakable Glass in Doors

Exterior doors must open to the outside; consequently, they are hinged on the outside. The same holds true for the doors on classrooms. In emergency situations students and staff must be able to push the door outward to escape. However, other doors in high-risk areas should be hinged on the inside so that the pins cannot be removed and the areas compromised. Visibility is assured by the viewing panels constructed in the doors; however, these panels must have nonbreakable glass to prevent unwanted hands and arms from passing through broken openings to unlock doors from the inside.

Burglar Alarms in High-Risk Areas

A review of all areas needs to be conducted, and a determination made as to what areas require alarms. Once completed, decide if a system that is connected to a twenty-four hour monitoring service is required. Perhaps an alarm that merely sounds internally is sufficient enough to scare off intruders. In certain situations this might be adequate. Other situations will require a system that sounds an alarm at the point of entry and in the boiler room. This will allow for personnel to respond without the cost of a system that is monitored by a security company.

Entry Areas Visible from Administrative Office

A unique advantage exists when administrators have the opportunity to work with architects to design schools. Most of us are appointed to a position in a district where the schools are already constructed. Many of these buildings will have a configuration that affords visibility from the main office to entry areas. If this is not the case, review the possibility of moving the office to an area that will allow this line of sight. Remember, the line will work both ways. When outsiders can see the main office, they too realize that they can be seen.

Metal Detector Wands or Walk-Through Detectors

Before deciding on metal detectors of any kind, meet with students, parents, staff, and community members. Some communities will resist this practice vehemently, viewing it as a violation of personal rights. Others will welcome metal detectors and consider them a technological tool to assist in creating a safe school environment. When a decision is made to use metal detectors, review your entry procedures and determine if the hand-held wands will be sufficient. If money is available and most are comfortable with the walk-through detectors, place them in a location that is visible to people outside the school. In this manner they will serve as another visible deterrent to outsiders. However, make them as unobtrusive as possible to students and staff.

Mirrors or Cameras in Hallways, Stairwells, and Cafeterias

Blind spots can create major problems for school security plans. A maze of corridors and stairwells provides myriad places for students to go unnoticed. Unless you have sufficient staff to assign to each corner of a hallway, at each stair landing or in every cafeteria, coverage of these areas will be impossible. The installation of mirrors, similar to those in large supermarkets, will provide a view of two hallways if placed at the intersection. A quick glance up at the mirror will provide a good indication of student activity in those areas. Video cameras will allow for one person to monitor many locations and provide a history of events. When students give conflicting information, a replay of the tape can provide accurate information about the incident.

Barriers or Gates at Strategic Locations

Pull-down gates or pull-across barriers that are permanently attached can provide flexibility for building usage. When the building is to be used for an evening event in the gymnasium, these barriers and gates can effectively block off restricted areas of the building. Visitors to the building will be channeled to the area of the event only, and students and nonstudents will not be able to roam in unsupervised areas of the school.

Configuration of Lockers to Provide Visibility

If you are able to design the layout of lockers in the school, ensure that the configuration provides for constant visibility. Lockers that are in areas with blind spots will attract illicit activity. These lockers would provide an excellent place for someone to plant an explosive device that can go unnoticed until it is too late. If lockers are in easy view, students will think twice about storing contraband in them.

Durable Yet Attractive Lockers with Lock Access for Administration

The gauge of metal used to construct lockers must be heavy enough to prevent easy bending and breaking in. The locks should be recessed to prevent the use of a pry bar to pop them off. For uniformity and security, combination locks with the ability to change combinations easily are desirable. A key system that allows the administration access without use of the combination will enhance your safety program. Post signs indicating that lockers are school property subject to search and place that message in student handbooks. Students will be less apt to place contraband in their lockers if they know that administrators can access them at any time.

Teachers Assigned to Monitor Cafeteria Area

Whenever large groups of students gather in one area, the potential for un-wanted events is increased. Add to this the elements of food and drinks, and you have the ingredients for a potentially dangerous situation. Furthermore, the cafeterias are natural settings for trespassers who enter the complex with the intent of affecting a large group. Proper supervision is essential in any school cafeteria. Develop a workable student-to-teacher ratio and supplement the assignments with an administrator or a teacher-in-charge for additional supervision.

Administrators, Teachers, and Security to Monitor Entry and Dismissal

Large groups of students moving from one location to another presents the occasion for unwanted incidents. Stationing administrators, teachers, and se-curity personnel at strategic locations while students are entering the building will set the tone for the day. Students and nonstudents will exhibit the desired demeanor of an orderly and safe egress when the same type of coverage is af-forded at dismissal. Additionally, you and your staff will be the last people the students see and talk to before going home. Parents who pick up their chil-dren will appreciate the visual presence of staff at the close of the day.

Administrators, Teachers, and Support Staff Conduct Daily Search for Unusual Items in Student Areas Before Students Enter the Building

A standard procedure for your safety plan should be the examination of all student areas first thing each morning. Teachers should report any unusual items discovered during this daily search. If a bomb threat is made, the safest places should be the rooms that have already been checked. The search team can then concentrate on other areas of the building while students remain in classrooms. Movement of students might actually put them in harm's way be-cause the explosive could be in any of the areas you are moving to or through. This search will also prevent perpetrators from hiding weapons in classrooms to be retrieved at a later time.

Restrooms Designed for Privacy with Partial Observation Possible to Deter Illicit Activities

Many unwanted activities occur in the seclusion of restrooms. A careful bal-ance must be maintained to provide for privacy while preventing illegal activity. Some restrooms can be converted to a "bunker-type" facility for terrorists. Meet with architects to design walls that wrap around the entry so that doors are not necessary. Stalls should be designed to provide privacy but allow visibility at the bottom. Metal mirrors can be installed to provide a double view of the restroom for monitors making their rounds.

Clearly, the first phase of any security plan is to recognize school problems. The twenty-six items on the checklist are generic, therefore, they are not completely comprehensive. However, they provide you with clues to areas of concern in your school. The information discovered by the use of this instrument will assist in your overall safety plan. This, coupled with a review of incident reports (to learn about problems) and surveys (to obtain a feeling for the climate in the school) are other pieces to the puzzle.

The surveys do not need to be restricted to students. Much insight can be obtained by surveying the faculty, support staff, and parents. All this information can be used when constructing your school safety plan. You can gain insights such as: the esprit de corps, maintenance of the school, the visibility of the administration, parental involvement, weapon possession, as well as drug and alcohol abuse. Once you have identified the problems you can move to the next logical step—developing objectives to address the problems.

DEVELOPING OBJECTIVES TO ADDRESS PROBLEMS

In constructing any objective, view the objective as an end of action or a goal. As such, efforts must be exerted toward the accomplishment or attainment of the goal. Remember that an objective or goal is merely a dream with a timeline.

When constructing any objectives there are guidelines to follow. First, the objectives must be obtainable. It would be fruitless to develop goals that are unrealistic. Review the concerns and develop objectives that are possible to reach. You can always set new goals once you have obtained existing objectives. Second, write the objectives in clear language that is specific in criteria. Measures, upon which you will judge whether the performance is achieved, are also necessary. Third, develop a timeline for the objectives and place them in rank order. Finally, make sure that the goals are measurable. This is how you determine if you have achieved the desired results.

To assist with the construction of objectives I developed a form that provides a template for the user. It is a simple and concise form that provides the school administrator with an excellent tool in the construction of the overall safety plan (appendix H). First, distribute copies to all members of the Crisis Management Team and let them work independently to construct objectives for the areas identified. Then conduct a roundtable discussion and take the best of each plan to develop the final objectives.

It is advantageous to divide your objectives into the physical security or the climate factors category. Then decide how you can reach the goals. Remember, you can be successful by improving existing measures, implementing new procedures, or by combining existing concepts with new measures.

Sample Objectives

Any safety plan depends on the daily maintenance of many factors. These factors must be designed to produce a positive, healthy school climate in conjunction with rational plans to reduce damage and secure the complex. During our four-crises year, we "learned under fire" about developing objectives to keep our school safe and supportive. We took knowledge and turned it into wisdom. Through a team approach, we were able to design objectives and meet them within our timelines. Support was evidenced from the board of education, central office, teacher association, parent groups, and city officials. We were able to analyze and synthesize our goals. However, the process is ongoing. Periodic reviews of our policies and procedures ensure that we maintain the safest school possible.

The following are two objectives I developed to address our concerns, one targeting security and the second to remedy climate issues. The first objective developed was based on a review of incident reports during the past three years and was fueled by a concern for more secure buildings.

A pattern of continual breaches of the panic locking system on our exterior doors was evident. With more than forty entrances, the opportunity for an outsider to compromise the system was apparent. Our own students, on occasion, would open doors from the inside to allow trespassers to enter our buildings. An additional problem was the ability of our students to leave any building through a multitude of exits if attempting to cut classes.

The goal of this objective was to prevent outsiders from entering the school unless they had proper clearance. Furthermore, we wanted to restrict the areas of entrance to the school. After considering many aspects and possibilities, the following objective was composed:

BHS Sample Objective Targeting Security
   To reduce by 90 percent the number of student entrances in the complex by November of 1997.

This single sentence clearly explains what is to be accomplished. An obtainable, specific, measurable objective with a timeline was developed. Because the objective was physical in nature, the percentage to be obtained was very high. It is far easier to complete these types of goals than those involving perceptions and attitudes. All that is required is the money to institute the change. We were not only able to reach our objective, we were able to exceed the goal and enhance the concept. By installing video cameras with buzz-in systems at two locations, we restricted entrance to the school for students and visitors. The decision to place mag-locks on all exterior doors virtually secured the buildings from the inside and the outside.

BHS Sample Objective to Remedy Climate Problems
By June 1997, 70 percent of students will demonstrate a high degree of respect for self, others, and their school environment as measured by a locally developed survey.

This objective targeted a smaller percentage as the goal for success. Here we were dealing with perceptions and attitudes, therefore, change would be more difficult. Programs had to be developed to teach the concepts we identified as essential to eliminate negative climate. New clubs and organizations were established. Advisors were trained in proper interpersonal skills and students were exposed to a caring and understanding environment. Proper cleaning of the complex and the removal of graffiti within twenty-four hours of discovery were some of the other strategies employed to help create the desired environment. We encouraged as many people as possible to become involved. The campus was spruced up with new shrubs and flowers planted by members of the environmental club. We also made a conscious effort to provide counseling for students and staff before, during, and after school.

As with the first objective, we were successful. In the six categories identified, 71 percent to 81 percent of the students surveyed had favorable responses. Their perceptions had been altered for the better. The climate of the school was more positive and getting better everyday. Once again, everyone was taking ownership and pride in our school.

The same formula can be used for all the objectives constructed for your school. Use members of the Crisis Management Team when reviewing the raw data. Visit schools that have incorporated the types of programs or facility upgrades you are considering. Incidentally, all measures will fall into three general categories. For example our security upgrade of cameras and mag-locks were physical changes. Climate objectives fell into the category of programs with on-going activities. The third category used to create a safe school was policy changes. This will determine the way you handle the actual crisis. Everyone will follow the rules and regulations stipulated in the board of education policy.

IMPLEMENTING A PLAN OF ACTION

The last component of my three-prong process is implementing a plan of action. You have already identifed the needs and developed objectives to address them. Place them in rank order and review the practicality of implementation.

By practicality, I am referring to the sensibility of incorporating each of the components in your school. Some options will be very costly; however, they might provide the greatest benefit. Others might not cost as much but will require a great investment of time by the administration and faculty. The Crisis Management Team needs to review the efficacy of options and choose those that provide the safest plan for the least cost. This is by no means an easy chore. Due to the severity of our situation, money was not an issue. The board of education and the community were willing to spend as much money as needed to make a safe school environment for their children. The superintendent and school business administrator provided all the support necessary to bring our plans to fruition.

As your team reviews the objectives developed, question if the items help only a few or a great number of students. Sometimes, even if only a small group is assisted, great benefits for the entire plan can be realized. For example, an objective could be designed to provide a counseling program for a small group identified as a "gang." Part of the objective could be to change behavior of this small group of students. When the objective is reached, the entire student body will benefit since the improved behavior of this small group will impact everyone. Furthermore, the money spent on vandalism could be drastically reduced by just affecting this small group of students.

The board council also needs to be involved when reviewing your plan. Some of the objectives might raise legal questions. By conducting a complete review of the current federal and state statutes, problems in implementation can be avoided. Remember, your safety plan cannot eliminate the rights of students and staff, however, it must provide a learning environment that is safe, secure, and free of intimidation.

When implementing any new policies or procedures, providing information to all the people involved is critical. Information is the key to success. All staff members need to know the particulars of any change. Once the information has been disseminated, the staff needs to be in-serviced regarding implementation of the policy. Only through open communication and involvement of appropriate staff will the plan be successful.

Next, the plan must be communicated to the board of education, students, parents, and the community. These groups will already have a working conception of the plan as they have been involved throughout the process. At this point, the administration is simply providing the final proposal developed from input furnished by all groups.

If you have been planning carefully, all stakeholders will understand that you have been developing a safety plan, not because there are problems at the school, but because you are proactive in developing precautionary measures. As the educational leader of the school, you are charged with providing a safe and secure learning environment for everyone. When you are in the information-gathering stage of planning, the groups involved will feel ownership. Therefore, they will provide support during the implementation stage. Their support will be solidified if you continually seek input to fine-tune the plan.

The Fourth Estate will be the last group you need to update regarding the safety plan. Provide the media with a copy of the plan and a written news release. Once received, a reporter assigned to the story might contact you for more information. Actually, it is important for the success of your plan if at least one item about it appears in the local papers. You should also develop a videotape that explains the plan and demonstrates the effectiveness of the procedures implemented. The tape can then be used at parent meetings and be broadcast on local cable access channels.

You can discover areas of concern in your school by conducting a comprehensive review of incident reports, completing the Physical Risk Reduction Checklist, and administering climate surveys. Then, by targeting security problems with risk-reduction procedures, and developing programs to combat negative climate, you can develop excellent strategies for school safety. As you review with your team all options and the cost effectiveness of each objective, you can implement the plan that will provide the best possible security and support for students and staff.

Chapter 7

What to Do When a Crisis Strikes

No amount of schooling can provide sufficient preparation when dealing with a crisis. However, review of existing information, practice with different scenarios, and meetings with the Crisis Management Team can ensure that personnel and procedures are ready to meet the needs of students and staff when a crisis strikes.

Tragic events can quickly escalate into a schoolwide catastrophe if handled poorly by the administration. Students, staff, and parents can buy into the frenzy of fear, sorrow, anger, and uncertainty. Rumors and chaos can run rampant unless the Crisis Management Team responds correctly. The response needs to be measured, as there is danger in doing too much or not enough. A careful balance is necessary to minimize the impact of trauma on the students, staff, parents, and community. Even with the best of plans and execution, the frenzy of the event can still have great impact on the school.

Generally, the crisis will acutely and negatively affect a notable segment of the school population. However, the Crisis Management Team needs to deal with the logistics of response and support for the entire school population. Staff members will need to cope with their own feelings while trying to meet the needs of their students. This is an extremely difficult task since the atmosphere of the school will be very strained, and if not properly prepared, the staff will not be able to respond appropriately.

The person who initially had firsthand information needs to bring it to the principal at once. This information is not to be repeated to any other school personnel. The principal needs to verify the information and convert it into a factual statement. Office staff involved at this step are not to repeat or give this information to anyone until instructed to do so. All inquiries should be directed to the principal or designee. If your school uses students to answer phones, assign adults to this task until the crisis has been contained.

If the crisis involves a death, the principal should contact the police liaison. In no instance is the administration to contact the family of the victim to ascertain the validity of the report. Get the facts quickly, distribute them, and inform everyone of the need for the family to go undisturbed during this trying time.

Once the tragedy has been confirmed and the superintendent activates the Crisis Management Team, all the planning will allow the school environment to return to normalcy more quickly and smoothly than when a crisis strikes and there is no plan in effect. A well-developed phone chain will facilitate the action phase of the team (appendix I). Almost immediately, the plan to respond and provide support will be in effect. Factual information will be shared via this initial call, and the team will assemble in the designated area at a prescribed time. Each member will know what is expected of him or her, as well as of the rest of the team. Depending on the event, sharing responsibilities may be appropriate, or additional support personnel may be needed to assist with the plan.

When everyone on the team has the necessary information, each can begin their specific tasks. Remember that at times these professionals will need to make decisions quickly and without input from the team or team leader. As a result, the daily debriefing meetings are essential to keeping the plan running smoothly.

Designate a specific room for the Crisis Management Team to conduct its meetings. This area will also serve as a gathering place throughout the day by various members of the CMT as well as the assisting outside resource people. Provide food and beverages at this location and keep it well stocked. Remember, these people will be working throughout the day without scheduled breaks.

INFORMATION GATHERING AND NEEDS IDENTIFICATION

Chapter 2 provided practical information on how we gathered information regarding the four crises during the 1996–97 school year. While each incident was different, the process for gathering information during a crisis has a common thread. If you have planned properly, your school will have a Crisis Management Plan in existence. Furthermore, you will have reviewed the contents so that you will have a general working knowledge of the document.

When the event strikes, you will first need to determine if it rises to the level of a crisis. If this review is necessary, the incident has already reached the level where notification to the superintendent is necessary. Once the superintendent has been notified, convene the Crisis Management Team. Review the event as it relates to a crisis situation to determine if the incident fits into the existing definition. The definition (developed by the Crisis Management Team) contained in your manual will serve as the guide for this process. It is possible that the event will not fit into your definition, but will still be considered a crisis.

Broad categories of situations that should be considered in your working definition of *crisis* for the school need to include threats, environmental catastrophes, and bereavement. The threat category includes threats to the physical safety of a student and/or a staff member. This would include events such as a collapse of bleachers resulting in injuries, the taking of hostages, and gunfire in the school. Environmental catastrophes would include natural disasters such as tornadoes, floods, and hurricanes. Fires can also be included in this category. Bereavement can be caused by the death of a staff member or student. There can also be occasions when the relative of a student or staff member can trigger the grieving process in the school. Sometimes a particular community member with strong ties to the school population can adversely affect a significant segment of the school population.

Rather than the principal attempting to evaluate all of the information, a team of trained professionals will weigh all of the particulars of the event. This will ensure that items will not be missed or misinterpreted. Otherwise, confusion or mishandling of the tragedy can result. Remember, the members of the team were selected because they were recognized as having good judgment and possess the ability to work well under extreme pressure.

When the determination has been reached, inform the superintendent of the team's classification of the event. Remember, the team is making a recommendation to the superintendent. Next, the superintendent will need to decide whether to declare that a crisis situation has been reached. If that conclusion is made, you will reconvene the team for full mobilization.

Time is crucial during the first few minutes of the tragedy. When notification is made, events will be set in motion dictating what course of action is to be taken. Misinformation is an adversary that can cause much confusion. Therefore, it is imperative that your information gathering procedures are designed to be effective and to provide accurate and timely data to everyone involved.

Those people gathering information should be careful to be compassionate, yet understand that certain facts need to be revealed for the team to respond properly. When interviewing, there are basic steps to follow. First, review reports that are pertinent. In most instances, only sketchy information will be received. The review by the team will help to clarify and add some data. Gather as much factual information as possible before sending personnel into the field to interview. Second, related facts will inevitably come up during the interview procedures. This might be as simple as determining who else was present during the event. Interviewers need to take copious notes, as their memory will be taxed to the limit during a crisis. Last, gather background information from everyone interviewed. Review the student folders or employee records for clues regarding the person's lifestyle and possible bias.

Remember why information is being collected. Naturally, you need data on the event itself. However, you also need to learn as much as possible about the circumstances surrounding the event. You also need facts about what occurred immediately after the incident. Additionally, you will need to gather information from the families of the victims. Data regarding their wishes on the type of visitation with which they will feel comfortable, as well as what information is to be shared with the staff and students may need clarification. Finally, insight into the immediate effects of the trauma on the interviewee can be discovered when interviewing. This will assist the counselors when they work with the affected students who are trying to overcome their traumatic experience.

A list of the people to be questioned must be developed as soon as possible. This roster will be the starting point for the interviewers. Many times when conducting an interview, new names will emerge. Students will refer to others who might have been at the scene. Parents could make references to friends of their children. Staff members will provide names and descriptions of the people present at the incident. Many of these new prospects may require investigation.

Do not think that interviewers will gain useful information simply because they are conducting interviews. Rarely will needed information flow effortlessly, unless the interviewers know what kind of facts the team needs. Consider setting the stage for the interviews. The psychology of the location for the interview cannot be understated. The person conducting the interview can have a great effect on the results; therefore, they should have no preconceived ideas concerning the event and must remain neutral when seeking the truth. Interviewers must speak clearly and make sure all questions are understood. They need to always ask open-ended questions and try to relax the interviewee. Interviewers should speak as little as possible while urging the person to talk. Finally, they should be cognizant of nonverbal signs, because researchers have determined that most communication is nonverbal. Sometimes witnesses to a tragedy will block out in their minds what has occurred. Body language can serve as a clue to when this might be occurring.

As each interview is completed, have the interviewers review their notes. Naturally, they will be short and sketchy. Instruct them to arrange the notes into proper form so they can easily refer to them when needed. Finally, have them write a short statement regarding their impression of the person interviewed. Consider if they were nervous, deceptive, distant, or nonresponsive. This will provide more clues when developing reports. It also will help to determine if a re-interview is in order. All these procedures, so vital to the healing process, will help to maintain the structure and routine of the school.

When developing your total crisis management plan, incorporate an instrument that will aid interviewers. The form can assist in gathering information on the incident while providing necessary risk-screening information for your counselors. The latter questions would provide a sort of mental checklist and provide a degree of risk quotient. Questions as simple as "Where were you when the event took place?" "What did you see or hear?" or "How do you feel about this?" can help to determine if further assessment or more in-depth intervention is needed.

Students who are identified as needing additional assessment or counseling should be referred to the counseling staff. If there is an overflow, the agencies identified in your crisis management plan can assist in the counseling chores. Remember, these individuals will be serving as adjuncts and if referrals are to be made to outside agencies, written parental consent needs to be obtained prior to the delivery of those services.

Once the raw data is collected, you need to structure a response to the crisis that will be read by teachers to the students (appendix J). Simple, easily understood, nonambiguous language should be used. The need will be different for various groups. Student, parents, faculty, and administrators serve as the initial groups in need of advisement. Various subgroups will emerge as the effect of the postcrisis trauma is felt.

The information needed by the central office will be different from the data that will be shared with the students. The police and/or fire departments will have various needs for information depending on the type of incident. Mental health agencies need to know the particulars of why their services are needed and if referrals will be made. Other types of agencies will need similar information, depending on their roles. The media and the community will also need to know certain information. Parents of those involved will ordinarily receive more information than parents in general.

When trying to identify the needs of all groups there are universal points to remember. First, there will be a wide range of emotions. There is no right way to feel. Second, the witnesses will probably need additional counseling. Third, classroom activities may need to be altered. Finally, students and staff will need time to grieve. A sudden death does not give time for preparation, therefore, reactions may be delayed. A violent and unpredictable event will be very frightening and the students and staff will feel violated.

Even if the crisis is not protracted, a written statement needs to be placed by each phone in the school. The importance of identical messages to be given by staff cannot be understated. People answering phones should also be instructed in the basic rules of providing the information on the statement sheet only. They should not deviate from prescribed conversations. They are not to provide their own viewpoints or opinions on the event.

IMPLEMENTING THE PLAN

The most important order of business during any crisis is to ensure the safety and well-being of the students and staff in your charge. The mobilization of the Crisis Management Team is the first step in ensuring this goal. If the incident occurred in or around school, call 911. Once the proper emergency services are on the way, activate the crisis phone chain. Have the designated person ready the crisis kit and notify the superintendent. Depending on the event, you may require a lockdown or a movement of students to predesignated locations. Turn off all bells and announce to the students and staff the plan that is to be followed.

If the event caused the injury or death of students or staff members, make sure that the families have been notified. This is not an easy task, but one that must be done as quickly as possible. The news of a loved one being severely injured or killed is devastating enough; however, imagine learning about it from the media. When notifying the family, do not go into any details. Merely state that there has been an incident at the school and that their child, spouse, or relative has been taken to the hospital. Someone from the staff should be at the hospital to meet with the parents. This should be a person they are familiar with such as the student's vice principal or guidance counselor.

After the review by the team, a determination needs to be made regarding the level of the crisis and subsequent response to it. The entire Crisis Management Team may not be mobilized for certain events. Alternative support or counseling approaches, such as working with select groups of students, may be sufficient in certain situations.

For example, just before the Thanksgiving break during the 1999–00 school year, one of our seniors was killed in a traffic accident. While riding his bike home, the young man was struck by a van. Just a few hours earlier, I had been enjoying a Thanksgiving feast that was prepared by the students in our culinary arts class. This senior was a member of the group who prepared and served the food. A large segment of the school population was devastated. However, remember that we are a large school and not everyone travels in the same circles. In fact, it is virtually impossible for every student to know every other student. The senior class normally has a population of about 500 students, so even seniors do not know everyone in their graduating class. Nevertheless, a large segment of the population did know and love this young man, especially the students in the culinary arts class. I was informed of the tragedy via the phone that evening. Because the call was from the police, verification was not necessary. I contacted the core team members of the Crisis Management Team to discuss our course of action for the next day. We developed a script to be read by homeroom teachers immediately following the

Pledge of Allegiance and National Anthem. The notice to all teachers advised them that a ten-minute extended homeroom would be conducted. We provided information as to the uniform procedures to be followed for student referrals to our counselors. I contacted a local caterer and ordered a food platter to be delivered to the family's home.

The message to be read informed everyone that one of our students was in a terrible traffic accident and was in the hospital. His name and homeroom were given and we asked everyone to pause for a moment to think about the student and his family. The accident took place on Thursday evening and we notified everyone the next day. Due to the severity of the injuries, the family made the difficult decision to terminate life support on Friday evening.

That weekend I again spoke with the core team to develop plans. Once more we believed the entire Crisis Management Team did not need to be mobilized. We chose the alternative supportive counseling approach, working with those affected students. We still followed all the steps involving the death of a student or staff member. I contacted the appropriate people to ensure that we had adequate counselors at the funeral parlor. I went to the funeral home prior to its opening to discuss the honor guard, busing, and counselor assignments. I met with the family, informed them of our plans, and told them to call if anything else was needed.

The family decided to hold the church service and burial on Monday. As a result, I needed to obtain the superintendent's approval to arrange for bus transportation from the school to the church on Monday. Additionally, I arranged for chaperones and counselors to be in the buses and at the church. I also reviewed the procedure for students requesting permission to attend the church services. In this way the students at the wake would have the proper paperwork on Monday.

I then developed another notice for the homeroom teachers and extended the homeroom period for ten minutes. The script was short and to the point. We informed everyone that the student had passed away. We then instructed everyone to pause for a moment of silence for our departed friend. In addition to the instructions on counseling services, we also explained the procedures regarding the arrangements for students and staff to attend the church service.

Once the determination is made that a full and immediate team response is needed, a method of notification to the staff and students is necessary. Some crisis management plans assign a code name for specific events. However, it is much easier and safer to use only one phrase such as "Emergency Announcement," to convey the importance of the message to follow. I have used Code Red for fire watch, Code Blue for bomb threat, and Code White to inform others that a nurse was needed. Inevitably, when I enacted one of the codes someone forgot the meaning. Therefore, it behooves you to develop one phrase for all emergencies. In this manner, you can easily gain the attention of everyone and tell them in simple terms what must be done given the current situation.

If you have selected the term "Emergency Announcement" as your lead, begin with that statement and then identify to all if you are in a lockdown, evacuation, or freeze situation. All of these scenarios need to be written out for the staff and practice sessions should be conducted.

Regardless of the specific situation, certain duties performed by members assigned to the Crisis Management Team will be universal. The chairperson is responsible to convene and conduct all scheduled and emergency meetings. This person must oversee the proper functioning of the team. The chairperson also must provide information to the superintendent throughout the crisis. In most cases, the superintendent will provide ongoing information briefs to board of education members. It is a good idea to enlist someone as the assistant chair to serve when the chair is unavailable.

One person will serve as the media liaison. This will be the only individual allowed to deal with the media. All statements will come from this person and all interviews with the media will be conducted with this representative. Carefully worded press releases must be developed. These releases will provide the school with a chance of getting the correct message to the community. Included should be information on the crisis, the way that the school personnel are responding to the crisis, and the needs of the students. Scripts for classroom teachers will be developed by this person with the aid of the individual overseeing counseling services.

The individual responsible for counseling will determine the extent and nature of the services to be delivered. Mobilization of auxiliary services from the community and neighboring school districts will also be in this person's domain. The number and location of counseling stations will be determined by this individual in conjunction with the CMT. Another duty can be supervision of the mechanism for dismissing students from school. These checkouts should only be permitted after initial counseling is conducted from a location away from the general population.

Someone to coordinate communications is essential. This person should be the individual who normally is responsible for answering telephones. A prepared statement that will be read to parents calling for information should be composed by the team. The communications coordinator will then be responsible for screening all incoming calls and maintaining a log of these calls. All in-house communications will fall under this person's jurisdiction. If more than one person answers phones, the script needs to be distributed to everyone with the same instructions on communications.

Managing the movement of students, the arrival of parents and media personnel, as well as crowd control is another responsibility of the CMT. The person assigned to this task will be working with the local police and fire departments in establishing the crowd-control plan. Evacuation plans and lockdown plans will also be the responsibility of this individual. Depending on the size and uniqueness of the school, co-coordinators might be necessary. In this manner, sections of the complex can be assigned to individuals with reporting responsibilities to the overall crowd management coordinator. This individual will need a complete knowledge of the entire school, campus, and surrounding areas.

The plan for crowd control needs to identify areas where students can be moved safely. Also, strategies to cordon off areas to protect physical evidence must be developed. Additionally, areas to assemble for distribution of information must be designated. Members of this unit need to be trained to recognize students in distress so that proper referrals can be made.

Another important person on the Crisis Management Team is the one responsible for keeping notes. Each meeting needs an agenda and someone to take copious notes. These notes will serve to clarify decisions that were made during the crisis. Remember, during this time people will be required to perform under extreme pressure. Decisions will be made that might have been made differently when viewed with the benefit of hindsight. Critiques of these notes will help to fine-tune the crisis management plan. Additionally, these notes will serve as the basis for the briefing and debriefing meetings with the staff.

These six individuals will be used in every crisis. The descriptions of their responsibilities are to serve as a starting point for your school. Depending on the size of the complex and student enrollment, certain responsibilities can be shared. This will allow you to keep the number of people on the Crisis Management Team small. However, take care not to overburden one member. The CMT members will need to work closely together for extended periods of time. It is easy for tempers to flare as the pressure mounts. Everyone must be supportive of the other's role and responsibilities. When the school returns to normalcy, you will find that there is a certain bond within the team and an overall strength in the school community.

Once the Crisis Management Team has been mobilized, the coordination of the plan and communications with all concerned will be prime issues. Obtaining as much factual information as possible in a timely manner is essential for a smooth operation. Rumors will run rampant and more misinformation than useful information will be generated. Unfortunately, there will be individuals on the staff who are into what I like to refer to as "crisis enhancement." These individuals, either through good intentions or the need to feel important, will stifle progress to contain rumors and quell adverse reactions. Communication of factual information in a timely fashion will help to squelch the negative effects of these individuals.

Preassigned roles enable the Crisis Management Team to perform functions in a manner that meets the needs of students and staff. The type of response will differ according to the particular situation. However, the support and control necessary for the school will always remain constant. Provide walkie-talkies or mobile phones to the members of the CMT for them to maintain constant communications with each other and the command post.

Convene a faculty meeting the first day of the crisis. Hold this meeting after school and provide as much information as possible. In some cases the police will require that certain facts be kept confidential until their investigation has concluded. It is also a good idea to schedule meetings each day after school to provide updates. While this is a strain on the principal, it will help to quell rumors, and important information can be shared. Many times these meetings will provide a forum for faculty members to reveal something that can be crucial to the police investigation or to the process of providing support to the students.

Communication with the media is necessary and will determine, in some cases, the protraction of the crisis. Sometimes communicating the nature of the crisis and what the CMT is doing about it can be almost as important as actually dealing with the incident. The media's agenda is not the same as the school's mission. By assigning one person to deal with the media, you will avoid confusion and ensure consistency. Do not allow any media personnel to come into the school or onto school grounds. An exception can be made if you are using a media room or auditorium for briefing, and movement in and out can be monitored properly. In this manner, you will at least be on your own turf. Student art work, a U.S. flag, or the school logo should be visible so that they will appear in the pictures of the spokesperson. These elements will serve as one of the anchors to stabilize the school environment.

Try to remember that media personnel are doing their job the same as you are doing yours. Do not approach them as the enemy. If some appear fervent and aggressive, they probably have a great passion for their work. They believe that the public has a right to know and some will report what they believe will make for a good story regardless of the impact on the school community.

A fact sheet can be prepared and kept for use as the occasion dictates. Include the name of the school, address, and phone number. Give the enrollment figures and grade levels. List awards or specialties of the school as well as any other distinctive features, programs, and achievements. Also include the age of the building as well as your name and years of service.

Whenever possible provide written statements. Propose a time and location for the news conference and answer questions in clear, simple terms that viewers can comprehend. Try not to be defensive and always tell the truth, even if it is embarrassing to the district or yourself. Never say, "No comment." If you are unsure of an answer, say that you do not have that exact information and that you will provide it at the next conference. As the spokesperson, you must be viewed as a leader who is decisive and credible.

Begin your conference promptly with an opening statement. Do not discuss specific details of the event nor your safety plan. Talk in general terms of how the plan is designed to provide help to those in need. This will keep the integrity of your safety plan intact and will not hamper possible police investigations. Describe the roles and activities of the Crisis Management Team and give the locations of outside counseling services that have been set up for parents and families. Then open the floor to questions. Some questions will allow you to rephrase the main points from your opening statements. Seize these opportunities and inform the media that updates will be provided when more information becomes available. Remember, you cannot control which segments of your copy or oral statements the press will decide to use. Your responses must be deliberate, factual, and measured.

FOLLOW-UP ACTIVITIES

Regardless of the type of crisis, some type of follow-up activities will be necessary. This might be simple, such as additional counseling for students and staff in need or at risk. Sometimes the activities might be as complex as long-term counseling for many, with a memorial program, and a one-year anniversary event. The crisis itself, combined with the resiliency of the students and staff, will determine many of the follow-up activities.

The Crisis Management Team needs to provide for ongoing opportunities to deal with the aftermath of the crisis. If a large number of students and staff were affected, consider keeping the outside resources that were used during the crisis on campus. A bond was already established with these groups, therefore, if they are able to remain, the healing process can be expedited. Otherwise, you can arrange schedules so that members of the school's counseling staff can provide the needed services. Consider having these people work before or after school for a stipend so their normal duties will not be affected.

Additional resources need to be made available to teachers who will be dealing with various student reactions. Prepared handouts explaining the warning signs for students at risk can be on file ready for distribution. In-service programs for the staff can also be conducted that will allow for a give-and-take approach on the issues affecting the school population. A library of reading materials covering a wide range of grief and recovery processes should be maintained. Depending on the event, a suggested reading materials list can be generated for students, families, and staff.

Do not overlook the importance of writing formal thank-you letters to the people and agencies that assisted and supported the students and staff during the crisis. Take the time to ensure that everyone involved is recognized for their efforts. This includes members of the school's staff as well as out-of-district personnel and community members. Do not forget members of the police and fire department, as well as members of special investigating teams who might have been called in to assist. Even if some of the personnel are still on campus providing services, formally recognize their efforts during the same time period of the other acknowledgments. Follow-up letters can be sent when their services are no longer needed.

Be alert to the fact that holiday time is often difficult for the students and staff who have experienced a loss. Also, "anniversary grief reaction" can occur as early as the next week or the next month on the day or date of the crisis. However, in normal situations after the one-year anniversary, additional programs are not recommended. If a similar crisis occurs in another school and is broadcast on the news, students and staff can regress, necessitating additional counseling.

If the crisis was not a suicide and the team determines that a memorial or special activity is appropriate, encourage the students and staff to become involved in the planning process. Whenever possible, you should provide mass transportation for large groups of students. A counselor should accompany the students on each bus. Counselors also need to be present at the special activity. The memorial could be conducted as an assembly program or tree-planting ceremony. Other venues include the yearbook, school newspaper, a memorial plaque, letters to the family, and the establishment of a scholarship fund.

Family members should be informed of the activities and invited to attend as guests. It is wise to discourage family participation in an assembly program during the first few months. However, if a scholarship fund is established, include it within your normal awards ceremony. Depending on the timeline, it is appropriate for a family member to make the presentation at the awards ceremony.

Many times a spontaneous memorial is established. Students will place flowers, cards, pictures, and so on, in tribute to their fallen comrade. Have the team decide when these should be removed and ask if the family would like to have the items. Normally, this should be accomplished within a few weeks of the tragedy. The goal is to return to normalcy as soon as possible.

During the follow-up time frame, reporters will try to gain access to the school to interview students and staff. They will be interested in focusing on how people are handling the situation, how the normal schedule has been affected, and what memorials have been established. Remind the media that the school community needs privacy and time for the healing process to occur. Do not allow them to enter the school or be on school grounds. Remind the staff that one spokesperson, and one spokesperson only, will deal with the media. Solicit help from ancillary personnel to alert you to media presence around the campus.

This is also a time that the school principal needs to be as visible as possible. Delegate tasks whenever possible so that you can walk the corridors and perimeter of the building. Walk through the cafeteria, gymnasium, and visit classrooms. This will let everyone know that you are a compassionate leader who is in charge of the situation. Take the emotional temperature of the school and meet with the Crisis Management Team to compare impressions as to the healing process.

As noted, the aftermath of a crisis will require varying responses. The crisis response team needs to be cognizant of natural stress reactions. An understanding of the responses to death and loss as well as developmental considerations, cultural values, religious beliefs, and family mores is needed. The CMT might determine that an informational meeting for parents needs to be held a few weeks after the crisis. At this meeting trained professionals should review the possible reactions of children to the trauma. These would include an unrealistic fear of the future, illness, sleeping disorders, and various other responses. District personnel should be able to handle this responsibility. Parents will respond better to familiar faces in these types of situations.

Although you have been holding regular debriefing meetings, do not overlook the necessity of counseling for the staff. Remember, they cannot adequately help students until their own needs have been met. Provide both short-term and long-term counseling. Make sure that everyone is aware of your employee assistance plan that could provide additional therapy for extreme cases.

Students who were victims or witnesses might experience difficulty in returning to school. They may need counseling to help them adjust to the regular school routine. Occasionally, a plan to make it easier for their return might need to be developed. This could include changes in class schedules or assignments made to home instruction until such time as the therapist believes a return to the normal school setting will be successful. Some students may need to be placed in a facility where they can be monitored full time. When they are released, school personnel need to coordinate a plan with the staff from the mental-health facility to make the transition as smooth and uneventful as possible.

A SCHOOL CRISIS KIT

As mentioned previously, a school crisis kit should be developed and kept in a place where it is accessible during a crisis, yet secure enough to prevent people from borrowing its contents. The contents of any kit will be a combination of generic items with specifics for your particular school and situation. I have developed a list of items that need to be included in a basic kit designed to meet various situations (appendix K). The following is the listing with its descriptions.

Communications Devices

When a crisis strikes, one of the most important aspects of gaining control in the situation is good communication. Communication is essential between school personnel and with outside agencies. High on the list are mobile phones and walkie-talkies. These two types of devices will afford the best type of instant communication between the command post and the areas of the school that are in crisis. However, if you are dealing with a bomb threat, this type of communication is prohibited. If there are explosives in or around the school, the radio waves could set off the trigger mechanism. Other considerations when using this type of system need to be addressed. Perpetrators could monitor these transmissions and keep one step ahead of your team. Also, the system could suffer a breakdown. Therefore, a strategy for conventional phone communication as well as a courier arrangement plan must be established.

Every member of the Crisis Management Team needs to be familiar with the use of the handheld communication devices you have chosen for your school. Tests should be done to determine if there are "dead spots" where this type of communication is impossible. Finally, the devices need to be fully charged and have back-up batteries on hand at all times.

Use of the conventional phone system may not be as easy as it sounds. When a crisis strikes, the trunk lines for incoming calls will probably be jammed with concerned parents and the press. Additionally, students will be clamoring to use the phones to call home. A written policy regarding the use of phones by students needs to be developed for your particular situation. This is not only for crisis management but also for normal day-to-day operations of the building. Many times parents will arrive at a school because their children called home with specific problems. The administration is unprepared for these visits because students normally do not share this information with the administration. Due to the convenience of the phones, they merely call home without the knowledge of school authorities.

Also, a policy needs to be developed regarding the carrying of handheld communication devices in your school. Not only for the previous examples cited, but to deter illicit activities and prevent the disruption of the educational process.

Lights

Natural disasters and some man-made disturbances can cause the power to fail in the school. When this occurs, the emergency lighting system should automatically engage. However, flashlights, propane lanterns, and candles might be necessary in certain situations. Remember to include a lighter or matches to light lanterns and candles. Even if partial power is provided, flashlights will allow members of the team to go into places that would be too dark to traverse without some illumination. If all power goes out, teachers should know to immediately raise all shades and disable other room darkening devices to allow for as much natural lighting as possible. Depending on the location of your school, a back-up generator to provide essential power might be appropriate.

Writing Supplies

Signs to be posted regarding the use of entrances and exits are just the tip of the iceberg regarding notices needed during a crisis. Depending on the event, some areas of the school might need to be designated as off limits. Notices informing the outside counseling teams of the check-in procedures will be necessary. A message board for ancillary personnel will also need to be established. Use posted notices rather than placing your staff in the position of answering a number of easy, redundant questions. Some of these notices can be made when you are stocking the kit. Others will be made as the need arises. Therefore, a good supply of markers and poster boards should be included in the kit.

Note-taking will be necessary during many phases of the crisis. Provide a large supply of paper, pencils, and index cards for members of the Crisis Management Team and support personnel called into the school.

Tape

Naturally, to place signs and notices around the school, some sort of tape will be required. Stock the kit with all types: masking, cellophane, and duct. Also, obtain a large supply of the yellow caution tape that is used to cordon off restricted areas. Additionally, keep a large supply of adhesive tape normally used by athletic trainers. The amount included in the average first-aid kit is not sufficient for more than a few minor injuries.

Cutting Instruments

Occasions will arise when the use of the normal desk type scissors will not be sufficient. Include a wide range of scissors sizes as well as some cutting knives and a few utility knives. These will be used to cut signs, tape, and rope as needed. Make sure that when storing these items in the kit, they are properly covered to prevent accidents during retrieval.

Hand Tools

Include a hammer with an assortment of nails, a screwdriver with an assortment of screws, staple gun, and a saw. Sometimes the signs made during the crisis will need to be placed on a tree or pole, staples or nails will hold better than tape. It might also become necessary to place signs in an open field, requiring a saw to cut stakes for the signs. There might be an incident when the screwdriver and hammer will be needed to remove the pins from hinges to allow access to locked areas.

Storage Materials

In an emergency, certain items will need to be stored quickly and separately. This might include clothing and personal items of students and staff. An assortment of plastic bags will allow you to contain items separately and label accordingly. Large plastic garbage bags should also be included for cleanup purposes. A good supply of plastic water containers and pails is also recommended. Water service could be disrupted or even contaminated. These vessels could be used to bring water from a safe area to be used as needed.

Miscellaneous

Your specific situation and geography will determine other items for the school crisis kit. However, include at least one first-aid kit, latex gloves, blankets, water purification materials, binoculars, and a supply of rope and string. When waiting for the emergency medical technicians or even the school nurse to arrive on the scene, the use of a first-aid kit could prove invaluable. Also, there will be times when minor injuries can be addressed with the contents from a first-aid kit rather than taking the attention of the nurse away from more pressing needs. When treating the injured and bleeding is noticed, make sure that everyone involved is wearing latex gloves.

Blankets can be used to keep victims warm—especially those in shock— until medical attention has arrived. Blankets also can be used to cover broken windows and other openings caused by explosions, carry materials to areas in need, or transport victims to safe areas.

If water service is interrupted or contaminated, purification tablets can be used to provide water as needed. Remember, there will be standing water in the pipes of lower levels of the school that can be retrieved. Bottled water in offices or cafeterias can serve as an emergency water source.

To obtain views of safe areas, binoculars will serve you well. Before moving students to athletic fields, you should visually scan the area for safety. This will be especially true if there is a hostage situation. From a vantage point on the roof, you might be able to determine the movements of perpetrators, which may serve as invaluable clues for the police.

Rope and string will be necessary for myriad chores. The string will be used to tie together plastic bags and perhaps hang signs. The rope can be use to cordon off areas and even haul materials from lower levels to higher elevations. If visibility is hampered, the rope can be used as a guide when moving students to safety. Everyone will assemble in a line and hold onto the rope to be guided by the lead person.

The items presented in this school crisis kit can be supplemented in many ways. Meet with the Crisis Management Team and have each member construct a list independent of each other. Then convene the team to compare lists. Make a composite list and share it with the police and fire liaisons. After a thorough review, fill your kit and check it occasionally to ensure it is always fully stocked.

As principal, the safety and well-being of the students and staff in your charge is your first responsibility. Knowing what to do when a crisis strikes will have a direct influence on how the students and staff react to the tragedy. Members of the Crisis Management Team can deal with the logistics of response and support only if they are fully trained. Time is crucial during the first few minutes of the crisis. Procedures on information gathering and needs identification must be clearly defined to ensure proper handling of the crisis. A fully stocked crisis kit will save time and energy, diminish stress, and spark ideas when responding to the catastrophe.

Chapter 8

Dealing with Threats to Security

During the past fifty years, the character of U.S. schools has changed drastically. More and more requirements have been mandated by the state legislators and federal government. Programs that were unthinkable a few decades ago are now commonplace in our schools. For example, courses on sex education, equal sports opportunities for females, breakfast programs, and classes for pregnant students were unheard of when I attended school.

While the composition of schools has been altered to accommodate the delivery of services beyond the three "Rs", the basic concept of teaching and learning is still in style. However, the modern principal must not only serve as the educational leader of the school, but as the coordinator and facilitator of myriad ancillary programs dictated by society. As if this were not enough, the school administrator must keep paramount the exigent function of providing a safe and secure educational community.

Schools were always meant to be safe and healthful learning environments for our children. When the public school system was established in this country, no one could fathom the need to provide security for our young. People of the past cherished the sanctity of schools and it was an unwritten law that all schools should be safe.

Only recently has the ugly face of terrorism entered the hallowed halls of our institutions of learning. Unscrupulous purveyors of drugs infiltrate the sanctity of our schools. Violence and vandalism seem to be accepted by a certain percentage of members of our society. Some students believe it is permissible to terrorize their comrades by cowardly acts while threatening death and destruction.

Historically, the principal was responsible for everything that occurred in the school. Today that responsibility has been extended beyond the confines

133

of the complex. Administrators are now answerable to the community for nearly any act committed by a school-age child. We are expected to correct any and all evils that exist in society. We are looked to as the last hope for the future of our nation. Truly an awesome responsibility, but one that the majority of principals have accepted as their charge.

As we lead our schools into the twenty-first century, the face of education will continue to change. The role of the principal will continue to evolve, and we, as educators, must be ready to meet the challenges set before us in a fashion that is visionary and far-reaching. We must rise to the call and ensure not only full educational opportunities, but safety and security so that all who come to school to learn, can do so in a pleasing and welcoming environment.

RESPONDING TO THREATS

Within any school, there exists a number of potential problems and emergencies that would cause turmoil and distress. Some events rise to the level of crisis requiring the response of the Crisis Management Team. Others will require the involvement of only the core members of the CMT. The policy and procedures you have developed for your school will determine into which category each event will fall. One of these categories is dealing with threats.

A policy needs to be developed regarding the procedures to be followed when dealing with threats. Once completed, have the policy adopted by the board of education. In this fashion, everyone will be on the same page when dealing with threats to security. Continuity for each event will be ensured by following the adopted procedure. The administration will also be protected from possible prosecution by adhering to the specified approaches.

As you develop these policies, it will be helpful to compartmentalize the offenses. Begin with a section on definitions. This part of the policy is designed to fix the limits of what would constitute an overt threat in clear and certain terms. When a situation occurs, reference to this section will determine if the school administration shall implement the procedures outlined in the policy.

Once you develop a working definition of a *threat situation*, it is helpful to divide the appropriate responses into three categories. Level 1 is the "Threat Situation," level 2 is the "Crisis in Progress," and level 3 is the "Aftermath." These general categories will allow you to respond in a measured and controlled manner.

Level 1 explains the procedures to follow when the threat is lodged. It outlines to whom and when the information is to be conveyed to the proper authorities. Specify that anyone becoming aware of a threat or knowing any details about the threat are required to report the nature of the threat to the principal without delay.

The principal should then isolate and contain the individual(s) reported to have made the threat. However, if the administrator believes that this procedure could jeopardize the safety of anyone, contact to law enforcement authorities must be made for assistance. If weapons and/or potentially dangerous materials are thought to be involved, follow the policies developed for these instances.

Convene a meeting of the Crisis Management Team or core team for consultation regarding the appropriate course of action. Such actions would include, but not be limited to: contacting the parents of the individual(s) involved, suspension of the student(s) pending further action, review by the child-study team or school psychologist, and reporting to the local police authorities. When a resolution occurs on this level, make sure that appropriate counseling services are provided to any individuals who might have been adversely affected.

Level 2, or a crisis in progress, demands immediate action. During the commission of an act of terrorism, police involvement is mandated. Your first responsibility is to notify the appropriate law enforcement authorities. They are trained in this type of response. Once notified, provide them with personnel and information that might be supportive and useful in resolving the crisis.

The Crisis Management Team will be assembled and briefed on the status of the situation. The team will act in an informational and advisory capacity. They will provide assistance and services to maintain safety, support, structure, stability, and control. They will extend this assistance service to students, staff, and the community.

During the aftermath, or level 3, when the situation is resolved, the CMT needs to determine the status of the student body, staff, and community. A plan to implement the necessary steps to reestablish normalcy must be developed quickly.

The team will make recommendations concerning individuals who are in need of referral to in-school or private counselors. A schoolwide faculty meeting should be scheduled as soon as possible to provide a debriefing. This will also help to allay concerns and fears. Additionally, it will serve as a time to review the policy and remind teachers of their responsibilities.

When a threat is received, a determination must be made as to the proper response. In the past, many threats were dismissed by the building administrator as hoaxes. One person made the decision regarding the safety and welfare of the students and staff. Often this decision was based on the creditability of the threat as interpreted by the principal. More times than not, the decision to ignore the threat was the result of a quick review in the mind of the principal. Today's climate dictates that every threat be taken seriously. Informing parents and guardians about your procedures to deal with threats can allay many fears (appendix L).

BOMB THREATS

Beginning in the 1960s, a favorite intimidation imposed on schools was the bomb threat. Normally, these warnings were received via the telephone and were made by students who wanted to disturb the continuity of the school day.

When such threats were received, schools were evacuated and a search was conducted. As students became aware that the school day would be disrupted, more and more calls were lodged. Unfortunately, the people conducting the searches were not really trained for this task. As a result, no one could really ascertain that a building was safe for return. Over time, school administrators began to develop strategies to deal with the recurrent telephone bomb threat. These included securing unused rooms, locking storage and miscellaneous areas at all times, requiring teachers to take roll books during bomb evacuations, and assigning staff members to search for students left behind.

As technology developed, caller identification apparatuses were installed on the phones in schools. These devices helped to apprehend many perpetrators using telephones to level threats. Once these individuals became aware of caller ID at a school, they began using public phone booths. Responding to this strategy, many schools contracted with the phone company to place blocks on these numbers. Today, I know of many schools that have extended this policy to include any caller that will not release their phone number. Using this type of system, these schools inform parents that incoming calls to the school can only be made from numbers that can be identified.

Normally, the people who receive a telephone bomb threat at school are secretaries or clerks. Sometimes it is a member of the administrative team. To assist these personnel, develop a bomb-threat checklist to be kept near the phones. Familiarize everyone with this form. Instructions should include trying to keep the person on the phone as long as possible while having another person call the police to set up a trace. Provide the opportunity for another to monitor the call so that the police will have two interpretations of the call. Questions that should be asked include: When is the bomb going to explode? Where is the bomb? Are you the one who placed the bomb? Why? What does it look like? What kind of bomb is it? Who are you?

Another section of the form should have a list of descriptions that can be checked off by the person answering the phone. Categories such as Caller's Voice, Type of Language, and Background Sounds can head these sections. Some of these descriptions could be very simple. Examples in the Caller's Voice category are: angry, excited, calm, slow, rapid, soft, loud, nasal, slurred, raspy, normal, disguised, accent, and whispered. Language classifications should include: irrational, incoherent, educated, foul, well-spoken, taped, and read. Background sound items such as: music, voices, street noises, static, clear, machinery, motor, animals, dishes, long distance, and phone booth should be included on the checklist. Other areas that should be added are: male, female, familiar voice, time of call, length of call, and exact wording of the threat.

Upon receipt of a threatening call, it is imperative to remain calm and listen carefully. Follow the instructions on the bomb-threat checklist you have developed. Remember to copy the number from the caller identification device. If your school does not have these devices on the phones that normally receive incoming calls, press star 57 (*57) immediately after the call. This will enable law enforcement personnel to identify the origin of the call.

When a bomb threat is received, the normal procedure is to instantly implement the school's evacuation plan and to immediately notify the local police department or call 911 to request assistance. However, many schools have developed policies to deal with recurrent bomb threats. For example, one district evacuates on the first call every time and conducts a search before allowing anyone to return to the building. However, if successive calls are received on that same day, they are ignored.

In my school we have developed a plan that is unique and effective. First thing each morning, teachers are to examine their classrooms upon entry. They are to bring to the attention of the administration any device or item that appears out of place. When a bomb threat is received, all bells are shut off and a coded P.A. announcement is made. This means that students are not allowed out of their classrooms and that the bells will remain off until an "all clear" is issued.

During this time common areas of the school are searched by school personnel. These include such areas as cafeterias, gymnasiums, stairwells, corridors, toilet facilities, and other gathering areas. In theory, the safest places in the school would be the classrooms that were already checked by the teachers. If we were to evacuate the building, we could be moving students into harm's way.

When I first implemented this procedure more than fifteen years ago, we virtually eliminated all telephone bomb threats. Students knew the school day would not be disturbed, consequently the calls ceased. As a result, perpetrators needed to discover other venues to cause disruption.

WRITTEN THREATS

Threats committed to paper are nothing new in society. It has always been one of the most popular means to intimidate. By writing threats, one is not in a position that could result in immediate physical repercussions. Terrorists hide behind written messages and even remain anonymous if they choose. Perpetrators can threaten and make demands without the fear of retaliation.

Adolescents may use written threats as a way to intimidate and wreak havoc in the schools. Unlike the telephone threat, a note or letter is unlikely to be traced. The most noticeable drawback to the written threat is the waiting period that the perpetrator must experience. Most adolescents crave instant gratification. When a written warning is mailed to the school, there is a waiting period for response. Furthermore, upon receipt of such threats, some administrators simply choose to ignore the message. Therefore, the students have little to enjoy because their efforts are never realized.

The mere action of writing the threat sometimes is enough to satisfy the individual. However, more often than not, the craving for revenge or reaction to threats becomes the driving force for these perpetrators. They want to see the results of their warnings. They enjoy the intimidation of fellow students or faculty. If they do not see results, they will intensify their actions. A favorite ploy is to send copies of the threat to not only the principal, but the superintendent, board of education, chief of police, and mayor. In this manner the terrorist ensures that some response is made. With so many officials receiving the note, it is impossible to ignore. Occasionally, the perpetrator will send a copy to the local papers.

All of these actions ensure a response and enhance the importance of the terrorists in their own minds. Believing they are in control, a series of hoops is positioned by these perpetrators through which they make school personnel jump. Each time we respond to ensure the safety of students and staff, the terrorist gains in grandiose delusions.

When receiving a written threat, there are procedures you can follow. First, try to limit the number of fingers that touch the letter. Some police forces will have the technology to retrieve latent fingerprints from the paper. Naturally, if sent through the mail the envelope cannot be used to lift prints, but save it, as other clues may be present. The date of the postmark and the city in which the letter was mailed are two obvious clues one can garner from the envelope.

Many times it is as simple as comparing the handwriting of the letter to writing samples of students believed to be suspect. Look to students who were recently suspended or have had a disagreement with a teacher or member of the administration.

What the threat says can also serve to develop a profile of the sender. A reference to a particular supremacist group can help you focus efforts on known members. If a particular teacher is targeted, a review of class lists will be your starting point. Speak with the instructor to gain insights to students who might be upset with a grade.

During the spring semester of the 1998–99 school year, we received a threatening letter that made specific reference to a timeline. The letter was placed in a guidance counselor's mailbox in the House Four office. This type of delivery is bold. Not only is it intimidating to the teacher receiving the note, the method also ensures response by school administrators. Some students believe if the threat is sent directly to the administration no response will ensue. This concern is removed when the message is sent to a staff member, as students believe discussion of the note will follow delivery. As more people become involved, perpetrators gain in their self-importance.

The terrorist threatened to blow up the entire school if we did not shut down in one day. He stated, "You will never know who this is because I'm not even alive . . . (in your eyes anyway)." The perpetrator went on to explain that the reason for the threat was that a fellow comrade of his was caught trying to follow his lead. He gave the first name and last initial of the other student and ended, "If you can't find the bombs by 11 A.M. on Friday, June 11th, your school will be just a pile of ash."

This particular case gave reference to a classified student (a fellow comrade) that we had apprehended earlier in the year for making threats to school security. In addition to his written, verbal, and telephonic threats to blow up the school, he called students at their homes informing them of his actions. He also threatened some of these students. Evidently, one of his friends was informed of his placement and felt the need to take up his cause.

At the time we received this letter signed, "The Reaper of Death," the special-needs student referred to was in a residential psychiatric treatment center. Upon further investigation, I discovered that he had been given phone privileges by his doctors and was continuing to make threats to other students from the hospital.

The letter was sent to the police for examination, however, as it was not in an envelope, specific fingerprints could not be expected. The letter was typed, so we could not try to match it with writing samples. The only venue we had was for the police to interview friends of the hospitalized student referred to in the note, a process that proved fruitless. I noticed that the message was typed in the Jester font, so I made mention of this to the police. I was hopeful that it was a jest and not genuine. Regardless, I ordered a search of the buildings and we held our breaths until 11 A.M. Friday morning. Luckily, no bombs were found and the day progressed without any incident or disruption.

Threats with a timeline have some advantage for school authorities. This way you can deal more efficiently with the intimidation. When the timeline has passed, the students and staff feel more at ease. If the threat were left open-ended, some people would continue to worry for days.

GRAFFITI THREATS

Adolescents have always written on walls and desks. At first it was a way to achieve permanence or be recognized. Then tags were used and messages were sent via graffiti. Now students use this venue to threaten and intimidate.

On Friday, 10 December 1999, two students informed a counselor in the Student Center that a threat was written on a stall wall in the third-floor girls' restroom in House Five. The counselor informed the vice principal who called me after he verified the threat. The message read, "D-Day, December 15th, 200 students will die by my hands."

After reading the threat, I locked the restroom. This was done to prevent other girls from reading the threat and to preserve evidence. We keep Polaroid and digital cameras in the office to take pictures of vandalism. Both cameras were used to record the threat. I contacted the police who also took pictures and examined the scene. Once the police completed the on-site investigation and cleared the area, I had the stall cleaned and painted over before reopening the restroom.

We then asked the girls if they knew of any others who might have read the message. They provided us with names and all of these students were sent to the Student Center for counseling. This was done because the graffiti message was life-threatening and could have emotional impact.

Rumor containment is always a concern, and when several people are involved, stories begin to circulate. Unfortunately, in this case, gossip was spreading like wildfire. Students and teachers were openly discussing the threat.

Some students claimed to have read the threat on the Internet. These students and our technology specialists went online and searched for the message hoping to find the author. These searches revealed only students communicating to others about the situation, not the threat itself. This serves as an example of how stories can be misinterpreted and how a rumor can gain a life of its own.

I convened a meeting with all vice principals, the director of student personnel services, the maintenance supervisor, those assigned to security, and the COPs In School officers. I reviewed what had occurred, shared the message, and outlined procedures for the upcoming days. We also discussed the problem of rumors and strategies to help students who were fearful.

Everyone was instructed to be as visible as possible, not only at the entry doors, but throughout the school day as well. Custodians were put on alert to increase their checks of common areas for unfamiliar objects. Security personnel were instructed to increase the random searches at the entry doors and the COP officers began to talk to individuals willing to share information.

Our loading area is frequently used. We prepare and deliver lunches to every public elementary school in the district. I needed to ensure that this area was secure. The cafeteria workers were instructed to monitor the area when loading and unloading, and to keep the security gate closed when their work was completed.

Unfortunately, someone contacted the local papers. It has always been a great disappointment to me that some deranged individual(s) feels the need to embarrass the school whenever possible. Even more disturbing is the concern that this person(s) could very well be a faculty member. Whenever something of this nature occurs on our campus, inevitably the local paper and sometimes the metropolitan television stations are contacted. I do not know of other school communities that are continually faced with this additional problem. I hope that the staff in most schools strive to maintain confidentiality and work hard to preserve the integrity of their schools.

In any event, the reporter contacted me regarding the graffiti threat. I answered his questions truthfully, taking care not to volunteer any information not requested. I would not relate the wording of the threat as to not impede the police investigation. However, I explained the security measures we were taking and the counseling that was available. Additionally, I shared the penalty for such an incident and explained that I had called in the K-9 unit to canvass the buildings.

I composed a memo to the staff regarding the procedures implemented and the process for referral of distraught students to counselors. I outlined the policy for dealing with students who were requesting a release from school due to the threat. This procedure includes directing the child to the Student Center with the appropriate pass, contacting the home by the vice principal to convince parents of student safety, and the requirement that a parent or guardian comes to the school to take the child home (appendix M).

Additionally, I wrote a script to be used by personnel answering phones. That message read,"The administration and security team at Bayonne High School are aware of the rumors and threats. Dr. Wanko has taken every precaution, including meeting with the police, to ensure the safety of every student. As always, counseling staff is available to discuss any concerns your child may have." My goal was not only to ensure a safe learning environment, but to keep disruption to a minimum.

I then met with various student leaders to try to defuse the situation. After informing them of the procedures I had implemented, I discussed the problem of rumor containment. I challenged them to serve as our ambassadors to spread the word that the situation had been addressed and we should not empower the perpetrator. Yes, we would continue to investigate as we do with any threat, however, we should not cause such an upheaval as to provide excitement for the vandal making the threat.

Even though the threat did not specifically mention bombs or firearms, I still arranged for the K-9 patrol to come into the school on the night prior to the designated time of the disaster. They had the dogs run the buildings and the search revealed no explosives. I secured the complex and waited to see what the next day would bring.

The headline in the local paper read, "Note in bathroom spurs tightened high school security." The reporter explained that neither the police nor school officials would disclose any specifics about the graffiti threat. He went on to relate that other threats have cropped up since the Columbine High School killings. He quoted me as saying, "Unfortunately, we are becoming much too adept at handling such security threats." This statement actually referred to how schools across the nation are responding to this phenomenon. As I continued to travel around the country presenting programs on creating safe and supportive schools, I came to realize how prophetic this simple statement had become.

The next morning I arrived early to oversee security and be visible to students as well as parents dropping off their children. Everything was running like clockwork. Students were entering the buildings in a calm and orderly fashion. We used the metal detecting wands on all students and found nothing unusual. As I watched this procedure, I became aware of the lower number of students arriving at the school. While I knew some students would seize the opportunity to stay home, I had hoped that our efforts would have provided a secure feeling for the majority of the students.

After homeroom I reviewed the attendance for the day. Forty-nine percent of the students were absent. Normally we have about 9 percent absence on any particular day. Almost 900 additional students decided to stay home on the day designated by the threat. A reporter from the local newspaper called to check the attendance and develop his story. Parents were calling the school to learn if the day would count toward their children's absence. It was evident that the people outside the school were reacting poorly to the threat.

Inside the school, the day went very smoothly. Children were in their classes and teachers were teaching. The staff was visible and everyone seemed to be acting normally. Anyone visiting the school on that day would not have been aware of any impending doom. The only thing they might notice would be a smaller population of students. The staff attendance was normal for teachers, custodians, and cafeteria workers. As the day drew to a close, I must admit that I breathed a sigh of relief.

The following day the local paper ran a story on the front page with the following headline, "Threat scares off 1,000 students." I was quoted as saying, "I am disappointed with those parents who did not express confidence that we could handle this situation." It was apparent that the parents were feeding into the frenzy. They were demonstrating a reflex reaction to what their children were telling them. Research has proven that when a school is cautioned regarding an incident, no injuries have ever been reported. Clearly we were warned and took appropriate action, yet, almost half of our population chose to abstain from school.

The article concluded with a statement from one of our senior students. He anticipated that many students would not return for the rest of the week. Fortunately, his prediction did not come to pass. We had normal attendance for the remainder of the week.

I met with the administrative team and the core Crisis Management Team to critique our performance and the reactions of students, staff, and parents. Everyone thought that appropriate and swift actions were implemented and that we had been prudent in our response. I explained my frustration in the number of absences and challenged the group to develop strategies to attack this problem. The result was the creation of a public service announcement to be broadcast on our local cable educational channel.

We gathered all essential people together and produced this message within three days. Upon completion, it began airing on our channel and seems to have obtained the desired results.

An effective use of camera and background music drove the message of "Talk to me," into the homes of our students. Panning shots of recognized and trustworthy faces floated across the screen with the missive, "We are here to listen and help, talk to us and take back your school." The message was simple yet effective. This was another venue for us to reach the students. Reminding them that it is everyone's responsibility to keep our school community safe and undisturbed.

The time period of this graffiti threat coincided with the release of a *Time* magazine issue on the "Columbine Tapes." As I spoke with fellow administrators, I discovered that similar threats were occurring at their schools. A chat-room threat closed Columbine High School on that Thursday and Friday. Once again the copycat mentality was triggered by the reports. Countless numbers of students were deprived of feeling safe and secure at their schools—a right that should be enjoyed by everyone.

E-MAIL THREATS

A new mechanism to lodge threats and intimidation that has gained popularity with adolescents is the Internet. Hundreds of thousands of children are growing up using this communication device as their portal to the world. Overuse has caused some of these young people to retard their ability to interact with people face to face. As a result, the perception of anonymity begins to over-shadow good judgment for these adolescents. They mistakenly believe that it is acceptable to do anything that strikes their fancy without fear of retribution. Consequently, threats and malicious comments are sent over the Internet to un-suspecting victims everyday.

About a week prior to the 1999–00 winter break, a member of the sopho-more class received an e-mail on her home computer. The message stated that there was a bomb in the school and that it would be detonated tomorrow. The sender went on to say, "I will let you live if you have sex with me." He ended with "kill, kill, kill, die, die, die."

This girl was experiencing difficulty with her printer and sent the message to a friend to print a hard copy. The next day she presented the note to her vice principal. She explained that her father wanted the school administration to see the note. The vice principal questioned the girl and brought the note to me.

I read the note carefully trying to gain clues as to the sender. It was signed with a tag name and sent via America Online (AOL). Occasionally students will use their real names on the Internet, however, tags are more popular. Look closely at these Internet identification pseudonyms, they can provide clues to the sender's identity. For example, if the last name is Herring or Cod, students might call themselves fish, or use another aquatic reference.

No specifics of when or how the school would be targeted was offered in this particular threat. On the bottom was the forwarding address used by the girl to obtain a print copy from her friend. This address used one of our school slogans, and while not part of the original message, I decided to include it in my investigation. It would expand the circle of students who might know the adolescents involved.

At the same time, I contacted the police department and gave a report. I re-quested that a warrant be issued so that they could trace the threat. A judge is-sued the warrant and the tracing procedures began. Concurrently, I continued our investigation. We interviewed both girls and obtained a listing of their male and female friends. We checked each class list for the girls to see if any of their classmates had a history of this type of incident.

The Juvenile Aid Bureau detectives asked to interview the girl who origi-nally received the note. We contacted the father to gain approval and the in-terview took place in the vice principal's office. This was done to make the process less intimidating. The vice principal who was the parent representa-tive remained during the questioning procedure.

Through the interview process some names were mentioned that were not on the class lists. These were friends, and friends of friends. One of the names could be a pseudonym for the tag that was used in the note. I brought this to the attention of the authorities and it became one of the focuses of the investigation.

About thirty-six hours into the probe, AOL ascertained the account of the sender, which provided us with a name and address. The last name matched the pseudonym for the tag. It was a male member of the sophomore class who was friendly with both girls.

He was brought to the house office and confronted with the evidence. He admitted to the incident explaining that it was just a prank. Following our policy on threats, we suspended the boy for ten school days and mandated counseling at our Student Center.

By all indications, the student was a fine young man. He was doing well academically and was involved in school activities. Evidently he was enamored with this girl and used this venue to express his attraction. When his parents came to school, all three met with our school psychologist. The child and family were mortified and were eager to make amends.

This is just one instance of an e-mail threat. Periodically, throughout the school year students and staff bring these types of messages to school. Some are related to school others are not. Even if the school is not targeted and the threat did not happen on a school computer, you can be of assistance to the victims.

By developing a procedure and a good working rapport with the police, you can help in allaying many fears and apprehensions for your students and staff. Information on the ways to proceed when the threat is not related to school can be shared with individuals receiving threats outside of school.

USE OF CANINE (K-9) UNITS

Certain schools have the luxury of close proximity to a Canine (K-9) Unit. Bayonne High School is one of these schools. Due to our location, a K-9 Unit from Newark International Airport can be on campus in about ten minutes. We have used their services on numerous occasions. Additionally, I set up assembly programs for the students and staff to witness how these patrols work.

The K-9 Unit uses specially trained dogs to detect explosives or drugs. The dogs and human partners both wear bullet-proof vests. Their role is to find the contraband. They are not responsible to remove firearms or explosives. Once a device has been located, a bomb squad must be called in to safely remove and dispose of the explosive.

Each dog is assigned to one specific officer. The dogs are trained to discover either drugs or explosives, therefore, you must request the animals trained for the specific task. The officers and dogs are partners and the dogs actually live with the assigned officer. Normally, a six- to nine-year work span is expected from each animal. Occasionally, when a dog is retired, the human partner will adopt the animal.

When the unit arrives, the dogs are taken by the officers to the areas to be searched. However, before the search an officer plants either some drugs or fireworks, depending on the reason for the inspection. This is called "putting out a hide." Upon questioning the commander of the unit, he explained to me that the dogs view their work as a game. This procedure not only serves as a motivation device (the dogs win), it also serves as a quality check of the unit's work.

EVACUATION PLANS

Every school has an evacuation plan for a fire emergency. Public schools practice fire drills at least twenty times every year. Given that threats seem to be a part of the day-to-day operations of a school, it is wise to develop plans to deal with threats to security that should include evacuation plans.

When fire alarms are sounded everyone leaves the buildings. Students are lead by teachers to a specific location. Teachers have roll books with them to check for accountability. Everyone moves in an orderly and quiet fashion to safety. Everyone knows what is expected and they behave accordingly. This is due in large part to the repetition of the actions. Education about the dangers of fire and smoke sets the tone for the practice drills. Administrators occasionally block off a designated egress with a sign reading "Fire," to determine if the teachers and students can move easily to the secondary escape route. At least once a year, officials from the Fire Prevention Bureau are present to monitor the evacuation and provide suggestions for improvements. It is a collaborative effort. Everyone understands the devastating effects of fire and they work together to ensure the safety and welfare of their comrades.

Every school should also have an evacuation plan for other emergencies. There might be a natural or man-made disaster that will require evacuation of the school. Sometimes these plans will be similar to the fire egress procedures. Other times the plans will bear no resemblance to normal fire-drill operations. For example, if it is believed that a bomb or other incendiary device is located in a certain area of a building, students and staff cannot be expected to egress through that area. Likewise, if a terrorist is present, movement away from that area is desirable. A hostage or even some bomb threats might require a lockdown rather than an evacuation. In every case a policy and procedure should be developed prior to the incident. This will allow for the administration to follow a prescribed plan to provide for the safety and welfare of those entrusted to their care.

Sometimes it is possible to designate other areas of the school as safe havens. If multiple buildings are located on one campus, it is conceivable that students and staff can be safely moved from the affected building to a structure that is unaffected. In this manner the students are contained inside and not exposed to the elements. However, a plan to provide activities for these students also needs to be developed. It is unrealistic to believe that they will sit in other locations quietly and docilely simply because an emergency occurred in another area of the school.

Arrangements with neighboring schools can be made to temporarily house your students. If no school is in close proximity, explore the use of other large facilities. When I was developing a crisis plan for another school district, I suggested that a movie theater located across the street from the high school be used for emergencies. An agreement to provide placement of the students in the event of an emergency was established. The screening of an appropriate film was also made part of the arrangement.

When developing your plans, try to list all possible reasons for evacuation. These would include events such as bomb threat, gas leak, tornado, hurricane, earthquake, flood, hostage situation, sniper, and power outage. A brainstorming meeting by the Crisis Management Team can result in a series of scenarios that could be specific to your school and location. Once the list is complete, the team can begin to construct an egress plan for each event.

Our schools must remain safe for our children and staff. By developing proactive plans to ensure the safety and welfare of everyone on the campus, this objective can be reached. The school administration must have policies and procedures already in place to deal with threats and intimidation.

In more than half of the school shootings during the past two years, one of the primary intents of the shooters was to take the principal or vice principal hostage. It is believed that this action was a type of retaliation. Part of your emergency response plan should include the principal and vice principal responding at opposite ends of the campus. This can serve to prevent this type of hostage situation from occurring.

Practice safety drills with the staff and students. They must know how to move to safety during emergencies. In the case of a lockdown, teachers must not allow their students out of their secured classrooms until a uniformed police officer or recognized school administrator tells them it is safe. If evacuation is decided upon, teachers must know the route for egress and the area that has been designated as the safe haven. They cannot overreact or underreact. They must serve as the conveyor of reason and stability for the students entrusted to their care.

By dealing with threats to security in a reasonable and prudent manner, your school can be perceived as safe. Furthermore, you will be viewed as a leader who can respond to the situation at hand. Confidence in the school's leadership will grow. Sometimes this will take time, especially if a crisis has already occurred in your school. Parents can easily fall into the terrorist's trap because there is nothing in this world as precious to them as their children. By keeping this thought paramount in your mind, you will develop a school that is not only safe, but caring and inviting.

Chapter 9

Perceptions and Conflicts

The United States still enjoys the mantle of being the most diverse nation in the world. Our country was built on immigration. We still welcome people from all over the world as they search for the land that will provide them with freedom and opportunities. The Statue of Liberty, which stands on Ellis Island just minutes from our school, has an inscription below it that reads:

Give me your tired, your poor,
Your huddled masses yearning to be free,
The wretched refuse of your teeming shore,
Send these, the homeless, tempest-tossed, to me:
I lift my lamp beside the golden door.

These words, written by Emma Lazarus, speak volumes about the mission and vision of our country. An intent that has even more meaning for our society today.

DIVERSE STUDENT BODIES

As the proliferation of immigration continues in the United States, our schools will reflect a more diverse student population. Over time, the staff of these same schools should also reflect the diversity of the communities where the schools are located.

New Jersey happens to be the most diverse state in the United States, and at Bayonne High School we embrace our diversity. There are about 8 million people in our state—the most densely populated state in the union. There are 130 languages spoken in New Jersey; however, 97 percent of Americans speak English. The English language has continually evolved drawing upon

149

the influence of diverse peoples. For example, of the 1,000 most frequently used words in English, about one-third are French in derivation.

The U.S. Census reported that as of 1 July 1998, 25 million U.S. residents were born in other countries. That equates to about 10 percent of our population. In the early 1900s most immigrants came from Europe. Today, most of our immigrants travel from Latin America and Asia. This trend has been developing over the past decade.

It is estimated that by the year 2050, the United States will be composed of 50 percent whites and 50 percent people of color. Currently, in the state of New Jersey 38 percent of public school children are minorities. Clearly, this country must embrace its diversity if we are to continue to prosper. However, much work is needed to move the current perceptions held by many toward this goal.

The Educational Excellence Alliance of Cornell University in Ithaca, New York, conducted a survey during the 1998–99 school year. The group surveyed 32,931 tenth-grade students at 130 schools in the Northeast about cultural insults and teasing at schools. They reported that 32.5 percent of male and 20.4 percent of female juniors surveyed responded that they were harassed either once a week or almost everyday. Schools with an 80 percent minority population demonstrated about a third fewer insults according to the survey. Clearly, diversity in schools is a worthy commodity in creating a safe and supportive school.

Many people will accept cultural schisms and chalk it up to xenophobia—a fear of strangers. Members of prehistoric tribes had a natural fear of any other tribe, especially if the tribe had different physiological traits. Even if hair color was the only different trait, the fear was expressed. Today, some people believe that this is an inborn trait, and we should accept the division in our schools as natural. Over the years this has lead to countless clashes among students.

I remember my first experience with bias. It occurred when I was in elementary school. At that time in Bayonne, children were assigned to schools by neighborhood boundaries. Due to the location of our home, I was placed in a neighborhood school that had a very high Jewish population. I was one of the Christian minority in that school. As an Eastern Orthodox, I was not in the Catholic or Protestant groupings. Not only was I in the minority, I was almost the sole member of my group. Members of my church celebrated Christmas and Easter following the Julian calendar. My Christian contemporaries used the Gregorian calendar. Therefore, when their Christmas arrived, I was off from school prior to the date that my group actually celebrated the birth of Christ. Then, on January seventh of each year, I needed to be absent to attend church.

My Christian friends would ask why I did not celebrate the "real Christmas." My Jewish friends asked why Christians had two dates to celebrate the same holiday. Each year I would explain to someone why we celebrated these holidays on different dates. While this type of bias seems inconsequential to many, it still illustrates how differences in culture can cause division in people. It demonstrates how groups and subgroups are formed in our society.

During that same time period, I remember my Christian friends talking about how they were treated differently in their own church groups. We did not use words such as *discrimination* or *equal rights*, however, these were examples of how a group can create a subgroup. When it was time for my friends, who were members of the Roman Catholic churches, to be confirmed, practices were held in the various churches. In every instance the students who were enrolled in the parochial school of that parish were seated in the front pews. All public school students were relegated to the back pews by the sisters in charge. This was a subtle form of bias imposed on members of the same group creating a subgroup.

So it is easy to see that whenever two or more people get together, differences in perception are bound to occur. Unfortunately, many times these differences lead to conflicts. Compounding this problem is the fact that perceptions can be influenced by past learning. If the perception is wrong, it will not matter to the individuals holding it as truth. Add the fact that human beings will actually confabulate, "fill in the blanks," when information is missing, it is no wonder that conflicts exist.

BIASED PERCEPTIONS

Perceptual "filling in" occurs daily. It is a constructive process that takes place on a visual level. As we view our world, we take bits and pieces of sensory information to create a reality in our minds. If there are visual gaps in the information gathering process, we tend to fill in the gaps based on our past experiences. Whether those past experiences are correct or incorrect does not matter, the results will be the same—reality for that particular person.

Phonemic restoration is the process that allows us to fill in missing auditory information. We do not notice phonemes missing from familiar words as we, the perceivers, fill in the gaps. Sometimes when phonemes are incorrect, we fill in the correct phonemes on the basis of what our past experiences with these words lead us to expect.

When a large group of students begins shouting at each other in a setting such as a cafeteria, bedlam almost always seems to ensue. Part of the problem is the inability for us to use dichotic listening skills when we are emotionalizing. Under the best of circumstances, it is difficult for students to demonstrate divided attention. Selective attention during an argument usually is directed to the person who is the loudest. A shouting match is inevitable as participants strive to get their points heard. The volume level rises and physical confrontation will result if the process cannot be short-circuited.

Plato discerned that we perceive objects through our senses with our minds. We select, organize, and interpret our sensations to construct the outside world in our minds. During this transformation process, each of us shades and tints the input data based on our previous experiences in life. When we perceive danger, an alarm reaction is triggered.

This alarm reaction was first described by Walter B. Cannon, an American physiologist in 1929, as the fight-or-flight response. Cannon saw it as adaptive because it prepares the organism to respond quickly to danger. It is an innate response to the perception of danger. When the alarm reaction is triggered, a number of physiological changes in our bodies occur. These changes are initiated by the brain and further regulated by the endocrine system and the sympathetic division of the autonomic nervous system.

The hypothalamus secretes corticotrophin-releasing hormone, which stimulates the pituitary gland. The pituitary secretes adrenocorticotrophic hormone (ACTH). ACTH acts upon the adrenal cortex causing it to release cortisol and other steroids that help the body respond to stress. This is done to fight inflammation and allergic reactions. At the same time the adrenal medulla is activated by the sympathetic division of the autonomic nervous system. This causes a mixture of adrenaline and norepinephrine to be released. The body then is aroused to cope with threats and stress by accelerating the heart rate and causing muscle tissue and the liver to release glucose. This means that energy is now provided for the reaction.

During this whole process pupils dilate, hearing becomes acute, lung capacity increases, the diaphragm locks, digestion stops, perspiration begins, and hands and feet get cold. The blood is rushing to the large muscle groups and organs to better prepare the body to deal with the perceived danger. This is where the saying "He has cold feet" is derived.

With all of these changes, the body is now ready to do battle or flee for safety. Our ancestors needed this response to survive. When a predator was spotted or heard, the fight-or-flight response began automatically. Throughout history disputes were settled in this same manner. "Might made right." Today's society is trying desperately to preach nonviolence; a concept that has still failed to take root with the masses. Yes, we have made great strides in trying to control violent reactions, yet we have a long way to go to make our schools safe.

PAST LEARNING AND PERCEPTIONS

Even if there is no real danger, students can perceive the situation as dangerous due to their backgrounds. Unfortunately, it does not matter if the danger is real or imagined, the perception makes it real and the response begins. Once a student begins feeling all of the physiological changes described earlier, something must occur. Normally, what results is a physical confrontation. That is why it is imperative that we infuse conflict resolution programs in our schools.

Countless students are raised in situations where violence is not only condoned, it is also encouraged. These children model the learned behavior and really cannot understand why they are punished by school authorities when they resort to violence. Add to this the fact that the parents or guardians of these children also do not understand why violence is not acceptable in school to settle disputes, and it is easy to see why we are experiencing problems.

Not only is there concern regarding children who come from abusive homes, perception variation is compounded by students arriving in the United States with vastly different cultural backgrounds. The diversity of experiences that accompanies growing up in different cultures can profoundly affect the way individuals look at the world and consequently, the way they label perceived events. What we consider to be unacceptable in this culture, may be completely normal for a foreign-born student.

Some cultures profess that when speaking, eye contact must be made with the listener. Other cultures dictate that the eyes must be cast down when speaking to someone in authority. Students who make eye contact could be perceived as threatening by other students. Although the intent was not meant to be aggressive, the receivers perceive danger. Even though the perception is incorrect, the fight-or-flight response begins and the "threatened" students react to the changes in their bodies. When the adrenaline is flowing, it is difficult to calm these students. Trying to rationalize with them during this time is almost impossible.

Many times altercations in schools are the result of misunderstandings. Perceptions based on the students' past learning experiences dictate reactions to current. It is as though the particular response is mandated. Anger will invoke anger. Fear and intimidation will cause students to either withdraw or lash out violently. Regardless, programs designed to bring students together to learn about different cultures can help to make schools safer.

FAULTY PROGRAMMING

The first thing we must consider when dealing with perceptions held by our students is the fact that many have faulty programming. When working with a computer program, if the software is flawed, the results will never be correct. What you expect to happen will not happen. The same is true for human beings. If the internal programming is flawed, time and time again situations will not have the desired results. Students believe that they will achieve the preferred results simply by repeating the same actions designed to accomplish their goals. Rarely do they examine the actions to determine if they are incorrect or inappropriate to the objectives.

Our society has used negative teaching from infancy. The first word recognized by infants is not *mother* or *father,* rather it is the most negative word in our vocabulary, "No!" Studies have proven children growing up in the United States will receive twenty-five negative statements to one positive remark. Think of that, a ratio of twenty-five to one. Now add this to our own self-defeating statements, such as, "I'm no good at that"; "I'm too old"; "If it weren't for bad luck, I'd have no luck at all"; and my favorite, "It's not easy being me," and it is easy to understand why we have problems with negative programming.

It has been estimated that by the eighth grade, students have witnessed 8,000 murders and 80,000 acts of violence via the media. Statistics reveal that they have been told, "You can't do that" 148,000 times. Clearly, our children have been exposed to negative programming that can result in faulty perceptions.

When we first roamed the Earth, survival was the lesson to be learned. As we became more sophisticated, altruistic lessons emerged. The mind is truly an amazing piece of God's work. Anyone who has watched an infant during the first eighteen months of life, can attest to this fact. During this time the baby is internalizing. The child is learning all by itself. The process is done by experimentation—discovery. If the child is trying to reach out and grasp a favorite toy, it begins by moving certain muscles. Then, through a process of trial and error, it finally learns which muscles need to be worked to move an arm so it can stretch out toward the toy. Through the same process, the infant learns how to grasp the toy and bring it closer.

After the first eighteen months of life, the child begins the cognitive process of learning. We now come into the picture, and with only the best intentions, begin to teach the child everything we believe it needs to know. From this point on, the child no longer can experience pure internalizing, and in a sense has become contaminated with the perceptions of others.

When our children enter schools that are still teacher-centered rather than student-centered, additional problems begin. Obstacles of effective functioning in a true teaching and learning interaction include: unmotivated, undisciplined students; lack of parental support; ambivalence and vacillation in government regulations; shifting societal priorities; and lack of home and school agreements, just to name a few. Poor nutrition, lack of proper rest, and a disaffected family life compound the problem, making the role of the educator extremely difficult. The immediate loser is the individual student who is excluded from full participation in, and contribution to, society. The ultimate loser is society itself.

The obstacles cited should not be an excuse for inaction, rather in light of pressing student needs, it is imperative that they be surmounted. If schools are to succeed, professionals and parents must respond to calls for maintaining educational standards via new approaches. Radical ideas need to be implemented if we hope to foster great minds in this country. No longer can we expect our children to succeed just because they are our children.

For decades, educators and psychologists agreed that the probability of learning would be enhanced if certain criteria were met. Of prime importance are proper stimulation and incentive. They further agree that learning takes place first on the conscious level, what they refer to as the cognitive learning process. Nevertheless, I believe that learning can also take place on the subconscious level.

Our learned colleagues have clarified that we learn first on a conscious level. The question then arises, "How does the subconscious acquire knowledge?" We know that all automatic, anatomical functions are inherent and instinctual to the human species. Activities are carried out by the subconscious without conscious learning. Functions such as breathing, the flow of blood, and the healing mechanism, are all inborn. Added to this are the movements that are taken over by the subconscious once they have been learned, such as walking, running, various sports activities, and other repetitive actions. These functions no longer require conscious thinking to be performed. They were first learned consciously, but have become learned activities of the subconscious.

These are examples of acquired knowledge, items our subconscious has learned and performs for us without our even being aware of them. For instance, we do not stop to think when climbing up a flight of stairs as to which foot should go where and how high to lift each foot to reach the next tread. If we did, disaster would probably be the result.

Then how does the subconscious learn these types of activities? The truth is that the subconscious can acquire knowledge in various ways; for example, repetition, emotion, and trauma.

Repetition

Repetition is perhaps one of humanity's oldest teaching techniques. The Japanese have used it for centuries with excellent results. In the United States, we also employ repetition for many learning tasks; for example, "Children, write each word ten times for homework." All types of responses can be established through the use of repetition. Well-meaning parents incessantly remind children to eat everything on their plates to grow up big and strong. Now, the adult children still clean their plates, subconsciously believing it is necessary to become fully mature. When this occurs, obesity may be a result. Through repetition, children learn a pattern of behavior to achieve a desired goal.

When things we do constantly become habits, eventually the subconscious takes over these functions. When this happens, the activities are performed at higher levels of proficiency. Every driver has experienced the following scenario: You have been driving for some time and become engrossed in talking to a passenger or in listening to the radio. Suddenly, you are miles from where you began and you do not remember driving the distance. Obviously, the subconscious took over while the conscious was absorbed elsewhere.

In my workshops, when discussing the subconscious, I sometimes use the analogy of shower amnesia. This is the process that occurs when you allow your mind to wander while in the shower. Suddenly, you cannot remember if you have shampooed your hair or washed a certain part of your body. It becomes necessary for you to take a sort of body inventory, trying to remember what you have washed. Once again, due to repetition, your subconscious knows what activities to perform to cleanse your body.

Think back to your days as a high school student. Remember the so-called natural athletes? These were the students who excelled in sports and seemed able to perform virtually any physical feat with little or no effort. Why were they so gifted and others needed to struggle to achieve even mediocre performance? First, the so-called natural athletes are endowed with certain physical attributes. Without the physical ability to perform, it is virtually impossible to excel in athletics. Second, since these students experienced success in physical activities early on, they programmed themselves through life as individuals who could perform physical feats easily. Usually, these children engage in organized sports such as basketball, football, and soccer. When the coaches recognize even just a small amount of athleticism, they praise those children. Furthermore, the coaches work closer with those individuals to ensure a winning team. The attention reinforces the children's perceptions that they are special and this feeds the notion that they can perform well athletically. The circle continues and success breeds more success.

If someone not as adept in sports tries to learn a new physical routine, much practice would be necessary. Mistakes and awkwardness would pervade the learning period. Self-doubt would rear its ugly head and make it even more difficult to learn the particular task. On the other hand, natural athletes know in their minds that they are naturals. Therefore, when faced with a challenge to learn a new physical activity, they believe they will be successful. If they have difficulty learning a new physical activity they simply tell themselves, "I can do this, I only need to perform the routine once again." Then, through repetition they master the activity.

They believe they can succeed, they believe in themselves—in their athletic prowess. If they are awkward in their initial attempts, they simply analyze the procedure and repeat the routine until it is mastered. They never believe it is too hard or impossible for them to learn. They perceive themselves as athletes and as a result are athletic.

Everyone has heard the term *second nature*. This phrase refers to the ability to perform a certain action without thinking. Just as in the examples of running up stairs or driving a car, athletes also acquire second nature when performing. Through repetition, or what is referred to as practice, athletes learn and then commit to memory, on the subconscious level, the desired routine. Once the subconscious learns the actions, it can "take over" in the competition and perform perfectly. However, when athletes begin to think about the actions, and the conscious comes back into play, that is when mistakes are made. When the conscious begins to analyze all the possibilities in any given situation, the pure action of the subconscious or what we refer to as second nature is lost.

I should mention at this point, the importance of correct practice. Vince Lombardi, former coach of the Green Bay Packers once stated, "Practice doesn't make perfect. Practice makes permanent. Perfect practice makes perfect." Consequently, no matter how hard we practice, if the practice is incorrect, the performance will be flawed. So too with the perceptions held by our students. If they are constantly exposed to the notion that a certain race or creed of people is inferior, they begin to believe that untruth. Through repetition, they are programmed incorrectly.

Almost a half century ago, the process of repetition was brought to a level that demonstrated how the learning process could be accelerated. In 1956, in a small movie theater in New Jersey, repetition was paired with a subliminal process that yielded amazing results. Advertisers became aware of a process called subliminal messaging, and tried an experiment during the screening of the movie *Picnic* starring William Holden and Kim Novack. To better understand this process, you first must be cognizant of how we see movement on the screen when viewing a movie.

The film upon which images have been developed is actually divided into smaller cells. These compartments vary in size depending on the type of film, and its intended use. For example, in the 1950s, home movies used an 8mm format. Whereas, the common size film for a movie theater was 35mm. To create motion on the silver screen, Thomas A. Edison used a process that relied on persistence of vision. He invented a machine that moved twenty-four frames or pictures past a light source in one second. As a result, people watching the screen would see twenty-four still images every second. However, to make the process work, it was necessary to separate each image from one another. To accomplish this, Edison constructed a device that came between the light source and the film every time a frame passed the lens. This resulted in his invention, a machine that projected twenty-four individual still pictures on the screen every second while inserting a black or void projection between each picture. Twenty-four times an individual picture and twenty-four times darkness each second.

Now, through the physiological process of persistence of vision, people see the illusion of movement as their eyes hold the previous picture until the next image is already on the screen. Advertisers discovered that a message could be placed on an individual cell of the film and would not be seen consciously. However, the subconscious has the ability to read and comprehend the message even though it was only flashed on the screen for one twenty-fourth of a second.

On that evening in 1956, a message that read, "Eat popcorn, drink Coca Cola." appeared on the screen throughout the film. However, no one in the audience consciously knew the message was there. At the end of the evening, a tally of the concession receipts found that sales skyrocketed 58 percent. People who were watching the movie were programmed to buy soda and popcorn without consciously being aware of the process.

When the Federal Communications Commission learned of the procedure, they quickly banned that type of subliminal advertisement. However, to this day, it remains pervasive in print advertising. During the 1970s, subliminal messages were placed on the music tracks played in shopping centers and malls. The messages were designed to encourage higher employee productivity and to discourage shoplifting. In the 1980s, entrepreneurs began selling subliminal audio tapes professing that one could learn or accomplish just about anything by using this method of instruction.

Upon close examination, one can determine that subliminal learning is merely a form of repetition. However, it is quicker and more powerful, as the conscious portion of the mind is not aware of the message being sent to the subconscious. When this occurs, the message is accepted more readily by the subconscious, regardless of the individual's own programming. This allowed people to reprogram themselves more quickly because the conscious is not filtering out what it considers to be unwanted messages. Therefore, when trying to erase an old message, it is not necessary to repeat a new message in quantities equal to or greater than the old message or for the same amount of time.

For example, if you have been a smoker for ten years and were using a plain repetition plan to become a nonsmoker, you would need to implant ten years of nonsmoking messages in your subconscious. The problem is compounded since the conscious believes you to be a smoker due to the ten years of repetition. The conscious resists nonsmoking information from entering the subconscious as the conscious holds as truth the idea that you are indeed a smoker. However, if the conscious is not aware of the message (subliminal), it can sneak into the subconscious. Once there, it can exert influence so that the message is accepted more quickly and reprogramming is easier and faster.

Faulty programming has clouded many students' perceptions of fellow students and the world around them. Parents instill their views of the world on their children. If the parents hold prejudices, the children most likely will maintain the same values. It becomes very difficult to reprogram the children when they are repeatedly exposed to faulty programming. A form of subliminal programming can also be achieved by parents if the messages sent are subtle in nature. Conflicts occur in schools as students come into a diverse setting where they have not been taught how to properly react or interact.

Trauma

Almost everyone can recall a time that they have warned a small child to be careful in the kitchen around the stove. Unfortunately, many children have been badly burned as a result of not heeding the warnings. A young mother tells her child not to put his hands on the stove when it is on because it is hot. The child listens intently, however, when the mother is out of the kitchen, the child places his hands on the stove and is burned. From that point on, the child never again places his hands on the stove.

The mother gave the child knowledge, but the stove gave the child ten fingers of wisdom. Once burned on the stove, the child will wince and pull away automatically, even if the stove is not lit. Consider how many times you have pulled your hand from the top of a stove after placing it there accidentally—even though the stove was cold. Trauma causes the event to be recorded not only on the conscious level, but also in the subconscious. From that point on, the subconscious forces you to act accordingly, without you taking the time to think of the proper response.

The prime directive of the subconscious is to protect the individual from harm, to keep you healthy and safe. It does whatever it believes is necessary to carry out this directive. The trauma of being burned coerced the subconscious to make a permanent record of the event to keep the individual safe. However, if the program is flawed or even somewhat incorrect, disaster could be the result. Taking the directive of survival to the extreme is presented in the following scenario.

A man is boating on a calm and serene lake. Suddenly, the weather turns bad. The wind begins to howl and rain starts to pelt the boat and lake. As the wind gains in intensity, great waves begin to swell on what was once a peaceful almost mirrorlike lake. The man becomes concerned because he never learned how to swim. He goes below deck and dons a life preserver.

At this point, the boat begins to rock with great intensity. The man tries to radio his position and predicament so he can be saved. However, the storm has apparently hampered transmissions. Now the man is beginning to panic. He goes on deck and tries to analyze his options. As he moves gingerly around the boat, looking frantically for the shore line, the boat lurches and he is swept overboard. The water is cold and very choppy. His inability to swim causes him more panic and he begins to swallow some water.

He frantically tries to get back to the boat so he can feel somewhat safe. After what seems to be a lifetime, he reaches the side of the boat. As he begins to pull himself up, his lifejacket becomes hooked on a grommet. At this precise moment, the wind kicks up and a great swell pushes him away from the boat. However, his lifejacket remains fastened to the boat. Immediately his panic increases tenfold. Shortly, he is swept beneath the violent waves never to be seen again.

An analysis of what actually occurred demonstrates the power of trauma and its influence on the subconscious. At first, concern was not too great, as the individual in the story analyzed the data fed to his mind. He knew certain facts, which he held as truth. One, he could not swim. Two, the storm was gaining in intensity. Three, the safety of the shore was not visible. The man at this point begins to hypothesize the data based on his past experiences. As he processes the information, he begins to develop a plan of action. When the idea of contacting someone by radio fails, he begins to panic, he is feeling isolated and powerless. He tries to gain some control of the situation by putting on a life vest and reviewing his options.

When he falls overboard, his emotions run high. He begins a process similar to confabulation. He begins to fill in the missing pieces to his dilemma. These pieces could be true or false; only time will tell. When in this emotional state, his reasoning faculties are somewhat distorted. He starts to react to events rather than becoming proactive and taking the initiative. He is panicking! Finally, when he falls back into the water without his life preserver, total fear engulfs him. As he goes underwater, he holds his breath as he knows on the conscious level that breathing will bring water into his lungs and he will drown.

At this point, an amazing thing occurs. He holds his breath so long that oxygen is deprived to the brain. Consequently, he begins to drift into unconsciousness. When he is unconscious the subconscious takes over the thinking process. Remember, the subconscious learns many lessons by repetition. It knows that the individual must breathe to live and the prime directive of the subconscious is to survive. It cannot think on the conscious level and analyze information. It merely reacts as it has been programmed. Therefore, it starts the diaphragm moving so breathing can resume. The result is water being brought into the lungs and inevitably drowning. As the subconscious followed its programming, the man died. The subconscious will always follow its programming regardless of the outcome. It is childlike and accepts whatever it is told as truth during the programming.

Most people can recall occasions when trauma has been used to teach. "Spare the rod, and spoil the child," was the driving motto of child rearing for centuries. Think about the methods animal trainers use to achieve the desired ends. Even today, in our so-called enlightened society, many people will argue that it is important to use trauma to shape desired actions in our youth. Clearly, trauma is a powerful tool used for centuries to train and in some cases to brainwash people. Inflicted trauma or physical pain are other ways to achieve permanent learning and consequently, are methods that cause perceptions to be formed in our youth.

Emotion

Emotion can be either pleasant or unpleasant. For example, many people can remember their first kiss. However, these same people probably cannot recall what they had for lunch just two weeks ago. This is because the kiss had a certain amount of emotion attached to the event, and unless the person eats the same lunch everyday (repetition) they will not remember what they ate. If the meal was a special birthday luncheon, the memory probably will be retained, otherwise the event will be passed into the deep recesses of the mind. By the same token, if a person ended a relationship with a special person while a particular song was playing, it is probable that whenever hearing this song, strong emotions will surface.

It is estimated that high school graduates retain only 30 percent of their lessons. Yet, almost all remember the theme song of their prom. Once again, we see the power of emotion when it comes to permanent recordings in the mind. Also, be aware that it is possible to record by emotion through various senses. For example, a certain perfume can invoke memories. Smell can dominate an emotional recall. Even unpleasant smells can evoke response, and many times an unwanted one.

While working my way through college, I had many part-time jobs. One was making pickups for a local funeral parlor. I will never forget the first time I went to a hospital morgue to collect a body after its autopsy. The sights and smells of that room were burned into my subconscious through emotion. Even three decades later, I still can vividly picture the event. Unfortunately, the memory is triggered by similar smells in comparable types of hospital rooms.

One scenario I present at workshops to help people understand the memory process is "The Filing Room." I ask the audience to imagine a long room almost like a wide corridor.

"There are no windows and only one door at the front end of the room. This is the only means of light for the room, since it is a secure information storage area. Lining both sides of the narrow long room are file cabinets. As far as the eye can see, the room extends until darkness precludes any true conception of its length. Each day, as we go about our normal routines we place our memories in file jackets, label them, and then put them into the files closest to the door. When it becomes necessary to retrieve a memory, we simply open the door and pull the information out of the file."

I explain that on the surface this is a very easy process. However, things become more difficult as we create more and more files. Every experience that we wish to remember we label and file. Therefore, on the next day, when filing, we move the material from the front files to the next file cabinet down the line. We keep current material close to the door for easy retrieval and where there is also light. Naturally, if some information from yesterday is to be used today, we keep it in the first cabinets.

The problem arises as we become overloaded with information. The data needs to be stored. If we keep moving the information farther back into the recesses of the room, it becomes more difficult to access. It is darker and farther away, making retrieval arduous. The problem is compounded if we label our files incorrectly. The information is in the file cabinets, only under the wrong category. Many times we cannot regain this memory upon command. However, sometimes it will "pop" into our consciousness at what appears to be an unusual time.

The truth is that it did not just "pop" into the mind, and it was not at an unusual time. It was retrieved in the same fashion we retrieve all memories. The difference is that it was placed in the wrong file. Therefore, when we were processing the information and pulled up certain files, we received the information within, except it was not the information we expected. The memory was called up based on the incorrect label. Our minds sent the information at the correct time, not an unusual time. We asked for it, only the file was not what we counted on, as we simply labeled it incorrectly.

Imagine that you work for a shipping company and you receive an order from a trucking firm. The name of the company is "Acme Movers." You collect the data and prepare a file folder. At this point you must decide if you are to label the folder Acme, Movers, Acme Movers, or even truckers. Whichever you select, the information will be of no value if it cannot be retrieved. You might label the folder "Acme Movers," a logical decision as that is the name of the company. The next week you are absent from work and your employer is looking for the file. He believes it should be filed under "Truckers" since that has always been his policy. Naturally, he cannot find the information at that location.

This is how we file data incorrectly. We place information in a folder and label it according to what we believe is correct at the time. Later, we tend to forget what label we put on that file. This is especially true if we process great masses of information and/or similar information. Adolescents in schools are not any different. Information is collected, labeled, and filed. When situations happen that require the use of past data, the information is retrieved. If the information was mislabeled, students cannot retrieve the data. As a result, the decisions made could be wrong. Also, if the perceptions held by the students are jaded, incorrect judgments are inevitable.

Sometimes we unknowingly file things so we cannot retrieve them at all. Most people can remember a time when they decided to hide something of great value. At the time we might say something to ourselves about hiding this valuable object so that no one can find it. Unfortunately, we are in that category of people that cannot find the object because the statement was "... no one will find it." We fall into the classification of no one; therefore, our subconscious, which interprets commands literally, prevents us from finding the item.

On other occasions, we place information in a file that is classified. This "top secret" file holds information that is too difficult or painful to remember. Psychologists refer to this process as repression. Usually only through therapy can these troublesome memories be recalled. This is because they were filed in the "Do not touch" cabinet as they were too painful for us to cope with at the time. Our subconscious was once again acting in a manner to protect us.

AMBIGUOUS VALUES

We perceive the world through minds that hold certain ideas as truth. If what we hold as truth is really not the truth, our decisions will be based on incorrect data. As a result, the decisions would not be correct. We must realize that some of what we hold as true may be untrue. People believe untruths to be true all the time. Take for example people who teach their children about Santa Claus. The children believe in something that is unreal. However, they are told by a loved one or authority figure that there is such a person. In addition, they actually saw pictures of Santa or perhaps even visited with him at a mall. Then on Christmas Day as they reveled in delight while opening their presents, the children saw more physical evidence of this man.

As these children grew older, they came to realize that there was no real Santa, so they changed their belief. Unfortunately, numerous students are laboring under many similar misconceptions: the notion that a certain group of students is inferior or that boys are superior to girls, and countless other demeaning concepts. Until they are willing to reexamine what they hold as truth, with the openness to make changes, they will be doomed to flawed decision making. When this occurs, conflicts ensue, violence can result, and schools become less safe.

Amazingly, the beliefs we have held from childhood still affect our actions. These beliefs act as filters through which we view the outside world. Consider a filter as something that prevents unwanted materials from passing through it to a containment vessel. Imagine the mind as the vessel and the filter as a barrier that prevents certain ideas to enter. What is held on the filter determines our actions and reactions. This occurs as the ideas on our filters are the principles upon which we base our lives. Everyday we view the world through a filter that may have faulty information placed upon it. Until our students realize that some concepts that they hold as truths really are faulty programming, they will continue to create problems in the school setting.

During my workshops I present a powerful demonstration representing the ease upon which our students can be influenced and receive flawed programming. After discussing the faulty programming and ambiguous values that many students work under in our schools, I review the basic training conducted by the military. In just a few short weeks, adolescents are trained to take orders without question and kill the enemy. I then transfer this notion to the concept of our children becoming influenced by gangs or cults.

To further illustrate this point, I conduct a group suggestibility test. All participants are told to sit in a relaxed position with the hands palm up or down on their laps with the legs uncrossed. I then instruct them to stare at a point slightly above eye level. At this point I begin giving instructions on the heaviness of their eyelids and general relaxation suggestions.

Participants are instructed to tense various muscle groupings for about five seconds and then to relax them for about twenty-five seconds. Everyone is to focus on the particular muscle group as we move throughout the body, tensing and then relaxing muscles. Four major groups are targeted. I begin at the feet and include the calves, thighs, and buttocks. Next I move to the trunk of the body and give suggestions about the stomach, lower back, and chest. The third group includes the shoulders, arms, and hands, and I finish with the neck, head, and face. Throughout the procedure, I give suggestions about relaxation and the feeling of well-being and security.

I then focus on narrowing the audience's attention and tell them they will experience a warm or tingling feeling in their hands and feet. Once I feel proper narrowing of consciousness is accomplished, as well as inertia and passivity, I begin to give suggestions similar to the following:

"Paint a picture in your mind's eye. In this picture you are seated at the table with your hands folded similar to when you were a child in grammar school. Clasp the hands tightly together. Look at your fingers and the way that they intertwine as your hands remain folded on the table. Now extend your index fingers straight out while your hands are still folded. Put the two extended fingers in a position where they are about one inch apart from each other, but keep your hands tightly folded together.

Now imagine that I am winding a rubber band around your outstretched fingers. I am pulling the band tighter and tighter. As the rubber band pulls tightly, your fingers begin to move toward one another. Shortly the fingers are so close that they must touch. They will move together as though they are in a vice and I am closing the vice pushing them together until they touch. Regardless of what you do, the fingers will move toward each other as though one were a bar of iron and the other a strong magnet."

After giving these suggestions I tell everyone that they are feeling fine and that their breathing will return to normal. I further instruct them that they will have a good night's sleep and will wake up tomorrow refreshed and ready to meet the challenges of the day. I count from one to three explaining that everyone is to open their eyes at that point to continue with our experiment.

Next, I explain what has occurred and tell everyone that their charge is to fold their hands, extend the index fingers, and keep them from moving together and touching. When everyone is in position I begin to repeat the suggestions about the rubber band, vice, bar of iron, and magnet. Shortly, gasps are heard as some people witness their fingers moving together and then touching. As I continue the suggestions, more people begin to see their fingers move and touch. Eventually, almost everyone in the workshop has their fingers touch.

The experiment is based on the relaxation technique developed by Dr. Edmund Jacobson. His book *Progressive Relaxation* was published in 1929. Since that time the technique has changed little. The underlying premise is that we cannot have the feeling of warm well-being in our bodies at the same time we are experiencing psychological stress. The technique causes the muscles to relax and the pulse rate and blood pressure to lower. Also, there is a decrease in perspiration and respiration rates. Jacobson contended that our bodies respond to anxiety-provoking events with muscle tension. He further argued that the same reactions would occur as a result of anxiety-provoking thoughts. As the physiological tension is experienced, the subjective experience of anxiety occurs. As physiological tension is incompatible with deep muscle relaxation, the anxiety is reduced.

When the mind and body are relaxed, we become more susceptible to suggestions. If the suggestions are carefully worded and are delivered with the proper pacing, most individuals will accept the suggestion and act accordingly. This is due to the conscious mind becoming somewhat lulled, and therefore not analyzing the feelings experienced. Then the subconscious becomes more alert and open to suggestion.

At this point I have moved the experiment from progressive relaxation to hypnosis. This is a state when there is a narrowing of consciousness accompanied by inertia and passivity. The audience now takes my words at their literal meanings. Hypnosis is nothing magical, it is a natural phenomenon shared by all humanity. It is a time of deep relaxation, both mentally and physically, a time when the mind is focused on one idea or suggestion.

We have all entered hypnosis without formal induction. When we lose ourselves in concentration or daydream, we are in a state of hypnosis. Prior to falling asleep and awakening we pass through a state of hypnosis. During this time we are highly suggestible. It has been argued that hypnosis is also a defense mechanism natural to all animals. When we enter the state of shock induced by injury, our skin temperature cools to minimize bleeding. Additionally, we automatically decrease movement and breathing.

After answering questions as to what has happened to the audience, I then review the experiment relating this short event to students and their perceptions. This serves as an extremely powerful tool in the understanding of how our youth can be swayed by a charismatic person. How someone just a little bit older or someone who has money or an individual who is viewed as special can develop a following. Unfortunately, this following is then indoctrinated in the narrow views of the leader of the gang or cult. The members hold the views of this leader as truth and act accordingly. As more and more of these groups develop, conflicts in the schools increase. Violence is the result, and the feeling of fear permeates our schools.

As our schools become more diverse and our students bring more biased perceptions to the classrooms, we will experience disagreements. These disagreements do not necessarily need to be harmful. Disagreements can invoke intellectual growth; however, until we develop and employ programs that recognize the importance of diversity, conflict will occur. Our students need to learn that everyone has a right to a free and public education, and this right is to be exercised in an environment that is free from fear and intimidation.

Much work is needed to devise programs that will teach our students about faulty programming, ambiguous values, biased perceptions, and how past learning can influence interaction. Once they are armed with intelligence rather than weapons, we will see a reduction of violence in our schools. A challenge that must be met by everyone involved in the rearing of our children.

Chapter 10

Job-Related Stress and Administrative Overload

I began my quest to learn more about stress management when I witnessed the death of some of my colleagues during protracted labor disputes. Many people are not aware of the potentially disastrous effects of workplace stress on their physical and mental well-being. Unfortunately, I learned this difficult lesson from a very close perspective. As principal, I make dozens of decisions each day that affect hundreds of lives. These lives, in turn, affect hundreds of more lives. The sense of responsibility is sometimes overwhelming.

During my tenure with the Bayonne Public School District, I have endured the illness and death of numerous fellow administrators and teachers. Exposure to this sad process is inevitable, as life is cyclical. However, in a relatively short period of time—eight years—we grieved the loss of an unusually high number of staff members. Four of my six vice principals were stricken with illness. One suffered a total of three heart attacks with the second heart attack taking place in my office, and the last one fatal. Another vice principal endured a stroke, and the other two administrators developed catastrophic diseases that robbed them of their lives prematurely. Additionally, one curriculum director was stricken with a disease that resulted in his death and another suffered six heart attacks, the last fatal. Finally, our school mourned the loss of four teachers, all to devastating disorders during the same period.

Coincidentally, protracted labor disputes took place during this same time span. We were exposed to various job actions and two strikes. Tensions were high and rifts developed among teachers, and between teachers and administrators. During the teachers' strike, middle management administrators suffered the most. We were torn between supporting faculty members and providing an instructional environment for our students.

In September 1987, the Bayonne Board of Education imposed teacher salaries which set a legal precedent for the state of New Jersey. The next few years were unpleasant, to say the least. Teacher leaders regularly brought their concerns to the community, and many teachers ceased supervising club activities and other special events.

We had to explain to students why certain programs had to be canceled and meet with parents who just wanted things to return to normal. As the days turned into weeks, and the weeks into months, and finally into years, I became increasingly aware of the toll being taken on everyone. Incidentally, there was no signed contract until June 1991.

I believe the constant stress of the workplace contributed to my colleagues' early deaths, and I vowed not to become a casualty. I began researching stress and stress-reduction techniques. I attended workshops, classes, and seminars. I read articles and books, and began to formulate my own theories about stress, its consequences, and the ways to contend effectively with difficulties.

THE NEED TO REDUCE STRESS

It has been said that the absence of stress is death. While it is true we need stress to function, we do not need to expose ourselves to undue stress that can result in illness. Stress is an everyday fact of life and the school administrator is no different from anyone else. Actually, the role of principal can be one of the most stressful jobs on our planet. As the educational leaders of our schools, we have been asked to do more and more with each passing year. We must not only ensure that our children learn, we must provide them with all the necessities that society demands and that many homes have stopped providing. Add to this the constant threats of lawsuits and the actions of various outside groups trying to impose their will on the school community, and it is no wonder that the principal is under severe stress.

It is true, we cannot avoid stress; however, we can control how we respond to stress. First, realize that not all stress is negative. Stress can be desirable and is essential to life. When you receive a promotion or buy a new house, the stress of change is felt. It can be exhilarating and motivating. It is only when we allow stress to turn into distress that problems will arise.

Some believe the actual word *stress* comes from the word *distress*. The theory espouses that the word came into common English usage from Old French and Middle English. It is thought that the first syllable was dropped due to slurring of the word. This theory has merit as children often use the word *cause* instead of *because*. Correct use of these two words has different meanings, because (since) and cause (reason).

Unfortunately, over the years we have come to associate the word *stress* with harmful results. Distress is always disagreeable; stress is not always harmful. It is only when we allow normal stress to become distress that problems arise. That is, when we become *distressed*. Think of stress as the demands of our lives. These demands are called stressors and the actual wear and tear on our minds and bodies is the stress.

I have developed an instrument to determine if the school administrator is suffering from severe job stress. The Principal's Job Stress Indicator can be self-administered and only takes a few minutes to complete (appendix N). It will provide you with a snapshot of your current situation, explaining if you are coping well with stress on the job or whether you need to take immediate steps to manage your job stress.

The stress that bombards us day after day is a natural by-product of life. Actually, a certain amount of stress is necessary for us to function properly. Understand that we experience stress from three basic sources: our thoughts, our bodies, and our environment. Clearly, only one-third of stress stimuli comes from outside sources. Therefore, if the internal two-thirds stressors can be controlled, our lives should be healthier, happier, and longer. In chapter 9, I presented information on how we perceive events in the environment. Our minds interpret and translate complex changes and determine when the fight-or-flight response is to be evoked. How we interpret, perceive, and label the experiences will either relax or stress us. The way we appraise the situation will determine what actions we take.

Stress is omnipresent in our bodies. Physiological stress results from the aging process, the rapid growth of adolescence, illness, accidents, menopause, and poor nutrition, to name a few. If you are worried about an event at your school the next day and cannot sleep well during the night, you have allowed the stress from your thoughts to affect your physical well-being. The lack of sleep will add physiological stress to your problems.

Stress occurring from the environment is interminable. The noise levels from students passing in the corridors, in the gymnasiums, or sitting in the cafeterias are stressors. Students crowding in the auditorium or on the stairwells causes us to experience stress. Performance standards imposed by the board of education, the superintendent, parent groups, or even ourselves can become overwhelming. Time restrictions and pressures, threats to personal security, and threats to our self-esteem can produce stress. Even the weather places demands upon our bodies that result in stress.

Stress is everywhere; however, we can plan our lives so that stress does not overwhelm us. When we mismanage stress, all problems will seem to be equal and stress will permeate the total environment. By working on simple problems first, then moving to the more difficult, stress can be reduced. We will actually see that progress is being made as we execute effective planning and set priorities. Stress can be the spice of life or the kiss of death; how we choose to manage it will determine our fate. Make the common stressors of the job the spice of life. It can provide us with energy and supply a zest for living.

Medical science has proven that the body's adaptability, or adaptation energy is finite. Therefore, more than just calories are lost when we are in distress. This reaction was first described by Dr. Hans Selye in 1936, and subsequently became known as the general adaptation syndrome (GAS). This is the biological stress syndrome, the set of organ changes caused by glandular extracts produced by various noncoms agents. There is a triphasic nature of the general adaptation syndrome. First is the alarm reaction. Here the body demonstrates the changes characteristic of the first exposure to a stressor. The stressor activates the body to prepare for battle or run to safety. During a school crisis this alarm allows us to spring into action, as we know it is imperative to act swiftly. Next, the stage of resistance ensues and we suppress the symptoms associated with the alarm reaction. This is when we become accustomed to the bodily signs characteristic of the alarm reaction. As a result, these signs virtually disappear and our resistance rises above the normal level. The final stage, exhaustion, follows long and continued exposure to the same stressor. Even though the body has become adjusted, eventually, adaptation energy will be exhausted. The original signs of the alarm reaction will reappear, but will not abate. We have reached the stage of exhaustion and our bodies are telling us to stop so we can recoup. Otherwise illness or death may follow.

Try to think of the three stages as being analogous to the three stages of life. During childhood we have low resistance and excessive responses to any kind of stimulus. When we are adults, our resistance is increased and during senility we experience an irreversible loss of adaptability. At the beginning of the crisis, we are hit directly with stressors. Similar to an infant unaware of impending danger—seemingly defenseless. We then rise to the occasion during the crisis; we are in adulthood experiencing increased resistance allowing us to perform and take control of the situation. Then, after a prolonged period of time, if we are not careful of how we expend our energies, we can reach the stage of exhaustion. If this occurs, we can no longer serve the students and staff of our school. Therefore, it is essential that we learn how to cope with stressors so we do not become distressed.

The human body was designed for physical use and actually gets better with proper operation, but abuse will lead to a breakdown. Every time we use a machine, it erodes a little. Just as a machine will wear out quickly if it is not properly maintained, so will the human body. We can learn to manage stress, thereby, the stress can be enjoyed as a challenge rather than dreaded as a threat.

Everyone has a certain amount of adaptation energy, which is determined by heredity. This is the ability for us to cope with stressors (either pleasant or unpleasant) and bring ourselves close to indifference which is the lowest stress level. Unfortunately, at this time, there is no objective proof that additional deposits of this energy can be made. Therefore, it is imperative that we use this energy with great care. Otherwise, one day, the storehouse will be empty and disaster will befall us.

Do not be fooled by the revitalized feeling you receive after a good night's sleep or a restful vacation. While these activities are essential to good health, they do not replace the adaptive energy lost to distress. We can restore our resistance and adaptability with these strategies, but not completely. The solution is simple, do not become distressed. Learn to relax and perform tasks in a controlled and measured manner. Allow yourself to save as much adaptive energy as possible, so it will be there when you really need it.

Everyone has a certain amount of energy each day. If you choose to burn up or waste energy on nonproductive activities such as worrying, you will have less energy for important actions. This results in stress. Set your priorities so that you can use your supply of energy on activities that will bring you closer to your life goals and the mission of your school.

Some general categories that use much of our energy are administration, mail, meetings, nonprofessional duties, organization, paperwork, parent conferences, pupil contact, supervision, and ourselves. Review these categories and chart how much time is spent on each. If you find that the smallest portion is devoted to you, there is a good chance that you are experiencing distress. Keep in mind that these categories do not cover family and social commitments, only work. Therefore, if the category devoted to yourself is small now, it will almost disappear if you add the other factors that compete for your attention. The lesson to be learned is to make time for yourself so that you can function at peak performance in all aspects of your life.

WAYS TO REDUCE STRESS

There are numerous ways you can reduce the stress in your life. However, first you must decide that you are willing to become an active participant in your stress-reduction program. Attending workshops or seminars designed to reduce stress is helpful. Look for programs that teach time management, controlled breathing, meditation, visualization, imagery, or even self-hypnosis. Any of these techniques will help you reduce your stress level. A trip to the local bookstore or time spent browsing the Internet will reveal a proliferation of books dedicated to relaxation and stress reduction. The following are some techniques and practices that can start you on your way to effectively managing your stress.

Make Time Work for You

Time is merely a sequence of events, but it is a nonrenewable resource. No matter who we are, how powerful we are, how wealthy we are, we all have the same twenty-four hours at our disposal everyday. How we use our time can determine whether we become distressed. The following provides some time management techniques that you might like to incorporate into your daily routine. Keep in mind that your personal "time use" philosophy must be congruent with your governing values.

Plan each day, leaving time for the unexpected while setting priorities among the items that must be accomplished. Then, work on the most important items during the time you have the most energy. Also, make sure you provide periods of rest or diversion. At work, handle each piece of paper only once and group telephone calls. Try to delegate tasks whenever possible and learn to say "no." Perform routine tasks at the end of the day, as they require little energy. Finally, devote some time each day to yourself. I have developed a shortened form, *A Dozen Time Tips for Principals*, that can be posted in your office (appendix O). By providing time for yourself, you will be able to function at peak performance in all aspects of your life. If you are not taking care of yourself, you will be of little value to others.

On-the-Job Vacations

Another strategy you can incorporate immediately is taking on-the-job vacations right in your office. Whenever you are feeling stressed, take a deep breath and while exhaling, close your eyes and say, "Relax." Now, with your eyes closed, try to create in your mind's eye a picture of your favorite vacation spot. Focus on all the elements that make this a pleasurable place. Concentrate on the sights, sounds, smells, and feelings you have experienced there. The more details you can create in your mind, the more relaxed you will become. Let go of the problems of the day and drift into a pleasant, safe, relaxing vacation spot.

If you are experiencing difficulty using your imagination, think back to a time when you were encouraged to use this amazing modality. As children we used our imagination everyday, we were excited to create with our minds. Think back to that simpler time and with just a little practice you will be able to resurrect this lost art.

Background Music

In 1695, William Congreve wrote that music has the power to soothe the savage breast. We often overlook the power of music on our psychological well-being. One of the most effective ways to reduce stress in your life is to play soothing background music at work, in the car, or at home as you go about your daily routine. Studies have indicated that a relaxing pace of sixty beats per minute can help relieve nervous tension.

As we listen to the music, either consciously or subconsciously, a pulse that is normally seventy-six beats per minute will begin to drop to match the slower rate of the music. This will occur without any conscious effort on our part. Some selections that play at sixty beats per minute are "Morning from Peer Gynt Suite No. 1" by Edvard Grieg, "Canon in D for Strings" and "Continuo" by Johann Pachelbel, "Concerto in F for Trumpet" by Johann Sebastian Bach, "Concerto No. 21 in C, K. 467" by Wolfgang Amadeus Mozart, and "Water Music: Lentemente" by George Frederic Handel. These selections are only recommendations, any music you enjoy that has sixty beats per minute and is calm and soothing to you will be just as effective.

Emotional Redirection

Throughout the day, many people will be pulling at you in all directions. Everyone will have an issue that they believe must be handled immediately. As the educational leader of the school you must respond, taking care to sort the items that need immediate attention from those that can be addressed at a later time. This delicate balancing act must also take into consideration the personalities involved with each issue.

The students, parents, and staff do not really think about the emotional strain they are placing on you. They simply expect results. You are there to do the job. This constant barrage can drain you emotionally if you do not take time to redirect some of that emotion. This technique is quite easy to accomplish with the use of pictures or props.

I have favorite photographs of my family strategically placed by my computer workplace. A quick glance at these pictures reminds me of what is really important in life. Additionally, I keep an oil painting of a tranquil seascape on the wall opposite my desk. When I begin to become stressed, I look at the picture and think of the pleasant times I have spent at the beach. In both cases the technique of emotional redirection is used. The strong emotion of family is easy to understand. The painting's redirection is enhanced because the picture has special meaning for me: Several years ago it was painted by one of the custodians and given to me as a gift.

Another element that can redirect emotion includes the use of a prop or special poster. Whenever looking at this object or placard it inevitably brings a smile to our face. This happens regardless of the harried pace of the day. Each of us has a poster of something or someone or some type of item that fits the bill. Bring it to the office so it can work its special magic.

Fixed Breathing

Proper breathing is an effective weapon against stress. If blood is not properly oxygenated, it can contribute to depression, fatigue, and anxiety. The first breathing exercise you can do is to simply become aware of your breathing. As you sit in your chair, scan your body and notice the mechanics of breathing. Locate the spot that seems to rise and fall with each breath and place one of your hands over it. Continue to breathe through your nose and try to ensure that your chest and abdomen are moving together.

The next exercise brings your breathing back to its natural manner, much the same as when you were an infant. Breathe in through your nose, filling the lower section of your lungs first, then the middle component, and finally the upper portion. Make this a smooth inhale. Then, hold your breath for a few seconds. When exhaling, do it slowly and pull your abdomen in slightly. At the end of the exhale, relax your abdomen and raise your shoulders gently.

The final breathing exercise I am presenting purifies your lungs. It can refresh you and may be familiar to women who have practiced for natural childbirth. First, inhale as described earlier, hold for a few seconds, then exhale a scant amount of air at a time, forcefully, through a small space between your lips. Imagine you are blowing through a straw. Continue in small forceful puffs, stopping between each until all the air is expelled.

FEELING OVERWHELMED

During my extensive research into the stress of life, I came across an element that was recurrent, but only during the past century of human existence. It is the feeling of being overwhelmed. Everyone has experienced this feeling many times over, and unfortunately, we will continue to feel this way at various times during our everyday routine. However, armed with information on stress reduction and with diligent practice, you will be able to diminish the occurrence of this phenomenon and lessen its effects when it occurs. Then, when a crisis strikes, you will have the emotional tools to lead your school through the negative effects of trauma, delivering the school community to normalcy.

What exactly is this feeling and why does it occur? It would be easiest if I relate an anecdote used in my workshops to illustrate. First, imagine a block of time from the birth of Jesus Christ until the year 1750. A fair amount of time in humanity's recorded history, but not a long period considering our total existence. However, it suits my purpose for this illustration. Hypothesize that you are living in the year 875, right in the middle of this chunk of time. Consider what you might do for a living. Perhaps you would be a merchant, a shepherd, a farmer, or even a teacher of sorts. Think of what your daily routine would be during that era. Life was very simple at that time. There were no deadlines as we now know them, no phones, no computers, no fax machines, no e-mail, and none of the so-called modern conveniences. You could be born, live your entire life, and die in the same village. In fact, Jesus Christ Himself did not venture physically more than thirty miles from His birthplace. During this span of time, it is estimated that our knowledge doubled.

Now imagine that you could be magically transported 500 years forward or backward through time. It is now either 375 or 1375. Would you be able to "fit" into the new society to which you were transported? Would your old job be available to you in the future or past? Of course, since the societies were agricultural in nature and technology did not develop greatly during the 1,700-plus year span we are examining. Your adjustment to life, half a millennium either way, would not be too difficult. Incidentally, during that same time span scientists and archaeologists estimate that humankind's knowledge doubled. This was a time in our history when not too many people felt constantly overwhelmed. They were worried about things such as feeding and sheltering the family unit, not when a certain fax was to arrive.

Let us now take another block of time. It will run from 1750 to 1900. During this span of only 150 years, the estimate is that humankind's knowledge doubled again. What took almost 1,800 years earlier occurred in just a century and a half. Think of all the development during this short timeframe, notably the industrial revolution and all the resulting societal changes. Now imagine being alive in the year 1400. If you were to be transported that same 500 years into the past to about 900, you could still make the transition with relative ease. However, if you were to move the same 500 years into the future to 1900, imagine the shock that you would experience. Assimilation would have been overwhelming. Society was no longer agricultural, it was now industrialized. Even the farm technology would be so alien to you that you might think you had been transported to another planet.

The first United States patent legislation was enacted during this time span (1790) and the U.S. Patent Office was created in 1836. Only seven years later, in 1843, U.S. Patent Office Commissioner Henry Ellsworth stated in his report to Congress, "The advancement of the arts, from year to year, taxes our credulity and sense to presage the arrival of that period when human improvement must end." This quotation would lead to the myth that the Patent Office was closed at this time. However, that was not the case. Ellsworth was simply using a bit of rhetorical flourish to emphasize the growing number of patents. The rest of his report outlined specific areas in which he expected patent activity to increase in the future.

The next time span we will investigate is from 1900 to 1960. Technology seemed to explode on the scene. Now flight was moving to outer space. Household technology took much of the drudgery out of caring for the home and more of that phenomenon called "leisure time" was evolving. Many families joined the ritual of the "Sunday afternoon drive" in the family car. Radio was pushed to the side in the 1940s by television. It was an exciting time to be alive. Things were changing so rapidly. During this span it is estimated that humankind's knowledge doubled once again. If you were transported from 900 to 1960, just sixty additional years from your last trip, there would be a huge number of adjustments you would be required to make. That feeling of being overwhelmed would now be dumbfounding.

Just think of what our grandparents witnessed in their lifetimes. They were taken from a time of horse and buggy, to a time of motorized vehicles, to a time of motorized flight. Almost everyday some new invention made its impact throughout the world. We were now able to fly, to speak over the air, and to travel underwater. The quality of life was becoming better and better.

If we examine the time from 1960 through today, we can readily see the onslaught of technology. Many people still remember eight-track audio tapes. Now vinyl records have gone the same route and compact disks are the state-of-the-art audio recording devices. Unfortunately, by the time many people master the nuances of their newly purchased computers, it becomes outmoded. Some people are reluctant to purchase anything high tech for this very reason. They are constantly waiting for the newer and better model so they have the "best." The obvious problem is that there will always be a newer and better model that will need to be mastered.

Things that many now take for granted are relatively new in our society. For example, if I tell one of my students that when I was their age, I made sure I was home at 8 P.M. on Tuesday nights so I could watch Uncle Milty (Milton Berle—The Texaco Star Theatre), the student would look at me in amazement, wondering why I just did not tape the program.

Scientists and researchers now estimate that due to computers, the doubling of knowledge will now take place every eighteen months. Overwhelmed? You will be confounded, there will be no escaping this feeling. Now imagine if you were born 500 years ago and were transported to the present. The adjustments would be so great that you would be highly stressed to say the least. Every day something new is developed and we must learn to contend with difficulties and adjust constantly. As we progress with more and more quickness, we will become dismayed more often. The key to surviving is to learn how to deal with this feeling of being overwhelmed and powerless.

Add to this the following data: Only 16 percent of today's families fit the traditional concept of family, that is mother, father, and children living together in a unit with the father working and the mother staying home to be the homemaker. Far fewer families have the extended family concept in practice. We seldom see families living together with grandparents who help in the rearing of children.

Today it is estimated that nearly half of all marriages will end in divorce. At my workshops, when I mention this statistic, I jokingly note that this means that fifty percent of all marriages end in death. Think about this statistic, just a few decades ago it was a social stigma to be a divorcee. Now it seems to almost be the norm. Add to the fact that households headed by women have doubled in the last twenty years and it is plain to see that our family unit is changing.

Without the support of family, individuals can become more and more stressed and have no immediate help to draw upon. More people and children are forced to rely on their own devices to solve problems. In the past, children as well as adults could turn to a family member for comfort, advice, and love. Finally, demographics project that 40 percent of all children born in this decade will spend part of their youth with only one parent. We, as a nation, no longer have the stability afforded to our parents or grandparents. Stability that equates to support and a feeling of well-being.

Evidently the feeling of being overwhelmed is here to stay. No patent offices will be closing. Things will not be getting any simpler. People will constantly need to adjust to the newer and better technology. It is estimated that within the next two decades, almost 500,000 new jobs will be created. Jobs that we have never had before. Jobs in a technology that do not even exist today.

Also, it is predicted that the average person will have five different occupations throughout their life. No longer will we see a great number of people spending thirty to forty years in the same occupation. Some of the jobs will disappear altogether, others will require extensive retraining. Schools need to begin looking at ways to teach students how to adapt and be flexible so they can cope with the ever-changing world of today and tomorrow.

If you wish to thrive as a school administrator and not just simply survive, review the information in this chapter carefully. Believe in the resolve of the human mind to grow and adjust. One way we can begin to become less stressed and not feel so overwhelmed is to learn how to take control of our lives.

TAKING CONTROL

Most school administrators would like to think that they are in control of their professions and lives. Many boast that they are "calling all the shots." However, the reality is that most merely react to situations; they are reactive, not proactive. They wait for an event to happen and then they respond. Unfortunately, many times administrators in this category are disappointed in the results of their actions. After reflection they feel disheartened, for they now have come up with a more appropriate action for the earlier event.

Hindsight is twenty-twenty, however, believe it or not, when faced with similar situations these administrators usually react in the same inappropriate manner, only to reflect once again and ask, "Why did I do that?"

Few administrators feel comfortable with the actions they take in various situations. These people are secure in the notion that they are in control. I am not referring to the administrator who is a compulsive controller. Rather, I am speaking of administrators who are very happy with the choices they have made in their lives. People who suffer from very little anxiety and stress. They balance their professional lives with their private lives. Administrators that most of us admire and try to emulate. People that we all can become.

We all have the ability to be happy, to make proper choices, and to gain control of our lives. However, as with everything else in life, you must first make the choice to gain control. By procrastinating, you are actually making a decision. Not deciding is actually making a determination. You are deciding not to do anything about the situation you are facing. You are deciding to remain out of control. Like a piece of driftwood in the ocean, you are letting the tides of life decide where you will go, and how and when you will get there.

In my workshops, I present a simulation regarding *Taking Control*. I explain that we only take command when the need is great enough. This concept is bizarre to many, so I present the following scenario.

I explain that I am planning to catch a flight after the presentation but that I need a ride. I offer a hundred-dollar bill to anyone who will drive me to the airport and ensure that I will make my flight. Let us say that the flight is at 5 P.M., and that is it now 1 P.M. The airport is about twenty minutes away by car. When someone agrees, I ask them when we will leave, reminding them that they only receive the money if I make my flight. Usually, the person will allow an extra hour or so for travel in case of heavy traffic.

Now, I begin to narrate our fictitious ride to the airport. We are en route, it is 3 P.M., and the highway is jammed. Traffic is not moving and there is no relief in sight. At this point, the person usually acknowledges that we cannot make the airport in time, and forfeits the $100. I raise the stakes by offering $500 to get me to the airport to make my flight.

With more incentive, the person begins to think of ways to get off the highway to an alternate road. I let this occur and the trip is resumed. After a few more miles, I explain that we now have a flat tire and there is no spare in the trunk. It is 3:30 P.M., and the road is deserted. Once again, the person acknowledges defeat and relinquishes the money. I again raise the jackpot, but this time to $10,000. The need now becomes greater and the person is ingeniously thinking of alternate ways to transport me to my destination. You would be surprised at the many innovative and creative venues that have been developed to ensure that I arrive on time. One man even offered to carry me on his back! The same situation prevailed, only now the need became great enough for the person to take charge of the situation—to gain control.

How many times have you decided not to act in a certain situation? Times when you felt the need was not great enough. Times when you believed it was easier not to reach a particular objective. Many people over time, developed a pattern of giving up—a pattern of failure. It became easier to give up, rather than work for a particular goal. Some people change the goal to something they feel is easier to obtain or worse, they forget it totally.

Keep in mind that it is perfectly acceptable to use subgoals. You should not have the impression that a review of goals and consequent modifications are undesirable. On the contrary, many times it is necessary to adapt to a new lifestyle or work condition. When this happens you should review your current goals. Naturally, if you list a goal that is unrealistic, you will meet with failure. Even if the goal is attainable but it is years away, you might become frustrated and quit. That is why it is important for you to develop subgoals.

If you possess a goal of becoming independently wealthy, there are many options you can follow to achieve this mark. You commit your goal to paper and list steps to achieve that objective. The steps could very easily become your subgoals. By developing a timeline for each step or subgoal, your entire plan is laid out before you. Now you can begin working toward your ultimate goal. However, make sure that you provide the necessities to aid in your quest. You must be willing to work to reach your objectives. This might require securing a part-time job to gain the necessary capital to invest in real estate or the stock market. It might require long hours and diligent study of the prevailing markets and research as to where your investments might reap the highest yield. Take care so that you do not fool yourself into believing you can reach your goal quickly and easily. Do not be like the character in the following story.

A man desirous of becoming rich, goes to his house of worship to speak to his god. He asks God to allow him to win the lottery. The next day he returns to ask again to win the lottery. This procedure continues for over a week with no results. The man then becomes frustrated and asks God why his prayers were not answered. Hearing no reply, he begins to leave the house of worship and he hears God's voice saying, "My son, at least you could have purchased a ticket."

This individual had a goal and a plan to reach the objective, however, he did not provide the materials necessary to reach his goal. He did not purchase the ticket that would enable his prayers to be answered in order to become rich. Therefore, you must ensure that you provide yourself with the tools necessary to reach your goals. Review your objectives and determine what is needed to assist in your quest.

To drive home the concept of being in control, I ask workshop participants to imagine that the walls of the room we are in represent two ends of a continuum. On the right, we have events that we can control. On the left are events that we cannot control. Everyone lives somewhere along the continuum that connects the two walls. Daily we move back and forth along the line as it suits our needs. I ask participants to remember when they felt more comfortable. Was it when they were closer to the "in control wall" or the "out of control wall?" Most people feel better when they are in control, closer to the right wall. People who are out of control have their backs against the left wall day after day. They are constantly frustrated and are probably the ones who eventually contemplate suicide. They have reacted and selected incorrectly.

Recent statistics tell us that one out of every four American teenagers has thought about or attempted suicide. This is alarming data for any country, let alone a nation such as ours that has so many resources, so much wealth and freedom. My theory is that these young people have their backs against the left wall all the time. They experience sentiments such as being pressured, hurried, inferior, and unworthy. They believe they have no control whatsoever, so they exercise control as to when their lives will stop. In their minds they finally have gained control.

Can you think of anything beyond your control? When I ask this question of my workshop participants many interesting answers are offered. However, inevitably someone mentions death, taxes, other people, and the weather. While it is true we have not yet learned how to cheat death, look at what has occurred over the past few centuries. The average life expectancy for a person living during prehistoric times was eighteen years of age. During the Middle Ages the life expectancy rose to forty years. Now life actuaries predict that we will live well into our seventies. We are still dying, but we are living longer and healthier. Through medicine, proper diet, and exercise we have begun to prolong life. It is estimated that within the next three generations, life expectancy can reach 300 years. This is due to the ability to locate specific genes on particular chromosomes. Through computers and medical science, our deoxyribonucleic acid (DNA) can afford us the ability to clone body organs and parts to replace worn, injured, or diseased portions of our anatomy.

Some people believe they have the solution to beat death. They have invested heavily in the science of cryogenics. This area of science professes that it is possible to freeze an ill person until a time in the future when a cure for the disease has been discovered. Then, the person can be thawed out and the disease treated. An individual interested in this science who does not possess enough money for the procedure can have only the head frozen. It is then hoped that the head can be attached to another body or a cloned body in the future.

On the other hand, we can exert some control over our taxes. Some people make their living as tax consultants. They provide information to consumers on ways in which they can reduce their taxable income. Furthermore, if your goal is to pay no tax at all, it can be accomplished by dissolving all assets or by moving to a deserted island and living off the land.

When it comes to the weather, it again seems that we have no control. However, when rain is needed we seed clouds. We have built structures in which we live and work that are climate controlled. Additionally, we now have sophisticated weather reporting and predicting procedures that warn us of extreme conditions so that we can take appropriate action.

Finally, can we control others? Basically, you can only control your actions and therefore, can only influence others. However, many people will admit they are controlled simply because they have come to believe it is so. It is easier for them to accept another will being forced upon them, so they do not have to make decisions. Think of the various cults that have seemly taken over numerous minds and controlled the actions of many individuals.

I am sure everyone can think of other situations that are beyond our control. Things we truly cannot command. However, they are few and far between. We have been conditioned to believe we are not able to exert control. Remember, we can take control when the need is great enough. The individual who was willing to carry me to the airport took control because he believed the need was great enough.

As a school administrator you can take control and provide the safety, support, stability, structure, and control necessary when a crisis strikes. You can also exert control in the day-to-day operations of the school ensuring that teachers can teach and students can learn. You merely need to set your goals, develop subgoals or steps to reach your objectives, and obtain the tools necessary to ensure success. Realize that a goal is just a dream with a timeline.

KEEPING IT IN PERSPECTIVE

Throughout the entire process of crisis response management, enormous stress will be thrust upon the building administrator. Likewise, stress will be prevalent among the students, parents, staff, and members of the Crisis Management

Team. It is imperative that, as the educational leader of the school, you maintain a balanced perspective.

This charge is not as easy as it may sound. People will be pulling at you from all sides, everyone has concerns that must be handled promptly and efficiently. To drive home the value of sorting out the mundane from the imperative, I present the following story.

Emile Coué was a pharmacist turned psychologist who had a clinic in Nancy, France. He lived at the beginning of the twentieth century (1857–1926). He developed many theories regarding the imagination and the will. It was Coué who coined the phrase, "Every day, and in every way, I am becoming better and better." This method of autosuggestion came to be termed Couéism. His belief was that the imagination was mightier than a person's will. He also believed that the imagination could affect how a person becomes ill and more important, how a person becomes well again. In addition, he was the first to use the analogy of walking across a plank with ease when on the ground, but falling when the plank was high in the air.

Since Coué first presented this analogy there have been many variations, the most powerful of which I use in my workshops. This particular variation points out the importance of willpower, imagination, and values; all of which revolve around the ideas of taking control when the need is great enough while keeping things in perspective.

Normally, I ask for a volunteer who has a child younger than eight. I then ask if they are familiar with the I-beam used in construction. These beams are in the shape of the letter "I" which provide optimum strength in architectural design. They are normally placed on the ends of two opposing walls to span the distance in between, thereby supporting the structure above that particular level. When everyone is clear regarding the relative concept of the beam, I describe one that is 200 feet long, 12 inches wide, and 12 inches high. Next, I ask if this person will be willing to walk from one end to the other when the beam is lying flat on the ground for a thousand-dollar cash prize. Naturally, the challenge is accepted, and I proceed with the experiment.

I now ask if the person will be willing to repeat this feat with a twist. This time the beam is suspended ten feet off the ground and I have raised the prize to ten thousand dollars. Once again the individual is willing to accept the challenge. The worse case scenario might be a fall resulting in a broken arm or leg.

At this point I discuss the importance of one's imagination and its role in the experiment. I explain that when challenged in such a manner, our minds begin a process of reviewing all data to determine if we can perform the task. We draw from past experiences and develop hypotheses as to the probable success or failure of the current challenge.

When the beam is directly on the ground, the task only involves walking 200 feet along a 1-foot wide surface. This surface is only 12 inches off the ground, therefore, the entire task is not threatening. It is something we believe we can accomplish. We also realize that if we lose our balance, we need only to step back on the beam to complete the task. Finally, we have a good incentive to motivate us, a prize of one thousand dollars.

The exercise involved our imaginations regarding what would happen to us if we attempted the feat; our willpower as to the ability to perform the challenge; exerting control when the need is great enough—monetary gain; what we value in life, i.e., the money versus the possible injury; and keeping it in perspective—deciding if the exercise is worth the effort.

When the beam is suspended 10 feet off the ground, some hesitation is evident. The mind is now reviewing the data and reports that injury may result if we are unsuccessful. This causes the person to be tentative in their walking strides as they are imagining what will happen if they fall. Nonetheless, the prize is more than adequate for the task and the volunteer usually accepts the challenge. The need now becomes great enough to attempt the walk.

Next, I inform everyone that I have hired personnel to move the I-beam from its present location to Kuala Lumpur, Malaysia, the site of the tallest buildings in the world. Furthermore, I have contracted to have the beam placed on top of the twin towers in such a fashion that it spans both buildings connecting one to the other with a 12-inch walkway. I explain that all weather conditions are mild. It is midday and about seventy degrees with no wind or rain. I now challenge the volunteer to walk the same 200 feet across the beam perched 1,483 feet from the street. This time the award is one million dollars. The imagination now paints a picture of the individual falling to certain death, a scenario powerful enough to resist the temptation of a large monetary reward.

Without delay, I change the circumstances. I now inform the volunteer that I am on the opposite end of the beam holding his or her child by its feet ready to let go at will. Furthermore, I explain that it is raining heavily and very windy. However, if the volunteer will cross the beam, I will not drop the child. As you can imagine, all volunteers were ready to cross the beam to save their children.

Immediately, the need became great enough for the volunteers to take control. They were no longer imagining what would happen if they fell, they were imagining what would happen if their child were dropped. By way of comic relief, I then explain why I specifically asked for volunteers with children younger than eight. One volunteer was experiencing difficulty with his teenager at home. When asked if he would walk across the beam to save his child, he yelled, "Let him drop!"

Throughout the crisis management process, take time to reflect on what is truly important during the current situation. Decide what is vital enough to risk crossing that I-beam. Keep these things paramount in your mind when sorting out all the other variables that will be bombarding you and the team. These will be the items that will guide you in the decision-making process. Everything else will really be inconsequential to the total picture. Yes, those items will probably need to be addressed; however, they should not occupy valuable time when decisions and actions must be made from second to second. By holding the I-beam image in your mind, you will discover that many of the things that you have previously held as valuable are not. They are of little consequence in life.

By this illustration it can be readily seen that we do have the ability to take control of many situations that we formally believed were beyond our control. Unfortunately, many administrators wait until the need is great enough before they decide to exercise this ability. When a crisis strikes, you must take command. The need will be great enough for you to be proactive. You will be able to cast aside your fears and doubts. You will provide the safety, support, structure, stability, and control necessary for everyone to move through the crisis and begin the healing process.

Ralph Waldo Emerson stated, "Do the thing you are afraid to do, and the death of fear is certain." These words uttered many years ago, ring true even today. The principal must set aside any personal fears and assume command of the crisis situation. Actually, there are really only two inborn fears, the fear of a sudden loud noise and the fear of falling. All other fears are learned responses acquired throughout our lifetimes.

If you take the time to think about your fears and try to remember their origins you will see that most are irrational. However, even though they have no basis in fact, they remain true fears. It really does not matter if the fear is real or imagined; it still carries the same impact for you. The same fight-or-flight response will be initiated. Also, if you believe in the fear, it becomes a true fear.

Some fears are necessary for your health and well-being. These trepidations are recorded correctly in your mind. For example, in the 1981 action adventure *Raiders of the Lost Ark,* the movie hero, Indiana Jones (Harrison Ford) had a fear of snakes. In his case, the fear arose while escaping from some dangerous individuals. During the chase he fell into a boxcar of snakes. Because he was a boy at the time, the incident caused him much fear. When this occurred, the subconscious made a record of the event and equated danger with snakes. This protective mechanism then remained with him throughout his life. Some would agree that this fear is legitimate since some snakes are poisonous. However, others would argue that snakes make wonderful pets and no fear is necessary.

Indiana Jones could not discern and separate his fear based on which snakes were poisonous and which were harmless. Therefore, he held a fear of all snakes, probably due in large part to the trauma and emotion that occurred during the original incident with the boxcar of snakes.

This is how most fears are learned, through traumatic or emotional experiences. Additionally, some fears were taught to us as when our parents instructed us to be fearful of strangers. Other fears are acquired. As children we may have watched horror movies. We then associate thunderstorms and darkness with danger and fear. The list is virtually endless. People can be afraid of almost anything, and the fear is real to those people affected.

Many principals have a fear of failure. By the same token, some are fearful of success. Fear is a knife that can cut both ways. Think back to a time when you were completely prepared for an examination in school. You studied arduously and had committed the material to memory. However, when you entered the classroom and began the exam, you panicked. Perhaps the first question was too difficult, or it was not in the material you studied. Whatever the reason, fear erased volumes of knowledge.

Do not take the concept of fear lightly. If we carry this notion to an extreme, it is easy to understand the problem facing a claustrophobic. People afflicted with this phobia suffer from apprehension of small, enclosed spaces. All indications are that at one time these people probably had legitimate reasons that fostered this fear. Perhaps there was a threat of physical or emotional harm in a very small place. The trauma of the event caused a permanent record to be established in the subconscious. Thereafter, whenever encountering confinement in a small place, the subconscious acts in a way it deems necessary to protect the individual. When entering elevators, these people consciously know there is nothing to fear. However, the subconscious, trying to protect the individual, does everything it can to get them to leave. Some become anxious, others begin to perspire, some even feel nausea. The subconscious does whatever is necessary to remove its precious cargo from the perceived danger.

Occasionally, fear is coupled with worry. Unfortunately, the school principal is not immune from this pairing. If you are concerned that something will go wrong in your school, you work to prevent the particular incident. It is a proactive exercise. You perceive danger and spring into action to ensure the safety and welfare of the students and staff entrusted to your care. However, when we spend countless hours worrying about a variety of concerns that may or may not happen, we can become debilitated. Worry solves nothing, it only burns up energy. It prevents us from engaging in productive activities. It serves no purpose. Still more people die from worry than from work, probably because more people worry than work.

Countless principals worry about mundane items. "What will happen if . . . ?" seems to be the mantra of this group. Do not fall prey to this mentality. Keep focused on the priorities you have set for the school. Remember what would cause you to cross the I-beam. You can take control of any crisis situation and guide your students and staff to normalcy.

Guilt is an emotion that burns up energy and serves no purpose other than to prevent you from repeating a certain action. After a crisis, the administrator will start to second-guess everything that happened. It is only natural to feel a certain amount of guilt, as you are the person responsible for everything that happens in your school. However, it is imperative that you not wallow in guilt. It will not assist you in helping your students and staff. Channel the wasted energy of feeling guilty into something constructive. Take action and you will feel better and so will the people around you.

William Shakespeare wrote, "Things are neither good nor bad, but thinking makes them so." When a crisis strikes we can use it as an opportunity to learn and grow from the experience. Out of crisis can come opportunity. By taking the challenge, we will learn about ourselves and our students and staff. We will grow from our successes and failures.

The lack of control over any job situation leads to uncertainty, frustration, and stress. Principals can become demoralized if they believe they are unable to meet the expectations of the superintendent or the board of education. If they feel the needs of students are not being met, they become disappointed. These and other factors have stressful repercussions. The special meetings, interruptions, bomb threats, phone calls, emergency repairs, and false alarms are only a few of the distractions pulling the principal from the school's mission. All jobs have difficulties; however, it appears that the role of principal requires a special type of person to perform effectively and deal with the stressors of the position.

Too much stress on the job is unhealthful. No stress on the job will result in boredom. Finding the right types and amounts of challenges to keep you well balanced is necessary. When properly stimulated, your performance will be enhanced without overloading you. Still, you will need to properly manage the distressing areas of the job.

Learn relaxation techniques. Engage in hobbies and physical activities. Eat nutritiously. Ensure a proper balance in your life. By adopting and integrating these components, you can become a more effective administrator. Ultimately, the students and staff in your school will reap the benefits of a revitalized administrator.

Chapter 11

Thinking Outside the Box

By this time, you are aware of the many factors that can cause stress. You are also mindful that stress will always be present. Learning how to deal with the everyday stressors of the job will make you a more proficient administrator. Furthermore, when dealing with a school crisis, stress management will allow you to perform at the level necessary to guide your school back to normalcy.

As a principal it is likely that you occasionally suffer from insomnia, have severe headaches, stomach disorders, feel tired when you should not, or even suffer from irrational fears. You might think you are not living up to your potential or that you are being overworked and taxed beyond your limitations.

Conceivably, there are days you wonder why you left the classroom. You feel as though you are entitled to more happiness in life. You believe that people rely on you too much. You might suffer from the "Lone Ranger" syndrome—the belief that only you can do the job correctly.

Yes, the role of the modern principal is far from what our grandparents and even our parents experienced. You are not only the lead teacher, you are expected to serve as a parent, police officer, physician, psychiatrist, contractor, accountant, confidant, and in a series of other roles that situations will dictate. Whatever the burden or agitation you experience, realize that you have more control than you previously thought. However, until you decide to take control, you will always fall short of your true potential. As a result, the staff and students will then fall short of their respective capabilities.

Millions of people never reach their true potentialities. They never live up to the maximum. They have settled for less. Their jobs, homes, and cars were merely accepted. Some have even settled on their spouse. These people have allowed the pervasive atmosphere of stress to direct their lives.

At times, everyone feels overburdened and would like to escape, especially in our highly technological society. As was pointed out in chapter 10, it is only natural to have these attitudes. The feeling of being overwhelmed is a type of brain overload. That uneasy sentiment one experiences when the pressures of the day seem too much to handle. When there does not seem to be enough time for all you would like to accomplish, and what is worse, there is not enough time for you to achieve what must be realized.

It would be wonderful to escape any time we wanted, without facing the consequences of our actions and without the students and staff being adversely affected. Escape to a place where everything is perfect—where you would be in control of your life. Everything would be secure, serene, and everyone would be happy. By dealing with items one at a time and practicing techniques to reduce stress, you can learn to live a healthier, happier, and more productive life. It will not be a place where everything is perfect; however, it will be a place that you can enjoy.

Not withstanding the pressures of daily reality, there are the obvious health concerns related to living a stressful existence. Study after study has demonstrated the health risks of existing in a constant state of stress. Researchers contend that too much stress can lead to certain diseases and even death. They further indicate that when people who are constantly stressed become ill, their recuperative period is longer than those of us who know how to deal properly with anxieties. If you cannot take proper care of your own health needs, you cannot be expected to function effectively as a school administrator. Furthermore, during a crisis situation, you will be one of the first to be adversely affected and perhaps become physically ill. You must be strong enough to lead the students and staff during those trying times.

You can dramatically improve the quality of your life in a relatively short amount of time. I have learned through observation, study, research, and application, the paths one can follow to reach life's goals. Over the past twenty years, thousands of people have received the benefits of my presentations on stress reduction and gaining control. I have combined that information with my research on school safety, resulting in a hybrid workshop for school administrators.

Many of the patterns and habits that govern your life have been part of your being for some time. Do not expect them all to disappear in just an hour, a day, or a week. You must be actively involved in your metamorphosis. Yes, it will require work on your part, but you will not be the only person to reap the benefits of those efforts. The students as well as the staff entrusted to your care will garner results.

First, you must learn to think differently—outside the box. Over the years you have developed certain patterns that govern your behavior. Unfortunately, many of these have limited your growth. Dr. Milton H. Erickson was a medical doctor who transformed hypnosis into an effective therapy for stress. He developed the theory that the cortical state in trance was one of intense focusing and concentration. He was very active in the popularization of hypnosis, forming the American Society of Clinical Hypnosis in 1957. Until his death in 1980, he was regarded as the foremost authority on medical hypnosis.

These were great achievements, however, they become more amazing when you learn that Dr. Erickson was stricken with polio and was on crutches or confined to a wheelchair since the age of seventeen. Currently, the New York Milton H. Erickson Society for Psychotherapy and Hypnosis teaches Ericksonian principles and techniques. They continue to redefine the hypnotic approaches developed by Dr. Erickson. He certainly thought differently.

One of his techniques demonstrates his ability to motivate people beyond the norm. While Erickson was working with the U.S. Olympic Rifle Team to increase their accuracy, he asked how many could hit the bull's eye. Naturally, everyone raised their hands. He then asked how many could hit the bull's eye five times. Now only a few raised their hands. When asked how many could hit it twenty times, no one responded. He then explained that if they could hit the bull's eye once, they could hit it as many times as they wanted. They had simply been limiting themselves due to their negative thinking. Modern psychologists refer to this syndrome as "learned helplessness."

Researcher Martin Seligman experimented with animals and human beings in the mid-1970s. He determined that oppressed people perceive control to be external and this perception may deepen feelings of resignation. People faced with repeated traumatic events over which they have no control begin to feel helpless, hopeless, and depressed. Then when faced with a similar situation that can be under their control, they react with a passive resignation—learned helplessness.

People in concentration camps, prisons, and some nursing homes are given little control. They experience a lowering of morale and increased stress. When given the ability to participate in decision making, noticeable improvement in morale can be noticed. Schools that provide opportunities for students to voice opinions and exert some control over small items, such as placement of chairs in cafeterias and painting of murals on walls, normally have higher levels of happiness among the students.

REPAVING THE ROAD TO SUCCESS

In chapter 9, I discussed the phenomenon of the so-called natural athlete. A theory on how they succeed due to not only natural ability, but also the mental attitude developed by success was covered. These individuals rarely fall prey to self-doubt when it comes to athletic performance. Think about all the times you may have fallen to self-doubt. When you allow negative thoughts to enter your mind, it severely damages your ability to perform at your optimum. It will prevent you from reaching your true potential and as a result, your lackluster performance will prohibit your students and staff from reaching their full capabilities.

Everything we accomplish is first created in our minds. Every picture that was ever painted was first seen in the mind's eye of the artist. Great works of music and architecture were also created in this manner. Even when we decide to drive to the store to shop for food, the same process takes place. However, when we are preparing to go food shopping we are not riddled with self-doubt. There is no question in our minds that we can successfully drive or walk to the store. We are not wondering if we will be able to take the food products down from the shelves and place them into our carts. Thoughts questioning our ability to take money in the proper amount from our pockets to pay for the goods do not enter our minds. All of these successful actions are proof of our ability to complete the shopping tasks. Activities that most of us take for granted.

Think for a moment about people who are physically or mentally challenged. The activity of going to the grocery store might be overpowering for them. They might experience that feeling of being overwhelmed. Frustration, fear, and anger are only a few of the emotions they might experience when going food shopping. The same emotions we might endure when we are not successful in our quest for success. Everything is relative. What is difficult for one person may be easy for another to accomplish. Each of us possesses certain attributes upon which we can build. However, many of us never reflect as to why we perform well in a certain arena. I contend that upon the first attempt with that particular task, we meet with success. We then believe that this particular task is easy for us to accomplish. With that in mind, when challenged with the same or similar tasks, we dive right in, believing that we will be successful—and we are.

Whenever you truly believe that you can accomplish something, it can be done with relative ease. If you have self-doubts and second-guess your actions, the results are less than perfect. That is precisely why people like to do what they do best. It is not burdensome to them. They enjoy what they are doing and they do it well. When we add to the equation repetition of performance, success will build on previous success. The cycle repeats itself with positive reinforcement.

Completing a task with ease and accomplishing it proficiently makes us happy. When people are cheerful they tend to work better. The cycle then perpetuates itself and the individuals reap the benefits. If you can provide an environment for your students and staff that allows for successful experiences, your school will become great.

This formula for success seems simple. However, do not misunderstand what I am professing. I do not contend that anyone can be proficient in any task they attempt. Specific physical and/or mental abilities are necessary to perform certain routines correctly. Each of us was born with innate abilities as well as limitations. My philosophy is to build from strengths. Learning what your abilities are and building on them is the way to advance. Discovering your limitations and working to improve in these areas will also add to your success. A person with average intelligence must work hard to comprehend quantum physics. While a person with above-average intelligence can learn and understand the same concepts with relative ease.

One of my graduates related an interesting story about his college days at Princeton University. During his first year, he noticed that his roommate studied only a few minutes each night. This was upsetting to my student, as he needed many hours to cover the same material. Finally, he asked his roommate what his secret was. Without hesitation, the roommate explained that my graduate could never expect to learn as quickly as he, since he was more intelligent. My student later found this to be true. As proven by their IQ tests, there was no doubt that his roommate was of higher intelligence. Almost thirty points separated the two young men. Therefore, the student with higher intelligence could grasp the same concept much more quickly and easily than the student with lower intelligence, even though both were of high intelligence.

My student, knowing his limitations, developed a tenacious attitude regarding his schoolwork and his life goals in general. He was able to divide his time accordingly so that he could master the work assigned. He also worked hard at meeting different people around the campus. Each day he would eat at a different table in the cafeteria. After introducing himself, he would talk with each of the students at the table. He ran a successful campaign to become president of the student council. He graduated from Princeton with the same degree as his roommate, even though it took him two or sometimes three times longer to complete his assignments. He was aware of his limitations, yet he developed a tenacious attitude regarding his life goals. He built on his strengths. As a result, he currently is the owner of a highly successful real estate business making an extremely comfortable living for his family.

The same holds true regarding physical attributes. Some people possess athletic abilities far superior to others. A person interested in mastering the sport of basketball can learn all of the drills, moves, and shots necessary to be successful, however, if he is not of sufficient height, he cannot dunk the ball. Anyone can be successful and reach beyond their limits, but they must be cognizant of their inherent limitations.

Yet, there are exceptions. Robert Hurley Sr. is the head basketball coach of St. Anthony High School, Jersey City, New Jersey. Upon questioning him about his team's national championship success, he points to his son, Bob, as an example. Many remember when Duke University won back-to-back national championships in 1991 and 1992. The team was led by Bobby Hurley who went on to play professionally for the Sacramento Kings in California. Coach Hurley explained that he merely taught his son the basics and then made him learn them to perfection. Bob Hurley is just six feet tall, very small as professional basketball players go, however, he was quite successful on the professional level until an auto accident. He knew his limitation in size and worked at a position of point guard, where he could be successful.

To be successful we must believe in ourselves. We must instill this attitude in our students. Hard work and tenacious efforts will reap benefits. Even the slightest change can alter our lives if compounded day after day. Albert Einstein once said that the most powerful element in the universe is compounded interest. By compounding the slight change in our lifestyles we can reap some of the benefits of this type of compounded interest. No longer will we just be reacting to events in our lives. We will become proactive rather than reactive. We will be in control of our destiny. We will decide what is in our best interests. Remember, others can only influence you, only you can control your life.

THE POWER OF THE SUBCONSCIOUS

Previously, you received information on the subconscious mind and how it can influence our lives. You learned how the subconscious sways our daily decision-making process and how the conscious mind really is not in full control of our actions. You read examples of how perceptions can influence student behavior and the difficulty in changing these attitudes. Now we will explore in greater depth the powerful driving force of the subconscious.

If the conscious portion of our minds were truly in control, no one would have bad habits, failed relationships, or a lack of money. We certainly would not consciously choose to have any shortcomings in our lives. Yet, we all know people who are unhappy with their lives, and many of us would like to improve our current situation. Our students are not any different. They have dreams and aspirations. Unfortunately, due to circumstance, some can never reach their goals. At an early age they have been driven down and consequently, have developed low self-esteem. Once they accept this type of programming, through repetition, they reinforce the concept and continue the self-defeating cycle.

Research has demonstrated that the subconscious mind plays a great role in determining how we react to various situations. It responds in a manner that is uncritical. It reacts according to its programming, and that is precisely the problem—faulty programming. If we feed imperfect data into our computers and then try to formulate a hypothesis, the results would be flawed. The same holds true with respect to our minds.

If you have ever thought about how your body knows what to do to heal a cut, digest food, or keep you breathing, you have begun to develop an insight into the subconscious. This powerful portion of the mind makes up almost 90 percent of the brain's use and is constantly working. All of our automatic and habitual activities are under the control of the subconscious. This means that only about 10 percent of the mind's activity is performed on the conscious level. When you begin to think of this disproportionate division of what I refer to as "mind labor," you can see how we have limited ourselves mentally.

I do not know of anyone who would purchase an appliance that only worked at 10 percent capacity. Yet, we all seem completely satisfied to use only this small conscious portion of our minds. Who knows what powers we might possess if we learned to harness the 90 percent of the mind's power hidden in the subconscious?

Division of Mind Labor

Everyone is aware that we perceive life through the five senses: seeing, hearing, touching, smelling, and tasting. However, not everyone is aware that we really do not see, hear, feel, smell, or taste with our eyes, ears, fingers, nose, or tongue. These are only receptacles that bring information to the brain. The actual realization occurs in the mind. We experience life through the conscious level using our five senses but the mind is the instrument that makes the experiences real.

Some people have difficulty accepting this concept; to them I offer an analogy to the dream world. When you experience a vivid dream you can actually see, hear, touch, smell, and taste. However, you are not experiencing this on the conscious level. Your *receptacles* (eyes, ears, fingers, nose, and tongue) are not bringing information into you mind. Rather, your mind is experiencing these senses based on its programming.

Protection from Harm

An important division of mind labor is the role of the subconscious to protect the individual from harm—the prime directive of keeping the individual safe and healthy. Previous examples of the child and the hot stove, as well as the person drowning, illustrate this role. To this end, the subconscious exerts what is called protective alertness. When this occurs, a sequence of thoughts is not necessary to perceive danger. For example, when you are asleep at home there are normal sounds that would cause you to awaken or continue sleeping. If the noises were ones that the subconscious recognized as normal or friendly (nonthreatening) you would continue to sleep. Conversely, if the noises are alien or threatening, the subconscious would awaken you so that you could investigate. It is following the directive to protect you from harm.

Taking the protective alertness concept further, imagine a new mother who finally gets the baby to nap. She is so exhausted from the challenges of the infant that she needs to rest herself. Upon falling asleep many noises of the day pervade the home. The garbage collection is made, and the bells of the local church loudly chime the time of day. Amazingly, through it all, the young mother remains asleep. However, when her infant begins to whimper the mother awakens immediately. Protective alertness can, and many times does, extend beyond personal health and well-being.

Involuntary Muscular Actions

The next division of mind labor concerns muscular actions. On the conscious level, we have the ability to move our legs and arms at will. We consciously decide how fast we are to walk or run, and when we will sit or stand. All of these muscular functions are at the beck and call of our conscious minds. At the same time, the subconscious is causing many muscles to perform without our conscious intervention. These are referred to as involuntary muscular actions. Some examples are: breathing, beating of the heart, dilation and constriction of pupils, yawning, sneezing, and blinking. If you stop to think about all the activities, you will be amazed at the numerous functions performed on the subconscious level.

Perception Through Intuition

On the conscious level, we experience life through the five senses. On the subconscious plane, we can experience the same sensations based on past experiences. Additionally, the subconscious can perceive through intuition. For years many scoffed at the notion of female intuition. Actually, both genders possess this ability. However, in the past, only females spoke openly of this capability. Intuition is nothing more than your mind processing information to develop a hypothesis. Given a particular set of circumstances, your mind can adequately predict what will happen in a similar situation. That is, if all things are equal and variables are not too extensive. Many people rely heavily on their intuition. Some will not make a career move unless it seems right intuitively. Many principals will make a decision based on what they refer to as "gut instinct." Problems arise if the programming is badly flawed. In those cases, the conscious portion of the mind is formulating its hypothesis based on faulty information stored in the subconscious.

Ability to Make Choices

The ability to reason or make choices and decisions is another division of our mind labor. For the most part, decisions are made on the conscious level. The subconscious does not make determinations. It accepts uncritically whatever is impressed upon it. This portion of our minds holds these impressions as truths. When making decisions, we use data that is stored in the subconscious. Poor choices could be made if the information stored is incorrect.

As was noted in chapter 9, subliminal advertising caused sales to rise 58 percent due to assaulting the subconscious with an idea. In this case, people did not make a conscious decision. Yes, they did review the information on the conscious level, but their decision was driven by the subconscious portion of the mind. The portion that received the advertiser's message and held it as a directive.

The audience reacted to subconscious programming, not to a rational, conscious decision. They were not aware of the process. They actually believed that they consciously made a decision, until they were informed of the influence exerted by the subliminal advertisement.

Protection from False Impressions

The last division of mind labor is the method used by the conscious mind to protect the subconscious from false impressions. The conscious portion is ever watchful. It is the keeper at the gate. It will not allow information into the subconscious that it believes is contrary to existing programming. The irony is that the programming held in the subconscious cannot be changed until new information is allowed in through the portal. So, while we are being protected from false impressions, what actually might be happening is that we are being blocked from receiving true information.

Training the Mind

At birth, we were unable to exercise voluntary control over bladder or bowel functions. Intuitively, we knew when it was necessary to expel waste. Through training, we placed these muscles under our conscious command. Great emotional or physical stress, unfortunately, can cause involuntary muscle reactions. If intensely frightened, severely beaten, or gravely stabbed, one can lose mastery of their bodily functions. When under great duress, our training of these muscle groups on the conscious level is replaced by the subconscious domain.

Prior to the late 1960s, it was considered impossible to voluntarily regulate the autonomic nervous system. Scientists have now discovered that some involuntary muscular actions that were previously thought to be uncontrollable can indeed be directed. The area of biofeedback is based on this premise.

Biofeedback is the scientific field that combines physiology and psychology. It is founded on three principles. The first is that an individual can regulate any neurological or biological function that can be monitored and amplified by electronic instruments and fed back to the individual. Second, every change in the physiological state is accompanied by an appropriate change in the mental, emotional state and vice versa. The third principle is that a meditative state of deep relaxation is conducive to voluntary control of body processes because it allows the individual to become aware of internal imagery, fantasies, and sensations.

The technique uses electronics to detect and amplify internal body activities too subtle for normal awareness. When we become excited, frightened, or disturbed to any degree, the sympathetic nervous system activates chemicals that stimulate physical changes to occur throughout our bodies (fight-or-flight response). Once we are able to become aware of these activities, we can use relaxation, meditation, and visualization techniques to modify them. By monitoring these results electronically, we know instantly whether our technique was successful.

Many modalities can be monitored via biofeedback such as heart rate, blood pressure, sweat gland activity, and skin temperature. Sensors evaluate the person's own nervous system actions and transfer the body's functions to light or sound readings and sometimes both. This way a physiological profile of how a person is managing their nervous system is available for review. With practice, we can control the body without using these monitoring devices.

Anyone who has seen the 1988 drama *Rainman* can attest to the amazing ability portrayed by the autistic-savant protagonist played by Dustin Hoffman. He had the ability to remember numbers that most of us would be unable to recall with the most diligent study. Yet, he was a human being with the same mind we all possess. However, one section of his brain was exceptional, while it lacked greatly in other areas of function. What causes these differences in our minds and our abilities? Albert Einstein, when asked about leaving his brain to science, informed everyone that they would find a brain no different from others. The physical makeup would be the same—however, Einstein had the ability to use more of the conscious mind than that mere 10 percent used by the general populace.

INSIGHTS TO THE MIND

The complexity of the human mind is boggling. Regardless of the enormous amounts of research completed, the brain is still a mysterious organ. The two hemispheres of the brain sometimes referred to as the "left brain and right brain," when working correctly, serve us well. The dominant left brain is somewhat more involved in intellectual undertakings that require logic and problem solving. This would include language, science, mathematics, and writing. The right hemisphere, usually nondominant, is concerned with de-coding visual information, aesthetic, emotional responses, and imagination. Here we develop fantasy, perception, and art and music appreciation. The hemispheres are similar enough that each can function well independently. When learning, both sides are educated together, even when instruction is in-tended to appeal to a specific hemisphere. The mind drives all functions of the body and physicians are again discovering the mind–body connection as it re-lates to healing.

The Mind–Body Connection

During the past century physicians have been treating the physical symptoms of their patients. Little was done to explore the healing powers of one's mind. An oversimplification would be medical doctors fixing the body, and psychologists fixing emotions, without an integral connection between the emotions and the physical substance of the body. Body and mind are two aspects of the same hu-man experience; the body is quantitative, the mind is qualitative. Physical symp-toms are a reflection, a mirroring, of emotional issues. The physical symptoms are directly connected to the emotions. The body is both physical and emotional. These two components are as two sides of a coin, inseparable, although one may be hidden from our sight while the other visibly manifests itself.

Prior to modern time, much emphasis was given to the healing powers of the mind. The model for the healing function of becoming whole was por-trayed more than 5,000 years ago in ancient Egypt. Recall the story about the god Osiris, who was murdered by his brother Seth. Osiris' body was dis-membered into fourteen pieces, each piece buried in a different part of Egypt. Isis, the wife of Osiris, collected these hidden pieces and brought Osiris back to life by re-membering him, by putting all the pieces together.

Following this thought, *remembering* would literally mean to reconnect one piece of the body to another. However, it actually means to recall, or bring an image or idea from the past into the mind. By combining the two no-tions, *remembering* then, is to restore ourselves to wholeness by recalling our unity and putting our mind and body back together. Imagery is the mental way of remembering and recalling. The act of seeing in pictures is to see in wholes and is the mental analogy to physical remembering. Surgery may be an attempt to re-member on a physical level. Imagery is the analogous process on the mental level and can affect remembering on the physical level.

The passport to imagery is the connection among emotions, sensations, and images. Emotions are not only feelings such as happiness, anger, and satisfaction. They are also our movement to stimuli. *Emotion* literally means subjective response or reaction. It also means to start out, to move out, to move away. Therefore, emotion equals movement, and movement is the essence of life. Sometimes our movements take the form of inner feelings such as happiness and anger. Physical actions, such as displays of surprise or fear, are discharged immediately. These are other examples of movement caused by emotion. We have an outward form of action and an inward form of feeling.

Emotions are intimately connected with images. Every emotion can manifest itself as an image. An image is the mental form of a feeling. The physical form is the sensations. When we are angry, often a constriction in the chest is felt. When we are happy, a sense of lightness can occur.

By creating the proper images we can change our emotions or sensations. You create and affect your experience. As you work on your images and change them, you simultaneously change and create the sensations and emotions that accompany them. Once the image changes, so do the emotions and sensations. As in the sides of an equation, emotion and image are equal, two expressions of the same reality, and sensation is attached to both. When you change the image, you change the whole equation. Then you will see that images are indeed a road to both physical and mental well-being.

In the ordinary world of cause and effect, everything is fixed and repetitive. There is no newness. A certain action always causes the same reaction. The human realm is different from the realm of physics. We live in a world that we create physically, emotionally, and psychologically. A world on the horizontal axis. Imagery work takes place outside the mechanism realm of cause and effect on the vertical axis.

When you use imagery, you recognize that human life obeys more than ordinary cause and effect. You have the capacity to make something new and to influence the physical material of your own body. All cultures and traditions have linked upward movement with transcendence, with myths of flight, with severing the bonds and limitations of everyday habitual behavior and activity, with finding new paths and new ways of being. Your imagery can produce real physiological effects. Currently, physicians are returning to the philosophy of treating the whole patient—body and mind. When stressed, you can create an image of a time when you were relaxed and calm. This will help you to handle difficult situations better on both mental and physical planes.

Functions of the Subconscious `

The subconscious is the source of ideals, aspirations, and altruistic urges. Functions of the subconscious can be broken down into six categories. It (1) serves as a memory bank, (2) controls involuntary functions, (3) is the seat of emotions, (4) is the center of imagination, (5) carries out habitual functions, and (6) directs energy.

Memory Bank

As the memory bank, the subconscious houses all memories and knowledge since birth, and many believe even before birth. The ability to retrieve information is based on how we labeled the information and how often it is used. Sometimes the information rises to the surface when we are not trying to recover the material. This is because we have mislabeled the data.

Involuntary Functions

The second purpose is the control and regulation of involuntary functions of the body. In addition to perceiving life through the senses, activities such as circulation, digestion, and repair of cells and tissue are just some functions of the subconscious.

Seat of Our Emotions

Next, the subconscious is the seat of our emotions. These emotions govern the strength of our desires and our desires govern our behavior. Again, we see that if the program is flawed, the behavior will not be as desired.

Center of Imagination

The subconscious is also the center of the imagination. Everything ever invented, every picture ever painted, every concerto ever written was first conceived in the mind. All creative imagination starts at the subconscious level. This portion of the mind is the source of our ideals, aspirations, and altruistic urges.

Habitual Conduct

The fifth function of the subconscious is to carry out our habitual conduct. Previously, I discussed the athlete practicing a routine and driving a car as examples of habitual activities. As mentioned, not only does the subconscious carry out habitual conduct, it actually does a better job when performing, as it does not make analogies and comparisons.

Directs Our Energy

Finally, the subconscious directs our energy. Our drive to fulfill our goals is directed by our behavior that is energy expressed. Energy cannot be destroyed; however, it can be directed. Think of the great amount of energy exerted as water is forced through the hose used to fight a fire. It takes several firefighters to control the hose and direct its energy effectively to fight the fire. If the hose were left on the street to its own devices, it would dart around with no direction.

The subconscious mind is the same. It must be directed. It was designed to be your servant, and consequently makes a poor master. Once an idea is fixed in the subconscious, it is fed back into daily behavior. It makes you what you are, therefore, proper programming is essential.

Characteristics of the Subconscious

Although the subconscious is very powerful, it can be harnessed if we are familiar with its characteristics. There is a complete absence of negation or doubt—it deals only in absolutes. It can host positive and negative viewpoints simultaneously as it has no sense of contradiction. It can hold information that is positive or negative as there is no logical conflict.

Even though we dwell in a time continuum, for the subconscious it appears that only the present exists. Ideas, viewpoints, and beliefs for different ages are all telescoped together into the present. What was held as truth at age five is held as truth today. In effect, it is truth for yesterday, today, and tomorrow unless we reprogram. What we believed in our youth can still have the same effect on us as an adult. An event may have happened when we were young that was recorded incorrectly. Immaturity sparked an inaccurate account of the incident. We were not knowledgeable enough to understand that the event was fleeting and specific to the event at hand. The mistaken record causes us to react incorrectly in the present as the subconscious holds the erroneous information as truth.

Carrying this further, it becomes evident that there is a constancy of emotional content. That is, a trauma experienced becomes a fixed idea that persists throughout life. The emotional quality of the generalized experience, not the event itself, is what we maintain.

A characteristic that causes many people great difficulty is that the subconscious interprets language literally. Our speech and thinking are riddled with ambiguous terms that compound this particular problem. If you constantly refer to a student as "A pain in the neck," chances are that when you see that child you develop a physical discomfort in the area of your neck. "She makes me sick," is a phrase that can evoke stomach disorders, headaches, and so forth. When you pronounce you are mad, you actually are telling your subconscious that you are insane. When you say someone causes you heartache, heartburn might be the result. My favorite cliché in this category is when parents tell their children that they are "sick and tired." Inevitably, the parents become ill and fatigued.

Children tend to repeat the behavior that adults recognize or praise. If we constantly recognize only negative behavior and then administer adverse enforcement, children will develop a pattern of unfavorable behavior. So be careful if you constantly tell your children that they are driving you crazy. First, you are programming your mind to that conclusion, and second, you are instructing your children to comply with your directive. They will do their best to obey, and you could end up needing psychological help.

Remember, the subconscious is the seat of our emotions and attitudes as well as our habits. It also houses all memories and knowledge since birth. Furthermore, it exerts such a tremendous influence over our conscious behavior and actions, that when there is a conflict between the two, the subconscious invariably wins.

INNER PEACE

Inasmuch as there is a good chance that your programming is flawed, so too, will be your actions. Therefore, the challenge is to learn how you can reprogram your mind to gain control of your life. When you are in command of your life, you can perform at an optimum level of professionalism. Once you accomplish this task you will have some claim on inner peace.

The term *inner peace* has been used by many groups to mean many things. In the 1960s psychologists began to study meditation. Here the practitioner focuses attention on a thought or image attempting to attain the goal of relaxation by clearing the mind. When meditating, they are driven to discover their own inner peace, believed to be a serene feeling of tranquillity.

While people in the field of meditation learn to relax without much physical exertion, practitioners in the martial arts use the concept of inner peace to supplement intense physical training. Even though meditation and martial arts seem alien to each other, their roots may be considered common. For instance, the origin of the martial art of karate remains masked in a cloak of mystery even to this day. Many theories have been expounded regarding its lineage, but its genesis remains a secret. Originally, the philosophy was believed to revolve around the process of realization of the mind known as meditation. This would allow the practitioner to keep the mind as a calm lake so that accurate reflections of the outside world would be visible. If the lake were turbulent, the images would be distorted and the individual's reactions would be flawed. Control of the self and toward others remains a vital ingredient in the art of karate.

I believe true inner peace is only gained when we exert appropriate control of the events in our lives. At that point we will experience harmony with ourselves, others, and the environment. Serenity and balance will enter our lives and we will be able to achieve our fullest potentials.

THE As, Bs, Cs OF TAKING CONTROL

Faulty programming, ambiguous values, and irrational fears are three reasons that we are not in control of our lives. I have arranged these reasons in a way that can be easily remembered, even during a time of crisis. By following the As, Bs, Cs of taking control we can reach our fullest potential. You now have the knowledge of why you are not in control, with work, you can become the master of your fate.

Admit that some of your programming is faulty. With this concession you must work to replace the incorrect data. Remember, you have been programmed from birth and much of that programming, while well-intended, is negative in nature. As such, you need to take the time and effort to correct this faulty agenda.

Build upon your true values and always keep them in focus. What would cause you to cross the I-beam? That is what is truly important in your life. Everything else is of little consequence. Take the time to sit down and commit to paper what is truly important to you. Then always keep your true values foremost in your mind and in your daily routine. By doing this you can easily build on your values and become the best person you can possibly become.

Concede that most fears are irrational and face or suppress them so you can grow. Recall that there are only two inborn fears and that we have acquired or learned all others. Some fears are beneficial as they protect us from harm. Most, however, are fallacious and need to be suppressed so we can move forward.

By following the As, Bs, Cs of taking control, changes in your lifestyle will occur. Life will no longer be merely a sequence of events played out day after day. You will be living and thriving, not only existing. Each change you make, no matter how small, will dramatically alter your course for the remainder of your life. It will be compounded daily.

Thinking outside the box will help you to perform at an optimum level not only in the role of school administrator, but also in your personal life. Once you realize that you can harness some of the untapped resources of your mind, new and creative solutions to old and persistent problems will become evident. As you grow as an administrator, the students and staff in your school will begin to reap the benefits of a dynamic and energetic leader.

Chapter 12

Conclusions and Summary

When I entered the teaching profession in 1969, I could have never envisioned the status of education in our nation as it exists today. The face of America's schools has changed forever. Creating safe and supportive schools has become the charge for all. Never did any of us think that we would be developing plans to deal with lockdowns, terrorist attacks, and crisis management. As educators these concepts were alien to us.

During the seventeenth and eighteenth centuries, U.S. schools were essentially private or church institutions. These schools were few in number and attendance was usually selective. Massachusetts passed laws in 1642 and 1647 establishing public education. However, not until circa 1800 was there a growing demand for public education in our country. Thomas Jefferson was among the first to propose a system of free public elementary schools with little success. Shortly after Jefferson's proposal, the public schools movement of the United States was launched largely due to the work of Horace Mann and Henry Banard. Early state laws permitted school districts to be created whenever six or more families desired to establish one. This district usually consisted of a one-room elementary school.

When our ancestors decided to establish a public school system (by the late 1800s most states had publicly financed schools) they were concerned with passing knowledge onto the youth of our new nation. These citizens were not thinking of security systems for the schools nor were they concerned with violence in the schoolhouse. The only violence was that of corporal punishment inflicted by the teacher to correct the behavior of unruly students.

In 1893, the prestigious Committee of Ten released the report that has driven the curriculum of the modern secondary school. This council comprised a group of college presidents convened by the National Education Association. Their charge was to recommend standards for college admissions. The committee was chaired by President Charles W. Eliot of Harvard University. They concluded in their report that schools should maintain a single academic curriculum for all students (four years of English and a foreign language, and three years each of mathematics, science, and history) even though at that time most of the students would not go on to college.

The curriculum was the national preoccupation throughout the twentieth century. While this concentration opened up the classroom to greater scrutiny, no examination in the past has rivaled the interest for safe schools. Curriculum debates would divide or unify the country depending on the issue at hand, while safety issues have united the entire nation.

The National Commission on Excellence in Education was established by U.S. Secretary of Education Terrel H. Bell in 1981. In April 1983, the commission released "A Nation at Risk." This report charged that the educational system was confused about its purpose and described a society that was no longer dominant in international economy. Education officials throughout the country began to reexamine their schools. Not since that time has there been so much focus on our schools as there is today regarding safety.

While many believe that our schools are in crisis, I contend that we are on the horizon of what can be our greatest accomplishment. We have the resources and the ability to develop programs that will lessen tensions among the various groups that are thrust together in our schools. Our greatest strength can be our diversity. We can learn from each other in a fashion that was unthinkable a generation ago.

Racial and ethnic barriers are collapsing. With each passing generation, the racist thinking and bigotry of past generations are lessening. The time is ripe for inclusivity. However, as great strides are made in racial harmony, divisions in social cliques have risen. Students choose their friends based on like interests. They also select companions for the type of clothing they wear and type of music they enjoy.

We will never be able to completely protect our schools from crisis. Whether it be the result of a natural or man-made disaster, incidents will occur. By preparing ourselves prior to the event, we can ensure that the students and staff entrusted to us will be as safe as possible. We will also be prepared to respond in a measured and controlled fashion when a crisis strikes to minimize the effects.

In the process, the role of the principal will be more important than ever. As the educational leader, you will set the tone for the recovery period. The manner in which you respond will determine how your students and staff will react to any crisis situation. Your ability to remain focused and strong will allow those in your charge to also maintain calmness. You will provide safety, support, structure, stability, and control.

As the characteristics of our country and family unit change, so too will our approach to education. When women left the home to join the workforce some individuals viewed it as the demise of the family unit. Similar concerns were raised when the extended family concept was eroding. Who is to determine what the family unit will be or should be? There are millions of happy, well-adjusted individuals who are contributing members of society who came from a family unit that was not considered traditional just a generation ago.

The human spirit is difficult to keep downtrodden. We have the ability to adapt to change, to rise from adversity, and to conquer our fears. This type of intestinal fortitude will be transmitted to the business of education. In the years to come, our educational system will become stronger and better. We will persist in our examination of teaching techniques and philosophies. We will continue our move from teacher-centered education to student-centered learning. Our schools will again become the focal points of our communities.

Yes, there has been too much violence in our schools. Death and destruction seemed to be rampant in the last decade of the last century in the last millennium. However, statistically more children are victims of violence in their homes than in their schools. We must not lose sight of the fact that schools remain one of the safest places for our children.

My situation was unique. I do not know of other schools that have undergone four tragedies in one school year. From a student suicide, sudden death of a faculty member, death of a student due to illness, to a homicide in the school, we lived through each tragedy. It was a chilling year for everyone involved. Death is difficult to deal with at any time; the death of a child is unthinkable. Yet, we must go on, and during our journey we must provide for those who are hurting. It is not enough to simply deal with the crisis at hand and expect everything to magically return to normal. Everyday, we at Bayonne High School live with the impact of that horrific year.

Responding to crises in an appropriate and effective manner is the duty of the modern administrator. The establishment of a Crisis Management Team is essential in any school. Proper training of the individuals responsible to provide counseling and other services to the students and staff of the school is crucial. The development of policies and procedures to employ during and after a crisis is not only good management, but it is also proactive administration.

A review of your school and the development of a safety plan must be done as soon as possible. Knowing what we know today, it is unconscionable that an administrator would not review, revamp, and ready the safety and security of the school. No one is scatheless. A crisis can occur at any time. It would be malfeasance for a principal to ignore the safety needs of the school.

Simple techniques and devices can be incorporated in any school to make it safer. Plans that require little resources can also be developed if money is an issue. Address the climate issues of the school concurrently with the physical security upgrades. Review with students and staff concerns relevant to the atmosphere of the campus.

Develop programs that celebrate the diversity of the student body and our nation. Incorporate lessons on values and the importance of all humanity. Reach out to the public to develop programs that create a bond with the community. All these activities will strengthen the character of your students. Review your curriculum and use it as a tool to aid in your school safety plan. This can be a powerful vehicle to extol self-worth in your students.

Contact agencies in your community to develop covenants before a crisis strikes. Share with these groups your vision and mission for the school. Discuss the goals of safe schools and enlist as much assistance as possible. Review with these specialists factors that would make your school safer. They possess the expertise regarding the environment surrounding the school. Develop a cooperative effort on the sharing of information for mutual benefit. Make the school available to these agencies to strengthen the bonds among everyone. Volunteer to serve on their board of directors so you can learn about their functions, and they can get to know you.

Do not forget the private sector of the community; it has much to offer. Remember this is the group that will be depending on your product (graduates) to fill vacancies. This segment wants you to achieve your goals as your accomplishments will allow them to be successful. Establish partnerships with your students so that they will witness positive role models.

Work at creating a climate of pride and ownership in the school. When students have high self-esteem and pride of ownership in their school, they take a vested interest. Everyone associated with the school needs to believe they are a key part of the school community. If the stakeholders possess pride, a safer environment will evolve.

As you develop your school safety plan, remember that nearly all of your students and staff will be suffering from faulty perceptions. Most of these erroneous ideas were implanted years ago. Be cognizant that people are not usually aware of these shortcomings. Diligent work is required to change defective insights. Over the years they become ingrained. With the proper encouragement, reinforcement, and monitoring, change will occur. The metamorphosis will be slow but steady.

The past learning experiences might include violence and degradation. Only through caring and supportive education will you be able to correct this faulty programming. When you establish programs that address misunderstandings at the most rudimentary level, success can be realized.

As never before, the potential for problems exists in our schools. However, only some will rise to the level of crisis. Regardless, the response of the Crisis

Management Team could be employed for smaller emergencies. Develop policies and procedures to deal with conceivable contingencies. One of these eventualities is dealing with threats to security. Clearly explicate procedures to ensure a proper and measured response to each type of threat. First, a working definition of a threat situation needs to be developed. The definition should be designed to fix the limits of what would constitute an overt threat. Second, establish procedures to follow when the threat is lodged. Third, define the procedures for dealing with a threat in progress. Fourth, determinations of the status of the students, staff, and community during the aftermath of a threat are necessary. This will allow you to deploy proper counseling services as needed. Finally, a plan to reestablish normalcy for the school and community should be constructed.

Do not hesitate to recruit outside assistance. The use of mental-health practitioners can help ease the counseling load of the personnel already on board. Provide training to the appropriate personnel so that all threats will be treated in a like fashion. Use technology to assist in apprehending perpetrators. When the message gets out that this type of activity will not be tolerated and perpetrators will be held responsible for their actions, a decline in threats will result.

Understand that many times we are dealing with perceptions. Unfortunately, the misunderstandings held by parents, students, and staff will frequently become realities. Also, there can be outside groups with negative opinions of the school. Work to educate the members of that group in addition to parents, students, and staff of the many wonderful things that are happening in the school.

The media will cover negative occurrences. Develop a good working relationship with members of the press, so that you will have the opportunity to share positive stories. Invite media personnel into the school regularly. Let them view, firsthand, the happenings in your school. When they perceive a positive and supportive learning environment, they are more inclined to cover stories reflecting this theme.

The climate you create in your school will determine, in great part, the success of your safe and supportive school plan. In the spring of the 1999–00 school year, we won our second Best Practice Award from the New Jersey State Department of Education. The commissioner of education noted that the program observed during a site visit was most impressive and significantly surpassed expectations.

The program, Student Connections, won in the Educational Support category. In addition to the monetary award to expand the practice, the program will be featured in a series of showcases and workshops so that other schools may replicate the program. Student Connections speaks to the positive, safe, and supportive climate you can create in your school.

This program empowers students to develop a series of activities designed to raise awareness of cultural differences, develop respect for diversity, and create greater understanding between student and faculty. One example espoused by this program is the creation of self-essays by incoming students. Their self-reflections are placed in guidance folders so that teachers can reach a better understanding of the children entrusted to their care.

Our country will continue to grow in its diversity. The U.S. Census Bureau predicts that by 2066 half of Americans will trace their roots to places other than Western Europe. As our demographics change, principals are challenged to meet the needs of an increasingly divergent population. On any campus, one of the most familiar sights is groups of students divided by cultural differences. Of these divisions, race is the most obvious. Everyone feels comfortable with and enjoys the company of like people. However, until we take the time to learn of others, we will tend to ignore the other groups.

Each person in a school needs to be treated as a valuable and contributing member of the campus. We must teach children to learn about themselves. When they discover what makes them unique, they can unearth similar characteristics in others. Then they can easily learn about those around them and view themselves as part of a school family. A result will be the development of mutual respect for people who are different.

To be an effective leader you need to tend to personal needs. If you do not take care of yourself, you will be of little use to others. The very people for whom you are sacrificing your health will not receive the benefit of your sage counsel if you become ill. Learn to eat healthfully and properly. Time for exercise is also essential. Additionally, part of the regime of good health is learning to reduce stress levels.

Discover ways to overcome that feeling of being overwhelmed. As assignments arise, take each task individually. Work at a pace that will ensure healthfulness and productivity. Delegate when possible. This will allow members of your staff to gain valuable experience. You will be empowering them. Make the proper choices regarding when to take control and when to give control. Keep paramount in your thoughts what is truly important in your life. This will help you keep things in perspective.

Be creative in your thinking. Do not stifle inventiveness by settling into a comfortable routine of doing things as they were always done. Do not settle for less, reach for the optimum. Learn to harness the untapped resources of your mind. Become aware of your strengths and limitations. Build from your strengths and overcome your limitations. Realize that your mind and body are connected. Allow them to work together for peak performance. You can grow in your professional realm and personal life by getting in touch with the connection between mind and body.

Develop a claim to inner peace. Learn to experience harmony with yourself, others, and the environment. Take control of your life and you will perform at an optimum level in all aspects of your essence. Everyone who comes in contact with you will reap the benefits of a dynamic individual exuding positive energy.

Learn to think differently. There are teachers who have had twenty years of experience, and there are teachers who have had one year of experience twenty times. The same holds true for principals. If you always do the things you did, you will always reap the same results. Look to creative and innovative solutions to common everyday problems. Believe that there are really no problems—only opportunities. Remember that everything we accomplish is first created in our minds. Use this knowledge to develop plans without restrictions of the physical world. Then refine the solutions so that they can be applied in the natural realm.

Face your fears and build on your abilities. Realize that some of your programming is faulty. Build on your true values, keeping them in focus and foremost in your mind. Take control of your destiny, and life will no longer be merely a sequence of events. Think creatively in all phases of your life and you will be amazed at the results.

When I am asked what I do for a living and reveal my occupation, questions inevitably arise. First, as everyone has gone to school, they believe they know all there is to know about education. We are the only profession that allows laypeople to direct our vision. We even empower our students to become part of the process. Can you imagine telling your physician how to perform an operation, or a lawyer how to argue your case? Nevertheless, after I explain what I really do, the questions eventually move to the area of student preparedness.

In this realm, people voice their concern about the poor quality of available employees. They complain that educators are not fulfilling their part of the equation, and that students are underprepared for the workforce and the world community. I explain that I work with students who will shape the future. I further elucidate that I am confident that the future is in good hands.

Opportunity can arise from crisis. We, at Bayonne High School, struggled arduously to ensure that favorable innovations resulted from a horrific act. The brutal stabbing in our school has left one family without a son. Another young male will not live as a free man for two decades and a third will carry emotional and physical scars for life.

The crises that befell our school community caused me to become stronger, sharper, more knowledgeable, and more humane. My confidence in the humanity of people grew, as the community came together to give help wherever dictated.

I knew that we would always be remembered for the random act of violence that befell our school. I wanted to ensure that we would also be known as a school community that learned how to deal with that tragedy and supported our students and staff appropriately and effectively.

Our school will never be the same. Everyday we live with results of that terrible day in March. Some of the reminders are subtle, such as the locked doors. Others, like the newly installed walk-through metal detectors, almost strike us in the face each day. Some bring back memories of a more cohesive time, such as the tree planted in Aubrey's memory. Yet, we must continue to move forward, to provide the best possible educational opportunities to the students entrusted in our care. To do any less would diminish our concern for the students affected and be unfair to the countless number of young adults who will become our students.

I will continue to spread the word of safe and supportive schools. Every child has the right to attend a school that is free of intimidation and fear. A place where teachers can teach and students can learn—a place like Bayonne High School.

S⁴C: Stabilization Plan

(See page 17)

- *Safety*

- *Support*

- *Structure*

- *Stability*

- *Control*

Appendix B

Crisis Preparedness Checklist

(See page 81)

Crisis Preparedness Checklist

To assess your crisis preparedness, check items that are already in place.

___ definition of crisis for your school
___ Crisis Management Team
___ training of Crisis Management Team members
___ person in charge during crisis
___ written policies and procedures for handling a crisis
___ Crisis Phone Chain
___ evacuation plan
___ alternate site for students
___ bomb-threat procedures
___ floor plans in the hands of police department
___ floor plans in the hands of fire department
___ spokesperson to deal with media
___ listing of community agencies with contact people and numbers
___ procedure to notify staff
___ method for sharing information
___ determination of what information is to be released
___ procedure to release information
___ plan to cover classes in emergency
___ law enforcement liaison
___ designated counseling area for students
___ designated counseling area for staff

___ designated meeting area for parents
___ referral process for additional counseling
___ accountability system to determine the whereabouts of students and staff
___ forms to assist in crisis management (scripts, checklists, classroom activities, etc.)
___ crisis response practice
___ legal review of crisis policies, practices, and forms
___ annual (at a minimum) Crisis Management Team meeting
___ annual staff in-service for updates
___ fully stocked school crisis kit
___ site communication systems evaluation
___ fire-alarm system evaluation
___ sign-in center for support personnel on campus established (with message center)
___ procedure to identify at-risk students and staff
___ incident reporting system in place
___ contingency action plan to deal with disruption and vandalism during crisis
___ procedure to release students
___ debriefing process
___ follow-up procedures
___ possible memorial programs
___ TOTAL

Rating Score: Add one point for all items with a check. If you score higher than 30, you are prepared; 30–24, you are ready, but should review blank areas; 23–17, you are doing well, but more work and training is needed; lower than 17, start working immediately to create an environment that is safe and supportive.

Appendix C

Vignettes for Crisis Team Training

(See page 82)
The following vignettes are to be discussed in small groups (6–10 people). The facilitator guides the groups by posing questions and providing information as necessary.

VIGNETTE 1

A nonstudent has entered the building before the start of school. He encounters a student and a scuffle ensues. Another student comes to the aid of his classmate. Suddenly, a knife appears and the two students are stabbed. One staggers for help while the other lies in the hall bleeding profusely. The intruder flees the school.

VIGNETTE 2

A popular athletic trainer at the high school is accused of sexual contact with a student athlete. He denies the accusations. When the story breaks in the papers other students come forward with similar allegations.

VIGNETTE 3

It is the second week in December. A popular teacher of thirty years suffers a fatal heart attack at home. His daughter is a senior at the school where he taught.

VIGNETTE 4

A junior is diagnosed with leukemia. She is placed on home instruction. During her senior year she succumbs to the disease.

VIGNETTE 5

A member of the sophomore class has apparently jumped from a bridge to her watery grave. Several of her friends were on the bridge at the time of the incident. Reports are that she was distraught over a breakup with her boyfriend.

VIGNETTE 6

Two students attack another student outside the school. They slash her face with utility knives. Both girls are arrested and placed in the youth house. Stories of gang-related retaliation sweep the school. The parent of the victim contacts the newspaper, claiming the school is not protecting her child.

VIGNETTE 7

Before the beginning of the school day, a teacher is shot three times as she enters the building. At the hospital, she identifies her husband as the assailant. Shortly thereafter, the husband is found dead in his bed at home—an apparent suicide. Rumors abound as to the reason for the shooting and suicide.

VIGNETTE 8

A week before the Thanksgiving break, a senior riding his bike is hit by a van. He is critically injured. His parents make the difficult decision to terminate life support. The newspapers run headlines about the tragedy. Students are requesting a memorial program.

Appendix D

Incident Fact Sheet

(See page 90)

Incident _____

_____

Location _____

_____

Time _____ Date _____

Description of incident _____

_____

_____

_____

_____

_____

Comments _____

_____

_____

_____

Person completing this form _____

Title _____ Date _____

Appendix E

Incident Response Guidelines

(See page 91)

PROCEDURES

Incident occurs
Phone call to superintendent (immediate)
Incident report (as soon as possible)
Fact sheet to superintendent (as soon as possible)
Narrative follow-up (details in a timely fashion)

CATEGORIES NECESSITATING IMPLEMENTATION OF RESPONSE PROCEDURES

Physical Confrontations

Weapon(s) used (Any object used to inflict or threaten harm)
Weapon(s) found
Premeditated assault

Threats

Overt threat to person or property
Overt threat to building security

Drugs and Alcohol

Intent to sell or distribute

Miscellaneous

Vandalism and/or theft ($1,500 minimum)
Explosives
Serious accident or injury
Media inquiry of a controversial manner
Any other incident the administrator deems serious enough to notify the superintendent

Appendix F

Incident Information Form

(See page 101)

School _____ Date of Incident _____

Time _____ Was it a Bias Incident? _____

TYPE OF INCIDENT

Check one or more categories:

___ **Substance abuse**	___ **Vandalism**	___ **Violence** ___ **with weapon(s)**
___ Distribution	___ Arson	___ Assault
___ Possession	___ Burglary	___ Assault (aggravated)
___ Use	___ Damage to property	___ Extortion
	___ Theft	___ Fighting
Type of substance	___ Other	___ Other
_____	_____	_____

LOCATION OF INCIDENT

___ **Inside school**	___ **On school grounds**	___ **On bus**	___ **Other**
___ Cafeteria	___ Athletic Field	___ Around bus	_____

220

___ Classroom	___ Courtyard	___ At seat	_____
___ Corridor	___ Parking lot	___ Boarding	_____
___ Lavatory	___ Perimeter of school	___ Exiting	_____
___ Stairwell	___ Playground	___ In aisle	_____

Description of incident (Specify costs, damage, injury, and so on)

_____

_____

_____

_____

_____

_____

Action by administration _____

_____

_____

Signature of administrator completing form _____

Signature

_____   _____

Title   Date

Appendix G

Physical Risk Reduction Checklist

(See page 103)

Review the items listed below and check if you have the security measure in place.

____ barrier or fence around campus

____ areas to hide eliminated

____ proper lighting of campus and trimming of foliage

____ signs for "Drug-Free School Zone" properly posted

____ video cameras in strategic locations

____ security personnel or police presence (patrol car or foot officer)

____ restricted access to parking

____ locking windows and doors

____ master key system

____ procedures for distribution and collection of keys (new and former employees)

____ exterior doors designed for egress only

____ restricted entrance areas secured by personnel

____ entry and high-risk areas secured with reinforced doors and jams

____ individual classrooms secured with locks

____ door hinges on the inside of doors and nonbreakable glass in doors

____ burglar alarms in high-risk areas

____ entry areas visible from administrative office

____ metal detector wands or walk-through detectors

____ mirrors or cameras in hallways, stairwells, and cafeterias

____ barriers or gates at strategic locations

____ configuration of lockers to provide visibility

___ durable yet attractive lockers with lock access for administration
___ teachers assigned to monitor cafeteria area
___ administrators, teachers, and security to monitor entry and dismissal
___ administrators, teachers, and support staff conduct daily search for un-
    usual items in student areas before students enter the building
___ restrooms designed for privacy with partial observation possible to deter
    illicit activities

Meet with your Crisis Management Team and facilities committee to develop
an action plan that will incorporate the omitted elements you believe will enhance security for your school. Assess the items you checked and determine
if they are satisfactory, given your current situation. Then compile a list of
particulars that need to be upgraded.

Appendix H

Writing a School Crisis Management Objective

(See page 111)

All objectives designed to meet the needs of the identified school problems are developed in the same manner. Whether to combat outside intruders or a negative atmosphere, begin by reviewing the results of the problems identified, then do the following:

- List these results in priority order
- Begin with the highest priority item
- Develop ideas to combat each problem

Remember an objective must be:

- Obtainable. This simply means the objective must be realistic. You do not have to reach for the stars at first. If necessary, start with an easily obtainable goal; you can write more objectives once you meet the easier aim.
- Specific. Write the objective in language that is as clear and precise as possible.
- Measurable. Definite criteria to measure the achievement of the objective is necessary.

Note: All objectives must have a timeline for completion and be shared with all people who are necessary to ensure its completion.

After a review of the incident reports or climate surveys, begin to target security problems or devise remedies to climate concerns using the following format:

The objective is to _____

Which will be accomplished by _____

And will be measured by _____

Within a timeframe of _____

Combine the above into a clear and concise written statement in the space below:

_____

_____

_____

_____

_____

Objective

Appendix I

Sample Crisis Management Phone Chain

(See page 117)

Person Initiating Call
(has knowledge of event)
Principal

Home Phone _____ Office Phone _____ Beeper _____

Principal calls police to verify, then calls superintendent. Superintendent notifies board of education. Principal then calls:

Crisis team leader(s), faculty phone chain, PTA president
(also director of student personnel services, if not a team leader)

Home Phone _____ Home Phone _____
Office Phone _____ Office Phone _____
Beeper _____ Beeper _____
Home Phone _____ Home Phone _____
Office Phone _____ Office Phone _____
Beeper _____ Beeper _____

Crisis team leader(s) calls:
Crisis Team Members
Home Phone _____ Home Phone _____
Office Phone _____ Office Phone _____
Beeper _____ Beeper _____
Home Phone _____ Home Phone _____
Office Phone _____ Office Phone _____

226

Beeper _____   Beeper _____
Home Phone _____   Home Phone _____
Office Phone _____   Office Phone _____
Beeper _____   Beeper _____

Crisis team members call:
Community resources (mental health, clergy, additional counselors)
Home Phone _____   Home Phone _____
Office Phone _____   Office Phone _____
Beeper _____   Beeper _____
Home Phone _____   Home Phone _____
Office Phone _____   Office Phone _____
Beeper _____   Beeper _____

Appendix J

Structuring a Response to Crisis

(See page 120)

Information to be included in the notification to:

Central office _____

_____

_____

Police and/or fire department _____

_____

_____

Mental health and/or other agency _____

_____

_____

Community _____

_____

_____

Staff _____

_____

_____

Students _____

_____

_____

Parents of those involved _____

_____

_____

Parents in general _____

_____

_____

Remember:

- Suicide: Not the result of normal adolescent stress; do not dramatize or glamorize the event.
- Homicide: A violent and unpredictable event; therefore very frightening.
- Sudden death: Difficult, as there has been no time to prepare; reactions may be delayed.
- General points: Expect a wide range of emotions (there is no right way to feel); talking about feelings is appropriate; witnesses may need additional counseling; classroom activities may need to be altered; students and staff will need time to grieve; after time, life will return to normal.

Appendix K

School Crisis Kit: Sample Contents

(See page 129)

Communication Devices
mobile phone, walkie-talkies

Lights
flashlights, propane lanterns, candles, matches

Writing Supplies
paper, pencils, index cards, markers, poster board

Tape
masking, cellophane, adhesive, caution, duct

Cutting Instruments
scissors, knives, utility knives

Hand Tools
hammer, nails, screwdriver, screws, staple gun, saw

Storage Materials
plastic water containers, large plastic bags, pails

Miscellaneous
First-aid kit, latex gloves, blankets, binoculars, water purification materials, rope and string

Appendix L

Letter to Parents

(See page 135)

BAYONNE HIGH SCHOOL
Selected by the New Jersey Department of Education as a
Best Practices Recipient
Blue Ribbon State Finalist
Star School

PRINCIPAL
Dr. Michael A. Wanko

(201) 858-5900

March 15, 2000

Dear Parents/Guardians,

During the past few years, various threats have been made against students throughout our country. Unfortunately, for whatever reason, some adolescents feel the need to frighten their classmates. Please be assured that whenever any threat is lodged at the students and/or staff of Bayonne High School, we respond accordingly. No threat is ever taken lightly.

Normal procedures include the following:

- Initiating an internal investigation
- Contacting the local police to launch an investigation
- Heightening security checks on students
- Searching student lockers
- Use of Port Authority K-9 Unit as needed
- Notifying Bayonne Fire Department when appropriate
- Any and all other procedures requested by police and investigative authorities

Every day all teachers at the high school are required to conduct a search of their classrooms before the beginning of the school day. Anything unusual is brought to the attention of the administration. Additionally, the administrative team is constantly vigilant regarding the safety and welfare of your child(ren).

As responsible parents, you should discuss with your child(ren) the negative ramifications of reckless acts such as issuing threats. Finally, please be advised that our counseling staff is always ready to meet with your child(ren) to discuss their concerns.

If you have any questions, please do not hesitate to call your child(ren)'s vice principal.

Sincerely,

Michael A. Wanko, Ph.D.
Principal

Appendix M

Containment of Rumors Letter

(See page 141)

BAYONNE HIGH SCHOOL
Selected by the New Jersey Department of Education
as a
Star School

Dr. Michael A. Wanko
Prinicipal

VICE PRINCIPALS

Richard J. Baccarella
Susan Hudacko
Timothy Mercier
John J. Skripak
Leo J. Smith, Jr.

To: All Staff
From: Michael A. Wanko, Ph.D.
Re: Containment of Rumors
Date: December 14, 1999

Since the tragedy at Littleton, Colorado, various threats have been made to schools throughout our country. Naturally, Bayonne High School has not been spared in this frenzy, and we have investigated fully each and every rumor to ensure the safety and welfare of our student body and staff.

Unfortunately, a pencil-written message was discovered yesterday in the third-floor girls' lavatory of House 5. I ordered a police investigation and the students who read this message were counseled in the Student Center. Today, I met with all vice principals, our director of Student Personnel Services, our maintenance supervisor, and our security personnel. We, in conjunction with Sergeant John Sucato and the "Cops in Schools" officers, as well as Detective William Opel and the Juvenile Aid Bureau will take all steps necessary to ensure a safe atmosphere and prevent future messages of this nature.

It is imperative that all staff react in a calm, measured, and thoughtful manner. Do not incite or initiate discussion of these types of occurrences. Otherwise we will be encouraging future incidents.

Any student who appears upset regarding any issues should be directed to the Student Center with the appropriate pass. Teachers desiring additional accurate information should meet with their vice principal rather than conducting open forums that could be overheard.

Finally, I met with all student leaders to provide them with accurate information to help us deal with this situation.

Appendix N

Principal's Job Stress Indicator

(See page 169)

Rate the items below according to how often they occurred for you during the past semester. Score the items as follows:

0 = never
1 = seldom
2 = often
3 = frequently
4 = always

___ My superintendent doesn't understand the problems of my position.
___ I am bored because I am underemployed.
___ Even small problems cause me to become agitated.
___ I do not have enough time for my family.
___ My authority is limited, preventing me from carrying out certain tasks.
___ I have little enthusiasm for my job.
___ Staff problems and needs do not concern or affect me.
___ I have suffered from a severe cold or the flu.
___ Even after a good night's sleep, I feel tired.
___ I have too much work assigned and not enough time to complete it.
___ My eating habits have changed in order to cope with work.
___ I have been caught in the middle of many conflicts.
___ My evaluation is not related to my performance.
___ The situations I experience lack adequate options.
___ I accept new responsibilities without delegating old ones.
___ The faculty and students do not appreciate my hard work.

___ I do not feel as though I am making a difference.
___ My values are different from those of my superintendent.
___ I am dissatisfied with my job.
___ My work is routine and not challenging.
___ I am concerned only with receiving my paycheck.
___ The community does not care about education.
___ I cannot concentrate as well as I previously did.
___ The teachers assigned to me try to take advantage of my good nature.
___ I am experiencing strained communications with my administrative team.

Add the scores of all items. If you scored 0–30, you are coping well on the job; 31–45, you are experiencing job stress; 46–60, you need to take action in order to prevent burnout; 61–100, you are heavily stressed and need to take immediate steps to manage your job stress.

Appendix O

A Dozen Time Tips for Principals

(See page 172)

1. Recognize that you cannot do it all.
2. Set priorities, goals, and deadlines.
3. Plan each day, leaving time for the unexpected.
4. Make a prioritized list of items to be accomplished.
5. Do the important tasks when you have the most energy.
6. Provide periods of rest and/or diversion.
7. Determine your best "internal" and "external" times.
8. Learn to say "no."
9. Delegate tasks whenever possible.
10. Group telephone calls.
11. Handle each piece of paper only once.
12. Perform routine tasks at the end of the day.

Selected Bibliography

BOOKS

Aldrich, Louise M. *Sudden Death: Crisis in the School*. Cherry Hill, N.J.: Aldrich, 1996.

American Academy of Experts in Traumatic Stress. *A Practical Guide for Crisis Response in Our Schools*. Commack, N.Y.: American Academy of Experts in Traumatic Stress, 1999.

Association for Supervision and Curriculum Development. *Quick Response: A Step-By-Step Guide to Crisis Management for Principals, Counselors, and Teachers*. Alexandria, Va.: ASCD, 1997.

Babbage, Keen J. *911: The School Administrator's Guide to Crisis Management*. Lancaster, Pa.: Technomic, 1996.

Blauvelt, Peter D. *Making Schools Safe for Students: Creating a Proactive School Safety Plan*. Thousand Oaks, Calif.: Corwin, 1999.

Bosch, Carl. *Schools under Siege: Guns, Gangs, and Hidden Dangers*. Springfield, N.J.: Enslow, 1997.

Brock, Stephen E., et al. *Preparing for Crises in the Schools: A Manual for Building School Crisis Response Teams*. Englewood, N.J.: John Wiley, 1996.

Day, Nancy. *Violence in Schools: Learning in Fear*. Springfield, N.J.: Enslow Publishers, Inc., 1996.

Dawson, Hal, ed. *School Security Screening*. Dallas, Tex.: Ram, 1998.

Decker, Robert H. *When a Crisis Hits: Will Your School Be Ready?* Thousand Oaks, Calif.: Corwin, 1997.

DiLima, Sara Nell, and Judy Marcus, eds. *Safety and Security Administration in School Facilities*. Gaithersburg, Md.: Aspen, 1998.

Goldman, Gary, and Jay B. Newman. *Empowering Students to Transform Schools*. Thousand Oaks, Calif.: Corwin, 1998.

Hill, Marie Somers, and Frank W. Hill. *Creating Safe Schools: What Principals Can Do*. Thousand Oaks, Calif.: Corwin, 1994.

Johnson, Kendall. *School Crisis Management: A Hands-On Guide to Training Crisis Response Teams*. Hunter House, 2000.

Lane, Kenneth E. et al. *The School Safety Handbook*. Lancaster, Pa.: Technomic, 1996.

Levitt, A. *Disaster Planning and Recovery: A Guide for Facility Professionals*. Englewood, N.J.: John Wiley, 1997.

Lichtenstein, Robert, M. Kline, D. Schonfeld, and D. Speese-Lineham. *How to Prepare for and Respond to a Crisis*. Alexandria, Va.: Association for Supervision and Curriculum Development, 1995.

McEvoy, Alan W. *When Disaster Strikes*. Holmes Beach, Fla.: Learning Publications, 1998.

National Association of Secondary School Principals. *Safe Schools: A Handbook for Practitioners*. Reston, Va.: NASSP, 1995.

Petersen, Suni, and Ronald L. Straub. *School Crisis Survival Guide*. West Nyack, N.Y.: The Center for Applied Research in Education, 1992.

Poland, S., and G. Pitcher. *Crisis Intervention in the Schools*. New York: Guilford, 1992.

Powell, Kenneth E., and Darnell F. Hawkins, eds. *Youth Violence Prevention*. Cary, N.C.: Oxford University Press, 1996.

Raider, M., and W. Steele. *Working with Families in Crisis: School-Based Intervention*. New York: Guilford, 1991.

Sesno, Alice Healy. *Ninety-Seven Savvy Secrets for Protecting Self and School*. Thousand Oaks, Calif.: Corwin, 1998.

Smith, Judie. *School Crisis Management Manual: Guidelines for Administrators*. Holmes Beach, Fla.: Learning Publications, 1997.

Stephens, Ronald D. *Safe Schools: A Handbook For Violence Prevention*. Bloomington, Ind.: National Educational Service, 1995.

Stevenson, Robert G. *What Will We Do? Preparing a School Community to Cope with Crises*. Baywood, 1998.

Trump, Kenneth S., ed. *Stopping School Violence*. Gaithersburg, Md.: Aspen, 1999.

Trump, Kenneth S. *Practical School Security: Basic Guidelines for Safe and Secure Schools*. Thousand Oaks, Calif.: Corwin, 1998.

Underwood, Maureen, and Karen Dunne-Maxim. *Managing Sudden Violent Loss in the Schools*. Piscataway, N.J.: New Jersey State Department of Education and New Jersey State Department of Human Services, 1997.

Wheeler, E., and A. Baron. *Violence in Our Schools, Hospitals, and Public Places*. Ventura, Calif.: Pathfinder, 1994.

Zeinert, Karen. *Victims of Teen Violence*. Springfield, N.J.: Enslow, 1996.

ARTICLES

Anderman, Eric M. "Victimization and Safety in Schools Serving Early Adolescents." *The Journal of Early Adolescence* (November 1997).

Blackburne, Linda. "Law on School Safety 'Lacks Teeth.'" *The Times Educational Supplement*, 13 December 1996.

Brandell, S. "A Time to Grieve, a Time to Grow." *Healing Magazine* 3, no. 1 (Spring/Summer 1998): 8.

Brandell, S. "Children and Death: Simple Journal Bridges Gap Between Past and Present." *Healing Magazine* 3, no. 1 (Spring/Summer 1998): 25.

Browne, J. Zamgba. "McCall Sees Errors in School Safety." *Amsterdam News*, 20 July 1996, p. 4.

Cantrell, R., and M. Cantrell. "Countering Gang Violence in American Schools." *Principal* (November 1993): 6–9.

Caudle, M. "Why Can't Johnny Be Safe? Eliminating School Violence." *The High School Magazine* (September 1994): 10–13.

Dear, J., K. Scott, and D. Marshall. "An Attack on School Violence." *School Safety* (Winter 1994): 4–7.

Dillon, Sam. "Cortines Wants 50 High Schools to Get Walk-Through Detectors." *New York Times*, 21 September 1994, p. B3.

Egyir, William. "Chancellor Shakes up Safety Division after Bad Report." *Amsterdam News*, 25 November 1995, p. 4.

Firestone, David. "Giuliani Creates Commission to Investigate Safety in Schools." *New York Times*, 11 June 1995, p. 1, 2bw.

Freidlander, B. "Violence and the Schools." *The High School Magazine* (September 1994): 18–21.

Furlong, M. "Evaluating School Violence Trends." *School Safety* (Winter 1994): 23–27.

Gaustad, J. "School Discipline." *ERIC Digest,* no. 78, 1992.

Goldman, L. "Helping the Grieving Child in School." *Healing Magazine* 3, no. 1 (Spring/Summer 1998): 15.

Grant, L., and B. Schakner. "Coping with the Ultimate Tragedy—The Death of a Student." *NASSP Bulletin* (April 1993): 1–9.

Grossnickle, D., T. Bialk, and B. Panagiotaros. "The School Discipline Climate Survey: Toward a Safe, Orderly Learning Environment." *NASSP Bulletin* (November 1993): 60–66.

Gutloff, Karen. "One Year After the Shootings: What's Happened to Make Schools Safer?" *NEA Today* 17, no. 7 (April 1999): 4–6.

Halford, Joan Montgomery. "Toward Peaceable Schools." *Educational Leadership* (September 1998).

Hechtkopf, Jackie. "Emergencies/School Safety." *School Library Journal* (March 1997).

Huff, C. Ronald, and Kenneth S. Trump. "Youth Violence and Gangs: School Safety Initiatives in Urban and Suburban School Districts." *Education and Urban Society* (August 1996).

Instructor. "Tools for School Safety." (September 1997), Vol. 107 Issue 2, p. 9.

James, Bernard "School Violence and the Law." *Education Digest* 60, no. 9 (May 1995): 17.

Johnston, Robert C. "Michigan Lawmakers Debate School Safety Bills." *Education Week* (1 April 1998).

"Keeping Weapons Out of School Is Everyone's Business." *School Safety Update* (September 1993): 3.

Klugman, J., and B. Greenberg. "Program Helps Identify, Resolve Problems in Multicultural High Schools." *NASSP Bulletin* (December 1991): 96–102.

Kongshem, L. "Securing Your Schools: Are Metal Detectors the Answer?" *The Executive Educator* (June 1992): 30–31.

Larson, J. "Violence Prevention in the Schools: A Review of Selected Programs and Procedures." *School Psychology Review* 23, no. 2, (1994): 151–64.

Metropolitan Life Insurance Company. *The Metropolitan Survey of the American Teacher 1993: Violence in America's Public Schools.* New York: MetLife, 1993.

Morrison, G., M. Furlong, and R. Morrison. "School Violence to School Safety: Reframing the Issue for School Psychologists." *School Psychology Review* 23, no. 2 (1994): 236–56.

Olson, Cheryl K. "Making School Safe." *Parents* 72, no. 11 (November 1997): 195, 2p, 1c, 1bw.

O'Neill, Barry. "Inventing the School Discipline Lists." *Education Digest* 60, no. 8 (April 1995): 4, 5p.

Purkey, William Watson. "What the U.S. Naval War College Can Teach Principals About School Safety." *NASSP Bulletin* (April 1996).

Reich, Denise, and Sarah Esberg. "Arresting Education: Should Cops Be in Classrooms?" *Amsterdam News*, 19 August 1995, p. 20.

Ricciardi, Diane. "Sharpening Experienced Principals: Skills for Changing Schools." *NASSP Bulletin* (January 1997).

Sabo, S. "Security by Design." *NY School Boards* (April 1993): 26–29.

Sanders, Mavis G. "School-Family-Community Partnerships Focused on School Safety: The Baltimore Example." *The Journal of Negro Education* (Summer 1996).

Sexton, Joe. "As Classes Resume after Student Shooting, the Subject Is Safety." *New York Times*, 17 September 1994, p. 27.

Stefkovich, Jacqueline A. "Students, Fourth Amendment Rights, and School Safety: An Urban Perspective." *Education and Urban Society* (February 1997).

Stephens, R. "Planning for Safer and Better Schools: School Violence Prevention and Intervention Strategies." *School Psychology Review* 23, no. 2 (1994): 204–15.

Stephens, Ronald D. "40 Ways to Safer Schools." *Education Digest* 62, no. 1 (September 1996): 13, 6p.

Stover, Del. "High Schools or High Tech Prisons." *Education Digest* 60, no. 1 (September 1994): 11, 4p, 1 cartoon.

Sunshine-Genova, Amy, Maija Johnson et al. "A Kid's-Eye View of Safety." *Parents* 69, no. 12 (December 1994): 40, 1–3p.

Toy, Vivian S. "Hearings Set on Examining School Crime." *New York Times*, 21 July 1995, p. B1.

"What You Can Do." *NEA Today* 13, no. 7 (March 1995): 6, 1/9p.

"Where Are Kids Safe?" *NEA Today* 14, no. 6 (February 1996): 27.

GOVERNMENT DOCUMENTS

Centers for Disease Control (CDC). *Youth Suicide Prevention Programs: A Resource Guide.* Washington, D.C.: U.S. Department of Health and Human Services, Public Health Service, National Center for Injury Prevention and Control, 1996.

Coordinating Council on Juvenile Justice and Delinquency Prevention. *Combating Violence and Delinquency: The National Juvenile Justice Action Plan.* Washington, D.C.: U.S. Department of Justice, March, 1996.

Dwyer, K., and D. Osher. *Safeguarding Our Children: An Action Guide.* Washington, D.C.: U.S. Departments of Education and Justice, American Institutes for Research, April 2000.

Dwyer, K., D. Osher, and C. Warger. *Early Warning, Timely Response: A Guide to Safe Schools*. Washington, D.C.: U.S. Department of Education, August 1998.

Kaufman, Philip et al. *Indicators of School Crime and Safety*, 1998. Washington, D.C.: National Center for Education Statistics and Bureau of Justice Statistics, October 1998.

O'Carroll, Patrick W. et al. *Youth Suicide Prevention Programs: A Resource Guide* (Summary). Washington, D.C.: U.S. Department of Health and Human Services, Public Health Service, National Center for Injury Prevention and Control, September 1996.

About the Author

Dr. Michael A. Wanko has been a teacher, coach, administrator, adjunct graduate professor, national lecturer, and workshop presenter. In addition to his baccalaureate, he holds two master's degrees, a Ph.D., six educational certifications, and an eighth-degree black belt in karate. He has been leaving his mark on education for more than thirty years.

As a result of his extensive pioneering efforts and vision, he has become a recognized leader in creating safe and supportive schools. In the spring of 2000, *USA Weekend Magazine* selected Bayonne High School as the national model of a safe and supportive school due to the programs instituted by Dr. Wanko. In just one year the incidents of violence, vandalism, and substance abuse at his school dropped by 42 percent.

Under his principalship, Bayonne High School has received much recognition and has won numerous prestigious awards. The state of New Jersey designated BHS as a Star School, the highest honor conferred by the state's Department of Education. Additionally, four separate designations for the Best Practices Awards by the state were also conferred under his leadership. The New Jersey Association for Supervision and Curriculum Development presented an Outstanding Curriculum Award; Chapter 154 of Phi Delta Kappa awarded two Exemplary Programs designations; and the National Association of Recording Artists and Scientists Foundation selected BHS as a Grammy Signature School. Also, the New Jersey School Boards Association conferred a First Place Award of Excellence in Communications and *New Jersey Magazine* selected BHS as an Outstanding High School.

He was selected as the New Jersey Department of Education and Dodge Foundation Visionary Leadership Principal of the Year and the NASSP/MetLife State Principal of the Year, and he received the New Jersey Principals and Supervisors Association's Golden Lamp Award, the National

Conference for Community and Justice's Silver Medallion, and the Hudson County Association of Retarded Citizens' ARC Angel Award. He was inducted into the Halls of Fame of Bayonne High School and the American Okinawan Karate Association. He was the national chair of the Larger Secondary Schools Committee for NASSP and president of the New Jersey Principals and Supervisors Association, the second-largest such organization in the nation. He is also the author of several articles that have appeared in national publications.

Dr. Wanko's innovative school initiatives have also been recognized by the media. He has appeared on network television, cable access, and radio, as well as in various newspapers. His programs have been selected to be featured in the textbook *Knowing Good Schools: A Guide to Rating Public High Schools*, by Dorothy Warner and William Guthrie. The authors remarked:

> It is obvious that Dr. Wanko is an active, visible, knowledgeable, and powerful force in the everyday operation of the school. We were impressed by his knowledge about the details of the curriculum. Dr. Wanko is obviously a person of action and not one to let any opportunity to advance the high school go by. As an example, he has used an entrepreneurial orientation to forge alliances with the community which have resulted in outstanding facilities. We were impressed with the emphasis on providing a safe atmosphere and Dr. Wanko's proactive leadership in this area.

Dr. Wanko, a consultant to various boards of education, provides information on creating safe and supportive schools. As a presenter, he brings excitement and enthusiasm to his audiences. Valuable research-based information, coupled with a bit of humor, allow workshop attendees to better cope with the topics at hand. His presentations to school communities have proven invaluable in supplying practical strategies for their organizations, as his model creates the framework for a safe and supportive climate.